perfect parties

perfect parties

the ultimate step-by-step guide

Alison Price

Kyle Cathie Limited

First published in Great Britain 1999 by
Kyle Cathie Limited
122 Arlington Road
London NW1 7HP
general.enquiries@kyle-cathie.com
www.kylecathie.com

This paperback edition published 2003

ISBN 1 85626 485 8

Text © 1999 Alison Price
Photography © 1999 Jeremy Hopley except as credited below
Cover photography © 1999 Jeremy Hopley except front centre (Joanna Plumbe) and back right (Will Heap)

Editor Sophie Bessemer
Copy-editor Samantha Grey
Design Vivid
Cover Design Paul Welti
Home Economist Dave Withers
Stylist Wei Tang
Production Lorraine Baird and Sha Huxtable

Alison Price is hereby identified as author of this work in accordance with Section 77 of the Copyright, Designs and Patents Act 1988.

A Cataloguing in Publication record for this title is available from the British Library.

Colour separations by Chroma Graphics Pte. Ltd., Singapore
Printed and bound in Singapore by Tien Wah Press Pte. Ltd

Additional photographic acknowledgements
page 14: Hulton Getty; page 26: Joanna Plumbe; page 37: Hulton Getty; page 54: Bill Batten; page 55: Bill Batten; page 59: Superstock; page 61: Hulton Getty; page 65: Superstock; page 67: Bill Batten; page 77: Hulton Getty; pages 111, 125, 128, 131, 132, 134, 137, 138, 140, 143: Will Heap

Dedication
To my mother for teaching me the love of good food, to my father for teaching me to be practical, I thank you.

Contents

Foreword by Sir Elton John 6

Introduction 9

Pre-Party 10

Prepare to Party 12

Fantasy Themes 16

Home or Away? 24

Invitations 28

Menu Planning 32

Hardware 34

Helping Hands 36

Room Transformations 38

Flower Festival 40

Candlelight 44

Table Settings 46

Formal Dining 49

New Ways with Napkins 56

It's Showtime 58

Party Etiquette 60

Food & Drink 62

The Party Spirit 64

Coolest Cocktails 68

Fresh Fruit Drinks 74

Practical Cooking 76

For a Cocktail Party 80

For a Buffet Party 94

For a Dinner Party 116

For a Supper Party 144

For Eating Outdoors 154

Cheeseboard 166

Basic Recipes 168

Essential Equipment 170

Acknowledgements 172

Index 174

Foreword
by Sir Elton John

When you've been to as many parties as I have, you tend to think you've seen it all before. Over the years, I've found that perfect and memorable parties require the host to blend the comfort of tradition with a fresh inventive spirit. It's where the expected and the unexpected meet. A successful party makes a guest feel completely comfortable yet never bored.

Alison Price has been responsible for some of the best parties I've ever given. She never ceases to amaze me. She always knows exactly what I want, yet never makes it feel stale or predictable. Whether it's a simple dinner for eight or a huge 50th birthday extravaganza for 400, her parties are always perfect.

With this book, Alison can help make your parties perfect too. I suppose I should be worried that she's given away her trade secrets. I'm not. I know that she will never run out of ways of creating the perfect party.

introduction

From a very early age, encouraged by my mother and father, I devoloped a great love for food, setting tables, making decorations and arranging flowers. To this day, I can recall the flavours of the wonderful soft summer fruits my grandfather grew, especially his loganberries. I remember sitting in his summer house in a garden full of scented flowers, surrounded by sweet-smelling summer jasmine, having afternoon tea. I also recall parties given by my mother. For Christmas, there were home-baked hams with roast capons and fresh vegetables, followed by Christmas puddings. I remember the wonder of watching my father light the brandy over the puddings and the bowls of brandy butter and home-made mince pies, filled with my mother's own mincemeat that I had eagerly helped her to make. On family picnics, there were flasks filled with home-made lemonade and bottles of ginger beer. Home is where I learnt about entertaining and the art of sharing.

I started Alison Price and Company in 1981 with my business partner, Terry Shaw. Our aim was to create a different style of food that would excite and amaze. Years of discovery followed, as well as extremely hard work. Terry and I would cook, wash up, deliver, do the accounts, write the menus and plan everything down to the last detail – all from a small flat in Bayswater, west London. Soon the business began to grow from personal recommendation and Gary Withers of Imagination offered us our first professional kitchen in his new offices. We have moved since there several times – we just keep outgrowing places!

We have always enjoyed running our business and have met enchanting people who have been generous in giving us the opportunity to be creative. Parties have taken us not only around Britain, but also abroad. What started as a two-person business has grown into a dedicated and loyal team of more than 20, who all contribute ideas, menus and planning.

We are perfectionists about food, wines and service and do not believe in gimmicky ideas –

simple, elegant entertaining is our company philosophy. Attention to detail is one of the

most important pieces of advice I can give. We always say failure is not an option.

Of course, at the beginning of our business venture, we had the odd disaster. I remember

a wedding that we catered for in the country where the water supply was from a well which

ran dry half way through the evening, leaving no water for coffee or to flush the loos. On

one occasion, power failed just as 350 guests sat down for dinner. We have even set off fire

alarms when sautéing foie gras. (These days we make provisions for such eventualities!) We

have, however, had years of great enjoyment creating memorable parties, every day bringing

new ideas and ways for the team to express their creative talents. In this book you will find

a wealth of practical advice resulting from all our experience.

Giving a perfect party is not difficult to do. Careful planning is required, whether you are

giving a small dinner for 10 or a large party for 100 guests or more. It is enjoyable, too, to

write a guest list matching new friends with old, think of different designs for invitations

and create table settings that will amuse and delight your guests. Choosing the food is an

excitement in itself. You may also want to create a memorable theme, in which case you

will find lots of ideas on pages 16–23. Remember that entertaining is your opportunity to

be as individual as you want to be.

I hope this book will give you all the ideas and enthusiasm you need. Whether holding an

impromptu supper in the kitchen with bowls of simple pastas, home-made sauces and fresh

salads or planning a grand dance, you will experience the unique pleasure of seeing your

guests having a fabulous time – and, what is more, you will have great fun doing it.

pre-party

If you have ever wondered what makes a successful party, the anwer is detailed planning and preparation. Remember the rule of the six 'p's, prior proper planning prevents poor performance; and think ahead to what must be done. For a party to be under control, someone must be in charge to make decisions.

prepare to party

If you have asked family or friends to help, be very clear what their responsibilities are. They can then proceed with as much enthusiasm as you, and listening to their ideas may help you to decide your plan of action. By devoting time and energy to organizing a party, you will ensure that it runs as smoothly as possible.

Be Aware of Your Budget

The budgets required by different styles of parties vary greatly, and it is vital to set a realistic budget for the type of party you are planning. Allocate the main part of the budget to the aspect of the party that is most important to you. For some people this is the wines and food, to others it is the decorations and entertainment. If you are planning a large, sit-down dinner, the cost of hiring tables and chairs can be very expensive. A drinks party is probably the least expensive form of entertaining. If you are providing the drinks, allocate half the cost of the food budget, although this will alter if you plan to serve expensive wines and champagne. Hiring a venue may be necessary for some parties. Venues come in a wide variety of forms and sizes, at vastly varying costs. You need to find one appropriate for the style of event you are planning, and allow for the hire cost in your budget. Always allow a little extra in the budget for unforeseen costs, too. Once you have finalized your budget, be very strict about keeping to it and do not be persuaded to spend more.

Perfect Planning

If you are planning a relatively large – scale party, such as an anniversary dinner dance, start by making a detailed list of the party requirements. These will include some or all of the following: invitations; food; drink; china; cutlery; glassware; furniture (also any furniture that must be removed from your home); venue (perhaps even a marquee); flowers; decorations; entertainment; staff. Write a schedule of events for the day, including at what time various deliveries are expected. Map out a sequence of events, such as the time

allocated to pre-dinner drinks and when to announce dinner, allowing time for guests to be seated before serving. Dinner should take about one and a half hours. If your party includes speeches, decide how many there will be and how long they are likely to take. If the meal is followed by dancing to a band, your schedule must include what time they will play until. Ask yourself whether your party will finish then, or if a disco will follow. If you have a finish time, allow about half an hour to three quarters of an hour for guests to leave. Making a detailed pre-party plan with a schedule that includes the timing of events will be of enormous help to you on the day.

The organization of an occasion such as a lunch, cocktail party, tea party or dinner may not be as structured, but most of the elements remain the same.

Setting the Date

Plan the date of the party as far in advance as possible. The dates you will celebrate important events, such as a 50th wedding anniversary or a 21st birthday are obviously set in stone. Otherwise, you need to take the following points into consideration when choosing the date.

Consider whether the date falls in the school holidays, as many families take the opportunity to holiday together – think how empty of traffic large cities are during August, early January and Easter. If you are planning a party during the Christmas season, remember that it is a busy social time and people's diaries fill up early. Final days of major sporting events are good dates to avoid, unless you want to hold a party to celebrate the event. Bear in mind, however, that while you may not

want to watch a final, the chances are that some of your guests will. One customer of ours actually hired large television screens for a marquee so guests could watch the World Cup final.

Good months in which to give a party are February and March since with Christmas and New Year behind them, people are refreshed and eager to enter the social scene again. Parties during these months, are a great success with very few refusals.

BEST FOR BUSINESS

DIFFERENT STYLES OF PARTIES ARE OFTEN BEST HELD ON DIFFERENT NIGHTS OF THE WEEK. WHILE FAMILY EVENTS OR WEDDINGS ARE POPULARLY HELD ON SATURDAYS, DID YOU KNOW THAT ONE OF THE MOST POPULAR NIGHTS OF THE WEEK FOR CORPORATE ENTERTAINING IS THURSDAY.

A Venue to Remember

If your home is not large enough for the number of guests you wish to invite, you may consider holding the party at a different location. Discover whether rooms in local museums, art galleries or large houses, or barns, boats or empty warehouses are for hire. We have even carried out the catering for parties in a disused Underground station in central London! Interesting and unusual venues are to be found everywhere – it just takes a little research. Make a list of suitable options, then make appointments to view the rooms and discuss arrangements. Most venues have an experienced events manager, who will be of great help to you. When you have made your choice, book as far in advance as possible because popular venues become booked up early.

Timely Invitations

Once the date and venue for your party have been decided on, invitations need to be organized. Although for weddings

and dances you ought to send invitations out two months before, for drinks parties and formal dinner parties, four weeks is enough. Indeed, particularly when it is a relatively informal affair, most people prefer to invite guests to dinner simply by telephoning them.

A HINT OF FUN TO COME

When giving a large party, such as a dance or birthday party, it is a lovely idea to send a 'save the date' teaser card to be followed at the appropriate time by the invitation.

A Musical Accompaniment

Music is essential to any party. For a drinks or dinner party, a compact disc player with suitable music can be all that is required. If you have a piano, you may like to engage the services of a piano player. It is worth contacting your local music school as many have students who, by arrangement, play at parties and other events. When planning a large dance, you may want

to hire a band. Choose the style of music for your party carefully, discussing your expectations with the band leader. Make your booking as soon as you have made your choice. This applies to discos and any other form of entertainment, too.

Food for Thought

Once you have decided on the date and location for your party, start to plan the menu and wines within your budget. Discuss the intended menu with your wine supplier, who will be able to make recommendations. When giving a dinner party, plan your menu wisely, thinking especially about what food will be in season. Think also of the dishes that you enjoy – tried and tested menus that you know work well and that guests will appreciate. Make sure that they can be prepared in advance. Always have a fall-back menu, too, in case certain foods are not available.

The Hardware

Once you have planned your menu, look carefully at your china, cutlery, glassware and linen. Decide on the plates, serving dishes, and so on, that you will use for each course. If you have silver cutlery, polish the pieces and buy tarnish-proof bags to store them in to prevent them from discolouring. Count your glasses to be certain that you have enough. Check that your linen is clean and pressed, then wrap it in acid-free paper and store in a bag laid flat in a cupboard or drawer. Alternatively, roll the linen and store it around a cardboard tube.

For Hire

You may not want to use your own china, glassware and so on for your party, or simply not have enough. In this case, there are many excellent hire companies offering a wide range of china, glassware, cutlery, linen, chairs, and even ovens and microwaves. Place your order as soon as you have decided on the style of your party and the number of guests.

Thinking Ahead to Table Settings

Making your own tablecloths and napkins can give your table a really special touch, but do this with plenty of time to spare. If you are arranging your own floral decorations, buy flowers that will be perfect on the day. Allow a few days in the warmth to open buds and bring blooms to perfection. Choose flowers that are in season and as with the menu, have an alternative plan. Consider containers, too, and select a style that will complement the table and the flowers.

The Morning After

When every detail of your party is planned – the invitations sent, the food, drinks, flowers and staff arranged, the house prepared, silver and glassware gleaming, garden tidied up and paths swept – have you thought of the next day? Do you want to be faced with a lot of dirty glasses and plates? Some people do not mind at all – I know a couple who enjoy post-party cleaning, when they like to discuss the night's events. Others recoil at the thought of facing the mess with a hangover. I recommend arranging for the house to be cleaned the next day – you will usually be able to find a local agency. Book a realistic time because you will not appreciate jolly cleaners turning up at 6.30am when you have only been in bed for an hour or two.

HELPING HANDS

IF YOU NEED TO EMPLOY STAFF BOOK EARLY TO AVOID DISAPPOINTMENT – ESPECIALLY DURING BUSY PERIODS SUCH AS SUMMER AND CHRISTMAS.

party plan checklist

Three to six months ahead
- Book venue if required

Ten to twelve weeks ahead
- If invitations are to be printed, start organizing them now

Four weeks ahead
- Invite your guests
- Decide what sort of food you will be serving. Will it be just canapés or will you be planning a full dinner?
- Book any staff
- Make a detailed list of all the items you require
- Plan any decorations; if you plan to hire any props, start looking now

Three weeks ahead
- Start to plan the menu, remembering the pre-dinner nibbles
- Check if any of your guests have special dietary requirements
- Order wines, decide on cocktails and soft drinks
- Make a time plan for the day before and the day of the party

Two weeks ahead
- Check the table linen is clean and pressed; wrap in acid-free paper

- Start chasing guests who have not replied to your invitation
- Check your tableware; now is the time to ask friends or arrange to hire
- Make a detailed shopping list for food, buying any unperishable items
- Make and freeze food that can be prepared in advance
- Start to make any decorations

One week ahead
- Chase any guests who still have not replied

Five days ahead
- Clean silver and wrap in tarnish-proof bags
- Check that you have ordered everything
- Buy flowers, cut the stems and store in a cool place in water
- Write your food shopping list
- Keep chasing those guests who have not replied

Two days ahead
- Make any dishes that can be refrigerated in advance
- If you are employing staff, write a list of what you would like them to do
- Place wines, champagne and soft drinks in the refrigerator

- Finish making any decorations
- Order the ice

Day before
- Remove and store any furniture.
- Write your table plan – memorize it if possible; if not, make a neat card for reference
- Write place cards and set the table
- Arrange the bar
- Prepare cocktails or fresh-fruit drinks if serving and place in the refrigerator to chill
- Prepare canapés if serving
- Organize hand towels for the loos and a coat storage area
- Arrange flowers

On the day
- Remove canapés from the freezer
- Finish preparing canapés and drink garnishes

Two hours before
- Remove corks from white wine bottles and the foil from champagne tops
- Chill the drinks
- Check loos have soap and hand towels
- Brief staff or helping hands
- Have a bath and relax

Before any of the practicalities can be addressed, at an early stage in planning your party it is vital to decide what, if any, theme your party will have. A little thought in this direction is well worth it – creating a theme for a party gives it an element of fun and can even add a sense of magic to an occasion.

fantasy themes

enthusiasms each person has. For a birthday party with a host who has a passion for musicals, we decorated each table in the style of a current West End show. These provided a wonderful talking point and, at the end of the evening, most of the table centres had disappeared – taken home by guests as keepsakes of a great party! On the following pages you can see what can be achieved at home for three very different themes. I hope they fire your imagination to make your party that little bit more memorable.

Style on a Shoestring

You do not have to spend a fortune to create a spectacular themed party. I find a glue gun and a staple gun are very handy for making decorations, and then you can do a lot with attractive leaves, pretty branches and fir cones. Other useful items to collect include cards, ribbons and tissue paper. Fabric remnants are wonderful for making your own tablecloths and napkins – even if you do not have a sewing machine, a friend will. All it takes is a little imagination and planning.

Think carefully about your chosen theme to be sure that it is the right one for you and will not place too much demand on the time you have available or over-stretch your budget.

Look in books and magazines and draw or make photocopies of ideas for room decorations, table settings or costumes. If the party you are planning is to celebrate a special occasion such as a birthday or wedding anniversary, think what particular interests and

Circus Skills

A children's, or even an adult's, birthday party could be enlivened by creating a circus theme with brightly coloured balloons, clowns' wigs and theatrical masks for guests to try on. Provide an assortment of items such as jack-in-the-boxes, juggling balls and hoops. Serve popcorn, toffee apples and coloured sweets to children and adults alike – most adults enjoy reliving the fun times of childhood.

Themed Table Settings

It is easy to create table settings that enhance your theme by using different tablecloths and tying or folding napkins in various styles. You could use carpets, brightly coloured blankets or quilts instead of tablecloths. For a 'last days of the Raj' party, we covered tables with lengths of jewel-coloured silks and used sari fabric for runners.

A French Feast

For people with an enthusiasm for the south of France we have brought to life a French theme by recreating their favourite restaurant simply with red and white checked tablecloths and large white napkins. In the centre of each table baskets filled with crudités were surrounded by bowls of olive oil and French bread tied in cloths, country-style. The room was lit by candles in hollowed-out artichokes and the music was typically French. Guests feasted on bouillabaisse served in large white bowls, followed by tarte tatin and crème fraîche. The evening was not only a great success, but the decorations and food easy to prepare.

Colour Co-ordination

It can often work well to plan a party around one colour, such as white, using white linen and white china with arrangements of white flowers in white or glass vases – even the guests can be asked to wear white. For this theme, simplicity will achieve the most elegant effect. Take care not to include food in such themes – it must look appetizing.

Summer Magic

Take inspiration from a summer garden for a natural theme, creating beautiful table settings with baskets or plant pots overflowing with summer flowers, herbs and fruit. Be inventive, perhaps using small garden forks and trowels (make sure that they are new and gleamingly clean) to serve food from a buffet. You could also bake bread in plant pots. Weave strings of tiny white lights through shrubs or trees.

Pool Party

For a pool party, cover tables with aquamarine-coloured tablecloths and place goldfish bowls in the centre – these could contain goldfish if you already keep them or have a suitable home for them after the party. Or, make centrepieces with piles of shells and pebbles covered with sand.

FESTIVE FIREPLACES

Collect fir cones to fill fireplaces that are not in use – they not only look decorative but give your home a warm and welcoming fragrance.

merry christmas

We all love to decorate our homes at Christmas, hanging wreaths on doors and garlands on mantelpieces. The decoration of the tree tends to be the most popular activity of all, and adorning it with home-made biscuits shaped into stars and half-moons looks particularly festive. Other favourite tree decorations include coloured glass balls and sparkling white fairy lights wound around the branches. Make left-over lengths of ribbon into garlands or tie them in bows on the branches. My friend Clare Signy searches antique markets for chandelier drops and balls to create wonderful decorations, and you can do the same.

Christmas is also the time to entertain family and friends over dinner. I like to spray nuts and fruits gold, then place them in bowls on the table. I tie my napkins with dark green velvet ribbon and make bread rolls in the shape of garlands. Prepare pomanders of oranges and lemons studded with cloves and pile them high on side tables; long cinnamon sticks arranged in vases also look festive. For a really enchanting display, place frosted pears on glass cake stands. If you have a glue gun – a useful tool for many crafts – make pyramids and balls of nuts to place around the house.

If you do want an ultraviolet effect, just replace ordinary lightbulbs with ultraviolet bulbs – the room will come to life. Food can be eaten off coloured plates or in napkins that harmonize with the colours of the paint. If you like, you can extend the input your guests have in creating the scene for their own party by letting them paint up their own original designs on the plates using the popular ceramic paints now available.

It is the application of a theme to the smallest details that really makes a spectacular party. For this street scene we wanted the serving dishes to have an industrial, down-to-earth feel to them. Consequently the beer and soft drinks stand in galvanized steel trays and even the salt and pepper (and of course mustard) are served from unfancy but utilitarian plastic containers.

street smart

This idea was developed for a party for teenagers a few years ago. The aim was to design something hardwearing yet suitably 'iconoclastic' and different. On that occasion the walls were splashed with ultraviolet paint. In fact, as these photographs show, with just a little artistic inspiration you can splash ordinary paint onto canvas draped over the tables and walls. It is most fun when you leave one wall or canvas free for guests to unleash their own creativity upon.

silks and spices

Inspired by the brightly coloured silks and aromatic scents and spices of the east, this room setting has a romantic mystery about it. Wooden bowls placed in the centre of the tables hold a selection of spices or fruit which not only look exotic but also release fine scents which can pervade a room (it is important to appeal to all the senses when creating a theme). As a further original decoration we filled silk bags with pebbles painted in colours that complement the colour scheme used for the napkins and the rest of the room. The hearts by every gleaming bowl then can be written upon to provide stunning name cards. To complete this theme, we removed the curtains from the windows and in their place hung generous lengths of pinkish silk (below) which can then catch the wind (and any draughts) to create a gently moving backdrop to the room. Using an inexpensive fabric such as coloured muslin would create the same effect.

Where are you going to hold your party? Will you be entertaining at home or at an outside venue? If your party is to be at home then take some time to work out how to arrange the space you have available. This may not always be readily obvious and involves a careful, lateral look at all areas of your home.

home or away?

Look at familiar, useable spaces with a critical eye to see how they could be arranged differently and how many guests they could accommodate comfortably. Changing rooms from their normal daily use is fun for the host and an interesting talking point for guests. Be inventive, using a large cupboard for a bar, placing tables in bedrooms, or a buffet or long dinner table in a large hall. Ask yourself practical questions: Where can you store coats for the evening? Is it possible to allocate separate bathrooms to men and women? For a large party I would suggest putting up signs for men's and ladies' loos so that you are not continually asked where they are. Also consider whether there is enough space in your kitchen to prepare the food you plan to serve, and whether your oven and refrigerator space will allow you to cater for the number of guests you want to invite. Plan where you will stack dirty plates, glasses and empty serving dishes.

Clearing to Create Space
If space is tight in your home, I advise removing some or all the furniture and storing it in a room (that you will not be needing) in the house, or in a cellar, garage or garden shed. If it is not possible to store it yourself, there are numerous furniture removal companies that will take away your furniture for a night and return it the following day. **Room for Manoeuvre**
For a cocktail party, arrange a few seats for guests, and make sure that there are clear surfaces to put down glasses and ashtrays. Do not place bars or buffets in areas that could easily become congested. If you are planning a garden party in the summer, place blankets and chairs on a lawn.

Sometimes the best solution is to reinvent space by turning a garage into a disco, or even a kitchen, for the day. For a disco, use ultraviolet lighting and cover the existing lights with coloured gels. In a garage, you can be adventurous with the decorations, draping the walls with fabric splashed with paint (see pages 22–3 for how we created the street effect with paint). Alternatively, rent a dance floor and supply your own music, perhaps with the help of enthusiastic family members.

LOOKING AFTER EVERYONE
REMEMBER WHEN PLANNING COCKTAIL PARTIES OR BUFFETS TO LEAVE SOME SEATING IN THE ROOMS FOR ELDERLY OR INFIRM GUESTS.

Cocktail Parties and Buffets
For cocktail parties and fork buffets, allow a space of 1.5m (5ft) per person. This takes into account a bar that will probably be in the same room and the removal of some of the furniture. For smaller parties you can get away with less than 1.5m (5ft) per person.

Are We Sitting Comfortably?
When planning a dinner party at home for a large number of guests, it is a good idea to make a basic scaled-up plan of the room, or rooms, you have chosen to use. Draw the shape of the room on a piece of paper – most rooms are rectangular – noting the measurements of its width and length. Indicate the positions of any obstacles, such as fireplaces, bay windows, recesses, immovable pieces of furniture, suspended light fittings and doors that open into the room (most do). Try to ensure that the windows are accessible so that they can be opened.

Take an average-sized reception room of 5.5 x 4.25m (18 x 14ft). In a room of this size, with no obstacles except for the door, it would be possible to sit up to 20 guests at two 1.5m (5ft) round tables, seating up to 10 guests per table. This would be cosy, but not uncomfortable. If you wish to have one long table, the important measurement to consider is that of the space between the floor edge and the open door. On some occasions, with space at a premium, we have removed the door for the evening. Ideally, the table should be 1.2m (4ft) wide to allow 50cm (1ft 8in) depth for the place settings each side, leaving 30cm (1ft) for decorations and serving bowls placed along the centre of the table. Allow 60cm (2ft) width of table for each guest, with a further 60cm (2ft)

The following is a guide to fitting guests at different-sized tables (at a rectangular table assume a width of 1.2m (4ft) with two people seated either end).

Table Size	Maximum Number of Guests
Round Table (diameter)	
1m (3ft)	6
1.2m (4ft)	8
1.5m (5ft)	10
1.7m (5ft 6in)	11
1.85m (6ft)	12
Rectangular Table (length)	
1.2m (4ft)	8
1.85m (6ft)	10
2.4m (8ft)	12
3m (10ft)	14
4m (12ft)	16

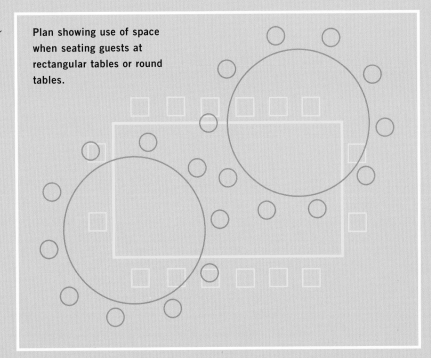

Plan showing use of space when seating guests at rectangular tables or round tables.

behind the chairs to give space for serving. The maximum size that the table should be in the average-sized reception room is 4 x 1.2m (12 x 4ft); with two guests at each end, this seats a maximum of 16 guests. It is worth noting that long tables tend to take up more space than round ones, so if you are trying to fit the maximum number of guests into an odd-shaped room, use a combination of different-sized round tables to utilize corners.

Glorious Garden Parties

For a summer party, set up a garden table as a bar for serving drinks. Your garden may present other possibilities, too, whatever the season, such as a greenhouse or conservatory for serving coffee and desserts. A candlelit summerhouse could provide an idyllic romantic hideaway. For outdoor parties, the weather plays an important role, so listen to forecasts beforehand and make sure you have drawn a contingency plan to cope with unwanted surprises. It may be possible to cover a garden terrace with a canopy or you may need to move everything inside – be open-minded about adapting your plan.

Playing Away from Home

If you are not able to accommodate the number of guests you would like to invite at home, you could consider a marquee in the garden if there is sufficient space, or look for a suitable venue.

Magnificent Marquees

Marquees can become an extension of your home, with the house used for serving pre-dinner drinks and canapés and guests having direct access to the marquee through doors that normally lead on to the garden. Sometimes, guests may not even be aware that they are sitting under canvas.

If you have decided on having a marquee in the garden, start your search for a marquee company by asking friends and family for recommendations. All marquee companies will make a site visit, armed with photographs and samples of lining – some even supply furniture. Ask if they are erecting a marquee with similar specifications to yours in the near future that you could visit. Take into consideration the area over which the marquee will be positioned. Some sites may require a scaffold structure to create an even floor. Tents today are

extremely sophisticated, with heating controlled by a thermostat, air conditioning, windows and patio doors. The colour and type of lining depends on your preference.

With the number of guests you are inviting in mind, decide how much space is required for a reception area, bar, buffet and dance floor. The marquee company will be able to supply a scaled-up plan setting out the different elements as you want them. If you are engaging the services of a catering company, they will require a service tent large enough for cooking and clearing away dishes to; also consider a separate staff area and a storage area for coats and bags.

The Light Fantastic

Lighting in a marquee can include night-sky ceilings, pin-spotted tables, and bars and buffets bathed in pools of light. Decorative features can be spot lit to bring them to life. If you want these effects, ask the marquee company to recommend a specialist lighting firm. It may be necessary for power to be supplied by generators, but these are now almost silent. It is worth the investment for peace of mind.

Practical Matters

Try to ensure that the marquee has windows on to attractive features of the garden, such as a beautiful flower border, pond or fountain. These could also be highlighted with outside lighting. You may need to arrange with the marquee company to have additional loos. These can now have luxurious touches, from designer wallpaper to scented candles and linen hand towels – your choice will probably be dictated by budget.

Expect your life to change while the tent is being erected, bearing in mind that some take up to a week to assemble and two days to dismantle. Check when the company will arrive to dismantle the marquee – you do not want to see them at six in the morning following the party. I would suggest a midday start, which gives you time to recover from the night before. Try to ensure that all equipment is removed from the marquee before they start to dismantle it. In addition, it is a good idea to have previously arranged insurance to cover any accidents, and most marquee companies offer this.

Bien Venue

The thought of having your home life disrupted for up to 10 days by a marquee company may lead you to decide to look for a venue. Your budget will point you in the direction of the appropriate place for you, from a grand house to the local village hall. The best space should be flexible but the more popular venues are booked up months ahead. Most venues have an experienced events manager who can give you advice. To help you to arrange the practicalities, make a list of questions that you need to ask (see right). Do be warned for the budgeting stage that some venues have lists of approved caterers and florists that they like to use who are accustomed to organizing food and flowers in a very tight time frame. This can be very important when you are, for example, hiring rooms in museums or art galleries that close at 6.00pm, with

your guests invited for 6.30pm. When you have made your choice of venue, write to confirm the booking as soon as possible and send your deposit. In most cases, you will be sent a contract detailing your arrangements. Check this carefully as you do not want any surprises on the day.

Asking the Right Questions

To help you choose the right venue these are the questions you need to ask yourself and the venue manager:
• Will the venue hold the number of guests you are inviting?
• Are there any restrictions to activities such as smoking, drinking red wine in certain areas or dancing?
• Is there easy parking – if not, can it be arranged?
• Are there telephones available (to call for taxis)?
• Is there cloakroom space for coats?
• If you are having a dinner, can pre-dinner drinks be held in a separate area?
• If using them, are you allowed to bring in an outside caterer and florist?
• Are there kitchen facilities and what are they like?
• Is there a food preparation area?
• Are you allowed to bring in ovens or hot cupboards, and is the power rating able to cope?
• What types of entertainment, including discos, are allowed?
• What time can you start setting up?
• When are the guests expected to leave and will overtime be charged for late departures?
• Is the lighting appropriate (some venues have much more sophisticated systems than others) – if not, would candles enhance the interior?
• Finally look at the loos and if they are not very attractive, make them more welcoming with floral arrangements, fragrant soaps and hand towels

ENCHANTED EVENINGS

IF YOUR PARTY IS IN THE EVENING, ARRANGE A VISIT TO SEE THE VENUE AT NIGHT TO MAKE AN INFORMED JUDGEMENT ON WHETHER THE MOOD WILL BE SUITABLE.

invitations

The success of a party depends upon attention to every detail. Well-designed invitations, in keeping with the style of your party, sent out in good time, will encourage guests to look forward to the event. Organized records of expected guests and an efficient seating plan will ensure that the occasion runs smoothly.

Making your Guest List

When making your guest list, you have to be sure that the number you wish to invite will fit in the space where you are planning to hold your party. As a host, inviting guests into your private world calls for you to be very thoughtful. You want to create a lively party with an interesting collection of guests that may include family members, friends and business colleagues. Choose guests who will be lively and even some with controversial views and conflicting interests to encourage discussion and debate. These days it is not so important to have a strict 50 percent male to female ratio, and you can mix age groups. For last-minute cancellations, have a list of friends who you know will not be offended if they are invited to make up the numbers.

Invitations

These days we live in a world where faxes and e-mail are dominating our communications. However, receiving a written invitation remains an important part of social etiquette. The thrill of opening an invitation followed by the anticipation of going to the party is something we all love.

Your chosen invitation design will set the style of your party. It can be traditional but, if you are giving a party with an unusual style or theme, try to be original with the design of your invitations, too. Interesting ideas include a tin can with an invitation label tied onto it, a CD or record with a recorded invitation, a cigar tube holding an invitation, and a small piece of glass with the invitation etched on. The invitation could also be added to fluorescent light sticks, a sheet of transparent film or an archive photograph. A simple and fun option is to fill the envelope with confetti, glitter or paper shapes that will spill out. People can become excited about going to a party that they know will be special simply because you have followed through the style of the party with your chosen invitation.

The invitation must include all the information your guests need to know: date, timing, dress, the type of hospitality being provided and where to reply. Enclose an RSVP card as this acts as a prompt for guests to reply. Some people can still be very slow in replying so, to be sure of numbers, do not be shy about telephoning them. Indicating to guests the style of the party will be appreciated as there is nothing worse than arriving in black tie to find that the remainder of the guests are in casual wear. If parking is almost impossible for your guests, give that information as well.

Rules to Remember

On formal invitations, the guest's name is always written by hand with a fountain pen, as is the envelope. Full titles, rank and any decorations are used when writing on the envelopes but not on the invitation.

Timing

Timing for sending invitations is as follows:
Two months before a wedding or a large dance;
Six weeks before a special celebration;
Four weeks before a formal dinner, drinks or buffet party.

the right size. Read the printers' proofs carefully, checking that the information is correct. Try not to agonize too much over the look of the invitations as changing your mind will mean a delay in sending them, and by then you may find that your guests have other social or business commitments.

The 'Yes' or 'No' List

I recommend that you compile a 'yes' and 'no' list for replies, making a note of daytime and evening telephone numbers for contacting people when you need to. Guests' names should be ticked off once they have been invited and replied. If you know about, or are told about, any special dietary requirements, write these next to the guest's name for later reference.

Allowing for Refusals

When more parties were given 30 years ago, 33 percent refusals were allowed for. These days fewer parties are given, so you can expect more acceptances. For private entertaining, allow 15 percent refusals for a cocktail party and 5 percent for a dinner. Refusals for business can be up to 30 percent for a cocktail party and 10 percent for a dinner. Refusals will vary depending on the time of year, the day of the week, and when invitations were sent.

MAPPING THE WAY

IF YOU LIVE IN THE COUNTRYSIDE OR YOUR HOME IS DIFFICULT TO FIND, HAVE A MAP PRINTED EITHER ON THE REVERSE OF THE INVITATION OR ON A SEPARATE CARD.

To invite friends to a dinner party, a telephone call is sufficient. Do this three weeks before and, if you like follow with a card or letter confirming the arrangements. If the dinner is for business, keep to formal invitations.

The Printed Word

Plan your invitations as soon as you have decided on the date for your party to allow yourself time. Printers will need at least four to six weeks before they are able to deliver printed invitations. During this time, after about two to three weeks, you will approve the design, style of the type and your copy. Ask for the envelopes before you receive the printed invitations as these can be written in advance. If the invitations will not fit in standard-sized envelopes, enquire how long it will take to make them to

Planning menus, no matter how simple or grand, requires thought. I always prefer to use fresh ingredients that are in season; then flavours are at their finest and prices at their most economical. Seasonal produce is also the most readily available and of course it gives you a starting point to your menu planning.

menu planning

When choosing ingredients, think about an interesting range of colours and textures. Imagine tasting all the elements you would like to serve, then consider whether they mix well together. Classic combinations, for example, include fresh mint with new potatoes and strawberries with clotted cream. Deciding what will complement each element is a good starting point when planning a menu. Try to keep the dishes you plan to serve simple, full of flavour and easy to prepare.

Tasting as Good as it Looks

Consider the visual appeal of the combination of dishes on your planned menu. For example, I would not advise serving scallops, followed by chicken with creamed potatoes and a dessert such as crème brûlée. Although each dish on its own is delicious, served as a dinner they are all the same colour. Think about how the colours and textures of the ingredients in each course will complement one another.

Perfect Presentation

When preparing and serving food, it is worth giving everyday meals a slight twist in the way they are presented. For a classic dish, such as a Caesar salad, try replacing the traditional croûtons with long, spicy ones. A casserole becomes hearty made with whole vegetables or delicate when the vegetables are cut into small dice.

Buying the Best Ingredients

When buying food, take time and care choosing each ingredient. Check for freshness and do not be forced into buying any item you are less than happy with. In large cities, it is becoming increasingly difficult to find a local butcher, fishmonger or green grocer – where I live in central London I have managed to find local shops and markets, where I have developed good relationships, but it takes time. Most of us are left to shop under one roof in large supermarkets. These generally have a have specialist fish and meat departments, so make the most of their staff's expertise by approaching to discuss what you would like to buy.

Be Kind to Yourself

These days we are bombarded with cooking programmes and new books, putting pressure on us to prepare food like three-star Michelin chefs. Be practical and accept that this is not realistic. Do not feel that you should prepare dishes that you sense are not going to work for you in the time you have available, otherwise you may be in the kitchen all night. Choose a menu that can be prepared ahead, that will require only minimum attention before serving. If you do not have time to prepare all the courses, visit a local delicatessen or patisserie for the starter or dessert. As long as the food you serve is fresh, why feel guilty?

BUDGET BLUES?

IF YOUR BUDGET ONLY RUNS TO A SIMPLE DINNER, SERVE A HEARTY SOUP WITH LOVELY WARM BREAD. FOLLOW WITH ONE CHEESE AND HOME-MADE OATMEAL BISCUITS, OR A FRUIT TART. GUESTS ALWAYS ENJOY GOOD, HONEST FOOD.

Variety is the Spice of Life

The best menus have a varied mix of flavours, ingredients, colours and textures. Try not to repeat any of the elements within a dinner menu. For a buffet or cocktail party, you can repeat some flavours and textures. If serving canapés before dinner, try not to include any of the dinner ingredients. For a buffet remember those guests who may not be meat eaters, and always allow a few dishes that do not contain any dairy products, fish or meat. You can be bold when planning the menu, and amaze your guests with bright and beautiful garnishes and serving dishes, but don't forget that classic simplicity can look effective too. Just keep within your own capabilities and choose a style which suits you and with which you are comfortable.

BREAK WITH TRADITION

DO NOT FEEL THAT YOU MUST ALWAYS FOLLOW TRADITION. THINK OF IMAGINATIVE ALTERNATIVES TO POTATOES LIKE RISOTTO, BEANS OR GNOCCHI.

No-Fuss Canapés

If serving canapés, plan bite-sized
ones with no messy bits to drop onto
carpets or spill onto guests' clothes.
They should be easy to prepare and
serve, and not so elaborate that they
can only be assembled at the last
minute. Also take into consideration
your range of kitchen equipment and
the storage space in your refrigerator.
Calculate that you are not over-
stretching yourself budget-wise. If
serving only a very few canapés, make
them memorably exquisite! (Try a
boiled quail's egg with celery salt!)

Remember the Vegetarians

Most parties nowadays will probably
include non-meat eaters and as host,
you do not want them to feel left out.
Before you start planning your menus,
ascertain how many, if any, of the
guests are vegetarians and then
consider whether to adapt a dish for
them or cook a separate course.

WINES WITH FOOD

Forget any 'rules' about the colour of
the wine you should serve – white and
red can both be delicious with fish.

Summing Up

Planning menus is enjoyable, and your
party is sure to be a success so long as
you keep within your time frame,
capabilities and budget. Take time to
present each dish with care, and
perhaps a little wit. Consider the plates
or bowls best for serving each course.
Also take into account practicalities
such as the room you will serve your
guests in, and do not plan elaborately
arranged food that must, for example,
be transported from the basement up
three flights of stairs – your beautiful
presentation could suffer!

If you are like me, you will have a diverse collection of serving dishes, plates bowls, cups, cutlery and glasses – what I call hardware. I enjoy mixing and matching china, and seeing the effect of combining different side plates with main-course plates to create an inviting table setting.

the hardware

Multi-Purpose Styles

I like to collect useful items that can have dual functions. Many years ago in Boston, I found jam jars that work really well as glass tumblers to serve beers or soft drinks in. Large white bowls can be used to serve pasta, a substantial main-course salad or a comforting winter soup. Bowls for vegetables or salads are also useful for desserts, such as a crumble or brûlée. Beautiful, painted Italian pottery is perfect for summer lunches in the garden, but also looks wonderful for serving breakfast in the kitchen or dining room. Most invaluable of all is simple white china, which fits any food and allows you to use tablecloths and napkins in a greater range of colour.

Mix and Match

It is not necessary for all your china to match, as different shapes and colour shades can complement one another. This is worth bearing in mind if you are giving a large dinner party, when you may want to borrow plates from family or friends. Try to collect pieces of china that will not date, keeping in mind your preferred style of table settings and food. I am always on the look out for new pieces and find that antique fairs are an excellent hunting ground. It is worth having a store of glass plates as they are ideal for serving desserts. I never buy anything that I cannot put in the dishwasher; this rule applies even to my collection of early blue and white china, which I use with great regularity.

BEAUTIFUL BUFFETS

To present plates in style at a buffet, layer them with napkins or tie up piles of plates with large linen napkins.

Choosing Cutlery and Glassware

The type of cutlery and glassware you choose should depend on your life – style. Even if you love silver, consider how much time you wish to devote to keeping it highly polished. This said, over the years I have put together a wonderful collection of beautiful silver cutlery from my various visits to antique markets and fairs. Using items collected abroad can bring back happy

memories – I have some pretty silver and mother-of-pearl fruit knives that always remind me of time spent in New England. When friends ask what you would like for a birthday present, why not ask for a silver dessert fork or spoon to add to your collection? The gift will last a lifetime.

Fortunately these days there are no set rules on which pieces of cutlery to use for certain dishes, although fish knives and forks have gone out of fashion, to be replaced by dessert knives and forks. Be imaginative – for example, horn spoons are ideal for boiled eggs. Serving spoons and forks will add interest to your table settings, and come in a variety of designs. Likewise, cutlery old and new can be found with classic wooden or bone handles, or jazzy plastic ones.

From stemmed glasses to tumblers there is a bewildering amount of glassware of all shapes and sizes to choose from – plain or decorative, it is up to your personal taste.

Serving

Collect serving dishes in interesting shapes and styles. Look around the house for large bowls, vases, flowerpots, baskets or any other item. Large fish platters, for example, allow wonderful arrangements of vegetables or salads. Steamer baskets look effective when piled high and topped with a bowl of noodles or rice. Footed bowls look delightful filled with salads, and hollowed-out Parmesan wheels, available to order from cheese merchants, are an imaginative way to present pastas or risottos. A one-pot dish, such as a cassoulet, is best served from the pot in which it was cooked – just clean around the edges first and check before you put it down that your table or serving surface is heat resistant.

ICE SPECTACULAR

ICE CREAMS OR SORBETS LOOK MAGNIFICENT SERVED IN ICE BOWLS. PILE THESE HIGH UP AND WATCH THEM CATCH THE LIGHT.

Stand and Deliver

Finally, if you do not own a large amount of hardware or do not wish to use your own plates, glasses and cutlery and serving dishes for a party, then hiring is the answer. There are many companies that specialize in hiring these items and it is worth arranging an appointment to see what is on offer. Ask if prices include delivery and collection, whether you will be able to return your hired items dirty and, if so, at what extra charge. Times you arrange for delivery and collection are, as usual, important – I suggest asking the company to deliver on the morning of your party and to collect the following day (allowing you time to recover). Bear in mind that if any equipment is damaged or lost a replacement charge will be made. (It is important to make this clear to any staff/helpers for the event.)

Frequently the number of guests you have invited to a party is too many to cope with single-handedly. In this case, your thoughts may turn to hiring waiting staff or asking friends and family if they are willing to lend a helping hand. Most people will be honoured and flattered to help, so do not be afraid to ask.

helping hands

Parties are, by their nature, a social occasion, so even a hard-pressed cook can usually find an extra pair of hands to help. Perhaps a family member or friend excels at cooking a certain dish – if so, they may be willing to make this for your party. Always make it clear exactly what help you need. For example, if you have a particular style of setting your table, demonstrate one place setting. As a professional, I always offer to help friends if they are giving a large party; sometimes they welcome the idea, but there are also occasions when they prefer to organize the evening themselves. The golden rule is never be afraid to ask for help.

Professional Help

When engaging waiting staff, I would suggest that you contact a reputable agency or ask friends whether they can recommend reliable staff – word of mouth is the best recommendation. If you contact an agency, it is important to be clear about what type of party you are giving and what you expect the staff role to be. Plan timings precisely so that staff have sufficient time to set the table and prepare the bar. For dinners and buffet parties, arrange for the waiting staff to arrive two hours before the guests and to continue for about half an hour after the last guest has departed. For drinks parties, the staff should arrive one and a half hours before guests arrive.

What to Expect

Give staff clear instructions – do not just expect them to start cleaning the silver and pressing linen on arrival. Be clear as to whether you would like them to wash up or load the dishwasher. If you are giving a dinner party, show them where the china, glassware, cutlery and linen is stored, and tell them what pre-dinner drinks and snacks you are serving. Experienced waiting staff will run your party, not only opening doors, taking coats and serving drinks, but helping you to place canapés on trays and perhaps even doing the last-minute cooking of vegetables, dressing salads, preparing cheese baskets and making the coffee and tisanes. Remember that they are there to help you.

LOOKING AFTER WAITING STAFF

If employing staff for over four hours, provide a light snack. You cannot expect staff to work late without food. If your party finishes after the last train or bus, it is standard practice for the employer to arrange and pay for a taxi.

Paying Practices

Waiting staff are paid by the hour to work a minimum of four hours. If using an agency, you can receive a bill or pay the staff direct, with the commission charged separately. If you engage staff without an agency, discuss fees first.

BEHIND THE BAR

When giving a drinks party with more than 25 guests, I would recommend hiring an experienced bar person, who will be worth their weight in gold. As with waiting staff, always provide as much information as possible.

Chefs and Cooks

When finding good chefs or cooks, the same principles apply as for finding waiting staff. Discuss with them your ideas for the menu as well as what dishes they like to prepare. They will be clear about the service that they will provide and what you will be expected to supply. Take time to show them the china and serving dishes you wish to use. They need to know in advance how many guests are invited, timings, how formal or informal the party will be, and whether there will be help serving the food and washing up. Charges are arranged in one of two ways – a flat fee plus the cost of food, or you can be charged on a per-head basis. Most chefs and cooks know good waiting staff that they work with regularly, so it is worth asking for their recommendation.

Mission Impossible

Do not expect cooks or chefs to create a dinner without proper ovens, hobs and so on. If you cannot prepare dinner without certain equipment then neither can they. Remember that, if necessary, you can hire ovens and hobs. Be realistic about your chosen menu, too. In a small kitchen, serving three hot courses may be very difficult.

The Morning After

We have all given parties, gone to bed then woken up faced with the prospect of cleaning up. If you are giving a party without any staff, it may well be worth arranging for a cleaner on the morning after – not too early, as the chances are that you will have had a very late night. Contact cleaning agencies about two weeks beforehand, giving details about what you require. Cleaners generally charge by the hour.

Dressed for Success

For formal dinners and receptions, butlers dress in striped trousers, a black jacket and waistcoat, with a white shirt and silver and black tie. For less formal occasions the dress code, which applies to both men and women, has changed. It includes a black jacket, trousers, waistcoat and bowtie with a long white apron. If your party has a theme, the staff could dress in accordance with this – although they must still be comfortable. Theatrical costume hire agencies generally have an excellent range of outfits.

Suggested Staff to Guests Ratios

Dinners One waiting staff per 10 guests
Drinks Parties One bar person and three waiting staff per 50 guests
Informal Fork Buffet Party One bar person and two waiting staff per 30 guests
Formal Seated Buffet Party One waiting staff per 10 guests
Afternoon Teas Two waiting staff per 30 guests

Information to Give Waiting Staff

• Timings, including arrival of guests and when the party is expected to finish
• Number of guests
• Menu
• Drinks and wines (do they need decanting?) and how they will be served
• Any guests who require a special diet or drinks
• Where the linen, china, cutlery and glassware are stored
• How you would like tables and bars to be set
• Where coats and bags should go
• Instructions to clear ashtrays regularly and replace them with clean ones
• Where the loos are for the guests, with instructions to maintain their tidiness during the party
• Instructions to tidy the reception area during dinner and to clear everything away and wash up
• Where coffee is to be served

In the decoration of the party space – be it a room or rooms at home, a marquee or a hired venue – your dreams and desires can begin to take shape. Much depends on the style or theme of your party which can be brought to life by your chosen decorations.

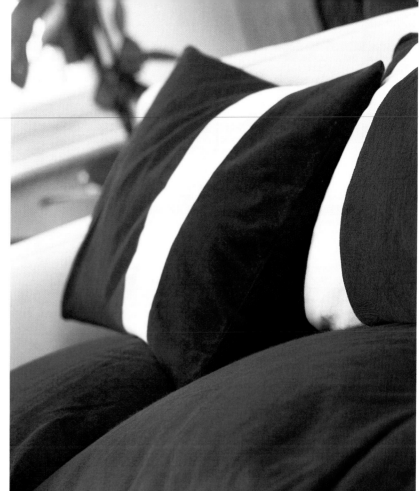

room transformations

In the early planning stages you will have started to think about possible themes for your party. If you are unsure about what might work well, discuss your plans with family and friends – they will enjoy sharing ideas. For example, you may like to recreate a style from a bygone era. Ask friends to give practical help, too, in decorating the party space. Most people welcome the chance to be creative and, if you give them clear instructions as to what you want, you will be amazed at the results. For ideas, look in magazines and books where a wealth of inspiration is to be found. In the midst of this planning do not forget your budget – if it is realistic, keep within it.

Changing Rooms

One of the easiest mistakes to make when decorating for a party is to get carried away with ideas and tend towards over-decorating a space. Be aware that you do not want the finished room to look fussy and become overpowering to guests. There are infinite ways to adapt any room very subtly with only a little bit of effort – for example, a Moroccan-style party is created by dispensing with chairs and replacing them with large cushions covered in richly coloured fabrics for guests to sit on. For any theme, draw attention to interesting areas such as windows and pretty corners of the room by placing candles

and small pots of flowers or plants on windowsills or other surfaces. For children's parties, cover the table with thick, plain white paper and fill paper cups with crayons so that children can amuse themselves by becoming artists. You may also like to write their names on balloons tied to the backs of chairs.

Magical Transformations in Marquees

Most marquees tend to be decorated with flowers. If you want to create a theme, a prop-hire company is a good source of interesting pieces. Take a look around at what they have in stock and it is bound to give you some ideas – you will be surprised at the effects

that can be achieved. Around the walls of a marquee, branches of trees cut and arranged to represent a wood or hedge look extremely attractive, as do climbing plants entwined around trellis – the plants can be transferred to the garden after the party.

Dance floors must be well defined, with small, round tables and chairs placed around them and the areas divided with a device as simple as low picket fencing or as grand as statues at each corner and an arbour of flowers. By scattering the floor of a marquee with lavender flowers or dried herbs, the scent will be released as guests walk over them.

WINDOWS ON THE WORLD

WINDOWS OF A ROOM OR MARQUEE CAN BE TRANSFORMED BY DRAPING INEXPENSIVE COLOURED FABRIC ACROSS THEM. IF YOU WANT TO PERSONALISE THE MATERIAL, GLUE ON FAKE JEWELS OR STENCIL AN INTERESTING DESIGN ONTO IT.

Food and flowers are two great passions of mine. Flowers bring warmth and life into the home. It is not necessary to have grand, costly arrangements – a single vase with a perfect bloom is just as pleasing. You can always gather up branches of blossom or put out small posies of fresh herbs to scent and brighten a room.

flower festival

Think carefully about the style of arrangement you prefer and your budget. There are many inexpensive ways to use plants, flowers and foliage to decorate a room. Try visiting flower markets early in the morning (one of my great joys) to see what is available. If buying from florists, place your order ahead of time to make sure that you have the flowers you want on the day of the party. Remember to allow time for the blooms to open, so that they are perfect on the day. Do not buy flowers on the day of your party that are not yet open because they will be at their best five days later. Always cut and split the stems, then place the flowers in fresh, clean water in a cool place until you are ready to arrange them.

SEASONAL SPECIALS

MAKE THE MOST OF YOUR MONEY BY ALWAYS BUYING FLOWERS AND PLANTS THAT ARE IN SEASON. THE EXCEPTION IS A SPECIAL OCCASION FOR WHICH YOU MAY WANT TO BUY SOMEONE'S FAVOURITES.

Blooming Beautiful

Garden roses arranged informally in bowls and silver beakers set a romantic scene at any table. Cut the roses on the day and scatter on the table any petals that have dropped. In spring, decorate the table with pots of bulbs such as paper whites, hyacinths or crocuses – these will continue to brighten up your home long after the

small pots or posies of sweet-smelling flowers. In a bathroom too, you can add sea shells and pebbles which will last long after the party.

Garden Glories

If you have a garden, look not only for flowers but for interesting foliage that could be used in your centrepieces or to create displays around the room. For example, berries, fruits, nuts and ornamental corn with colourful foliage make enchanting autumnal arrangements displayed in pumpkins which can be surrounded by hollowed-out baby squashes with night lights glowing inside. Ask yourself whether any of your friends or family have a large garden that you could raid.

Pots of Style

Small terracotta pots filled with a mixture of inexpensive plants or herbs look stunning placed along the centre of the table. Grouping together pots of herbs in saucers or baskets also looks very attractive. In summer, try trailing geraniums or lavender or a foliage plant such as Mind Your Own Business. After the party, they can be transferred to the garden or to window boxes.

Hiring a Professional

If you are planning a grand party or wedding for which you need the services of a floral decorator, discuss in detail the type of flowers and arrangements that you would like. A good floral decorator will be very creative and stay within your budget, no matter how large or small. If you are holding the party in a marquee, discuss the colour of fabrics you will use and have a sample of the lining available. Remember that flowers must complement the style and colours used for table settings and interiors.

PRACTICALLY SPEAKING

WHILE TALL LUXURIANT ARRANGEMENTS ARE FASHIONABLE ON A TABLE, YOUR GUESTS WILL BE HAPPIER IF THEY CAN SEE TO TALK TO THE PERSON SEATED OPPOSITE.

party. The very reliable and flamboyant gerbera looks stunning in a single vase or try an assortment grouped in a few narrow vases for a colourful effect. A wonderful, and inexpensive, idea of Simon Lycett's for displaying gerberas is to wind colourful pipe cleaners around the stems and group them in the centre of the table – they look like

they are on springs! For flowers with bare or unattractive stems, glass cube vases are very versatile. Fill them with gravel or small stones to hide the stems, add water, then arrange your chosen flowers or plants. Aside from the room in which the festivities are held, guests will also visit the bathroom so think of adorning this with

During the last decade, candles have once again come into their own. Who cannot recall the joy of lighting candles during a power cut and seeing pools of glowing light transform the room?

candlelight

In the 1980s I worked with the floral designer Ken Turner and found using candles within displays an education in the romance of candlelight for parties. Today candles are available in many styles and colours, with a vast range of pretty containers. The effects that can be created are almost infinite – but it was Ken who first lit the way!

A NECESSARY NOTE OF CAUTION
REMEMBER NEVER TO LEAVE CANDLES UNATTENDED, ESPECIALLY INDOORS.

Candlelit Dinners
When planning your party, consider using candles to light rooms and tables. Their flickering light dances over table settings and interiors to give a warm, sensuous and magical atmosphere. For formal dinners, long candles in tall candlesticks with small shades on top look wonderfully elegant. They cast a warm glow over the table, creating reflections on the silver and glassware and bringing them to life.

CREATING A CENTREPIECE
FOR AN ENCHANTING FOCAL POINT, GROUP CANDLES IN VARIOUS SHAPES, SIZES AND COLOURS IN THE CENTRE OF THE TABLE.

Scents of Occasion
For a dinner party, it is best not to use heavily scented candles on the table as they will interfere with delicious food smells. On the other hand, lighting scented candles does helps to neutralize any tobacco smells if you have smokers at a party. Scented candles also make a world of difference in a marquee, since they can complement the fragrance of flowers and removing the musty smell that sometimes pervades a tent.

Clever Candleholders
Ideal candleholders can be made by cutting patterns in hollowed-out fruit and vegetables. Try with oranges, lemons, apples, artichokes, pumpkins

or squashes. Such candleholders will add wit and humour to a table or terrace. Other decorative options include wrapping thick pillar candles with sheets of sushi seaweed secured with raffia or pins, or placing small candles in your favourite shells or inside hollowed-out coconut shells. At Christmas, surround candles with cinnamon sticks tied in place with gold cord. For a soft, feminine effect, wrap candles with paper doilies tied with ribbon. Alternatively, to create a tropical look, cut snake grass into lengths and tie it around candles using thick garden twine. For further impact, make holders from thick bamboo cut into varying lengths to surround the bases of tall candles.

THEATRICAL EFFECTS

To create a sense of drama, stand tall, wrought-iron candelabras in corners of the room or on tables. (Use only non-drip candles, and keep them away from draughts.)

Outdoor Lighting

Using candles along paths and drives is a wonderful way of welcoming guests. We place thick pillar candles inside brown paper bags filled with fine builder's sand to light the way. Or, on a summer's evening, hang lanterns from trees. These are easy to make from tin cans in which you pierce holes to form a pattern of perforations. Place a night light inside each one, attach loops of wire to the tops and hang them from trees and shrubs to create areas of glowing light in the garden.

Extra-Special Night Lights

When using night lights in glass holders, try wrapping the holders with pretty leaves, flower petals, grasses or herbs. Or spray the holders with glue so that you can decorate them with nuts, spices, and dried lemon and orange slices. To create lively splashes of colour, wrap cellophane around the holders. For table settings, place cards tied around night lights look very pretty.

Flowers and candles bring a touch of enchantment to table settings. Cover uninteresting tables with attractive cloths that you already have at home. Look in cupboards and drawers for interesting fabric items such as a pretty sheet, blanket or rug if you are short of ideas – it is surprising how good these can look.

table settings

Gather together your favourite pieces of china and glassware and arrange them on the table to see the effect. If you have a long table use lengths of fabric as a runner down the centre, or along the sides to replace traditional place mats. You could take the theme further by tying napkins with fabric strips to match the tablecloth or runner. Napkins can be cut in any shape or size from matching or contrasting fabrics. Other options for improvised napkins include scrim, jacquard tea towels, or scarves – let your imagination run riot (see page 57 for more ideas). Large tropical leaves, such as banana leaves, can replace place mats.

PLACE CARDS

ONE FUN WAY TO PERSONALIZE YOUR TABLE IS TO PREPARE PLACE NAMES FOR EACH GUEST SO THEY KNOW WHERE THEY ARE SITTING. KEEP IT LEGIBLE AND YOU CAN BE AS ORIGINAL AS YOU LIKE – WRITE NAMES ON LUGGAGE LABELS, GLOSSY LEAVES, MASKS, BALLOONS OR PIECES OF PAPER TUCKED NEATLY INTO FOLDED NAPKINS.

Ringing the Changes

Sometimes when entertaining informally, I get inspired to do something out of the ordinary with my table setting – some ideas take very little effort (and can be surprisingly practical). Why not use different china, glassware and cutlery for each course. If you need extra linen or tableware, ask friends if they could lend items that will match your theme. In place of flower arrangements on dining tables, piles of smooth pebbles with tiny nightlights look delightful and create a soothing mood. In winter, make piles of spices such as star anise, cinnamon and cloves, placing nightlights inside hollowed-out oranges. For an autumn theme, fill bowls with polished horse chestnuts, some still in their prickly, citrus-green shells, and golden leaves.

Edible Decorations

Baskets of vegetables and herbs or figs and whole or halved pomegranates look stunning or, in summer, pile glowing, deep-red cherries in bowls. Alternatively, bowls of sweets in a myriad of colours, shapes and sizes look fun and attractive. Salt and pepper can be presented in an assortment of interesting containers, from shells and tiny flowerpots to large wooden bowls and hollowed-out miniature vegetables. Butter can be rolled into balls, mixed with herbs if desired, and placed on edible leaves or small, round glass coasters, or smoothed into coloured-glass nightlight holders. On buffet tables use fruits and vegetable decorations to emphasize the food you are serving. Tall glass vases filled with lemons and limes enhance bars greatly. Hollowed-out pumpkins make enchanting natural holders for food; warm them in the oven for hot food. Banana leaves look stunning shaped into serving bowls, but do not use them for liquid food as they will leak. I also love disguising serving bowls inside baskets.

ORIENTAL SETTING

MATCH YOUR TABLE SETTING TO YOUR FOOD – AT AN ORIENTAL MEAL SUBSTITUTE CHOPSTICKS AND RICE BOWLS FOR CUTLERY AND PLATES AND PLACE SAUCERS OF SOY AND CHILLI SAUCE ALONG THE TABLE.

formal dining

For a large, formal dinner party, display table numbers, letters or names on stands so that guests can identify their table. If you are theming your party, you can have fun naming the tables and designing the name cards. We arranged a 4th July party for which each table was named after an American state and the name cards on the tables were shaped like the state they identified.

You may have a friend or relative who has wonderful handwriting, or wish to engage the services of a calligrapher to write the cards. Ask how long they will take to complete the job and, as for the printing of invitations, allow for this in the time plan for the party. Supply the correct information for guests' names. A copy of your guest list is useful. Remember to give guests their full names, not simply 'Mr and Mrs William Smith' – give Mrs Smith's name. The style of place cards and menus should complement that of the invitations.

A STEP TOO FAR
NEVER THEME FOOD COLOURS TO MATCH THE TABLEWARE AND LINEN. DO YOU REALLY WANT TO EAT PURPLE FOOD OFF A TABLE SET WITH PURPLE TABLEWARE AND DECORATIONS? I KNOW I WOULD NOT!

Successful Seating
Seating cards are essential for large parties. Write the guest's name on a small envelope and place a card inside indicating the table where they are seated. Arrange the seating cards on a reception table or counter in alphabetical order so that, as guests arrive, they are given or pick up their own card. In this way, guests can keep their card in a pocket or bag to refer to and there is no crowding around seating plans causing congestion at entrances. Giving out seating cards also provides a good guide to the number of guests that have arrived. If you need to make any last-minute changes to the seating plan, nobody will be the wiser if you write some new seating cards, whereas changing names on seating plans can look a mess.

ON THE MENU
FOR A FUN TALKING POINT AT THE START OF THE MEAL, GIVE YOUR GUESTS A MENU WRITTEN WITH GOLD OR SILVER MARKER PEN ON BRIGHTLY COLOURED, THICK CARD.

Menus
When arranging menus for the tables allow one between two guests. If it is a very special occasion, give the date and, if appropriate, the hosts' names or the name of the person that the celebration is for. If grace is being said, the name of the person saying grace should be included. Other menu information that can be included is the wines to be served, food courses, including coffee, and the speeches (with names of speakers).

classic elegance

To create an elegant and opulent table setting for a truly formal dinner, it helps to stick to a fairly simple scheme based on classical colours and styles. Here, on top of a beautiful white Italian linen tablecloth the fine gold and white china is picked out by the sparkling gilt-tinged crystal glasses and the rich gold napkin rings. These rings can be made very easily with tassels and cord from any fabric shop, and for your own fabulous fine linen tablecloth to use again and again, just edge good quality linen sheets with runners of lace. To echo the gleam of the polished silverware, you can offer all sorts of accoutrements for the traditional dinner table such as silver salt cellars and pepper pots, candles and beakers. Any manner of personal touches may be added to suit the mood of the occasion – the gorgeous full-blown roses in this case offer glorious luxury and romance while, to me, the wistful young boy gazing into the salt (below) injects a mischievous sense of humour. Once the candles are lit you can be sure that a table like this will positively shine.

contemporary chic

There are times for a less formal occasion when you can create a setting made up of very individual place settings. A genuinely contemporary table need follow no rules and you can achieve a fantastic explosion of pattern, style or colour – the choice is endless. It is easy to mix and match plates and cutlery and you'll find that with just a little care for the juxtaposition of colours you will still achieve a brilliantly coherent setting.

Wooden handles of inexpensive cutlery can be dipped in paint and then you can have great fun painting your own designs or a single-colour wash on the plates and bowls with ceramic paints. Why not get each of your guests to design their own plate – it is easy to arrange. Plates lined with tropical leaves or bowls adorned with a single flower will ensure each guest feels his or her place is special.

mostly moroccan

Sometimes you may want to do something a little bit different with your table setting. This table shows how, with a little thought to the theme and style of your party you can create a stunningly evocative table that can become a talking point in itself.

Inspired by the wonderful flavours and colours of Djery's Moroccan food on page 100 we have chosen here to recreate the vibrant originality of North African eating. Blue and green tiles on the floor replace the traditional table, and plump cushions make a comfortable alternative to chairs. If you are unwilling to eat off the floor, then a low coffee table could be just as effective.

Colourful Moroccan plates and tea glasses can be hired, but are worth purchasing since they are beautiful and original enough to use when serving any food or drink. If serving Moroccan food, then you could also provide small clay bowls on the table filled with appropriate 'extras' – not just salt and pepper but also almonds, prunes, olives and of course harissa. Finally, a few rose petals scattered around the table or in a bowl on the table can be a sensuous touch of decadence.

new ways with napkins

Napkins can change the look of your table setting in almost an instant to create a formal or informal, witty, colourful or even daring statement. To enliven your table settings and complement different themes, try some of the following ideas: tie napkins with ribbons, raffia, lengths of ivy, skeins of hops, gold cord with a fake jewel or heavy cord in a nautical knot or decide on a style and vary it slightly for each.

There are many types of napkin to buy or make yourself, including traditional linen napkins with hemstitched borders, antique giant French damask napkins, scarves, scrim, tea towels, bandanas, or even pieces of fabric trimmed into shape with pinking shears. You can fold napkins into elegant shapes such as fans or tall cones, drape them or tie them in one of the ways suggested

above, stand them in glasses or make huge piles of bright colours. Whatever you do, the secret of success is to ensure that they are in keeping with the table setting.

HAPPY BIRTHDAY
MAKE A BIRTHDAY LUNCH OR DINNER EXTRA SPECIAL BY FOLDING THE NAPKINS TO LOOK LIKE PRESENTS.

Selecting the right entertainment for your party will set the mood for the night. The choice depends on your budget and the style of your party – you may want to enhance a relaxed atmosphere or create an up-beat mood that could be witty and even a little daring, requiring your guests to enter into the party spirit.

it's showtime

Whether it is playing charades or booking a 14-piece dance band with singers to supply the music at a grand dance or wedding, consider what is appropriate to your party. If you are looking for music there is much on offer, from a string quartet, jazz trio, wind quintet, a pianist creating subtle background music or strolling players catching guests' attention to a lively disco. Musical quartets and pianists set the scene perfectly for larger drinks parties. If the room is small a quieter form of live music, such as a harpist, is recommended.

SETTING THE MOOD

WHEN I GIVE A DINNER PARTY, I CHOOSE THE CDs WITH CARE – JOLLY BUT NOT LOUD AS GUESTS ARRIVE, EBBING TO A QUIET CALM DURING DINNER. IT IS NEVER SO INTRUSIVE THAT GUESTS ARE UNABLE TO CONVERSE.

A Walk on the Wild Side

For table entertainment, magicians are popular, as are caricaturists, palm readers and even face painters. This style of entertainment also helps to break the ice. To make a large event even more memorable, look-alikes to the famous are very amusing and circus performers such as jugglers, fire-eaters, hot-coal walkers and stilt walkers can greet your guests on arrival. A display by tango or salsa dancers, with the great rhythm of the music, is ideal for persuading guests on to the dance floor.

Disco Dancing

Choosing a disco is just as important as selecting a live band. The disc jockey needs to be experienced enough to judge the mood of the party. Discuss the music that you would like carefully and be prepared to accept advice – disc jockeys know the popular music that makes parties go with a swing and keeps guests dancing through the evening. The best means of finding a good disco and disc jockey is always personal recommendation, although it may take some time, energy and research. When planning a large party, such as a wedding or dance, start your search as soon as you have finalized the date and the party venue. A venue's events manager should help – seeing a more acts than most, they are in a unique position to offer advice.

Finding a Band

In your search for a band or any forms of other entertainment, you could consult an entertainment agency who can suit your budget and taste. When considering a band, to see how they present and hear their style of music, try to see them performing, or ask if they have a demo tape or video. Discuss your taste in music and with the bandleader – check that your favourite tunes are easy to dance to. Most bands and entertainers have a list of past customers and it is a good idea to contact one to confirm your choice.

Asking the Right Questions

You will be asked to sign a contract, so make sure that you have discussed every detail and check that you know the answers to the following questions:
• What time does the band start and finish playing?
• What time do they intend to set up?
• Will they require a sound check? If so, when? (Not in the middle of pre-dinner drinks!)
• How long is each set, when are the breaks and how long will they last?
• Can the music continue during the breaks with just a few band members playing, or music from a disco or stereo?
• How much will it cost to extend the entertainment beyond the agreed time?
• Are the singer or singers you have chosen named in the contract with the number of band members?
• Does the band require a sound system and, if so, who supplies this?
• Who decides on the playlist and can you order the songs to encourage people on to the dance floor?

Looking After Entertainers

Most entertainers will require plenty of soft drinks and food, as well as an area to change in. Venues normally have a designated space for this. If the party is in a marquee, arrange for entertainers to have the use of a small area behind the stage. At home, set aside a room large enough for a few people and specify whether smoking is allowed.

The etiquette of party giving and going can send terror into the strongest hearts. For a party to run smoothly and for an atmosphere of conviviality to remain throughout, it helps for host and guests to bear in mind some basic rules of etiquette and good manners. These are some of the more common dilemmas.

party etiquette

Duties as a Host

Your main duty is to give your guests a relaxed and enjoyable party. Some guests will arrive early and, if you have not finished in the kitchen, invite them to join you, give them a drink and finish those last-minute jobs with relaxed conversation. You must be confident, never apologize for yourself, the food or draw attention to guests who do not drink alcohol or are vegetarian. Never drink too much before guests have arrived or before you finish cooking – you need to be in control. If you appear relaxed and confident, then this will rub off on your guests.

Arriving Late

If you are delayed when a guest, always try to inform your host and give an indication of your expected arrival time. As a host, if you know the guest is going to arrive later than the time you planned to serve dinner, I suggest you carry on with your original time plan – people are very understanding.

Making Introductions

We can all recall times when we have walked into a room of strangers and discovered that there is no one to introduce us to other guests. I know some people who have left parties because they have felt excluded. As a host, the importance of introducing your guests to each other cannot be

underestimated. At a large party, make your introductions early. Use your ingenuity to introduce people with common interests and remember which guests have situations, friends or relatives in common. Start your party near to the front door so that you can greet each guest and facilitate introductions. A good host is able to put guests at their ease by being a good listener and supplying relaxed and amusing conversation. If you have one guest who does not know many people, wait for an appropriate break in conversation and introduce them to a group, staying for a while to make sure that he or she feels comfortable. If you see that a guest is overwhelmed by someone and feeling trapped in an unwelcome situation – you may receive pleading 'help me' looks – wait for an appropriate moment to rescue them by saying something such as 'You must come and say hello to George. He has been asking if you have arrived.'

Awkward Silences

It is the duty of the host to overcome those moments of awkward silence when a few seconds can feel like hours. A useful 'trick' is to remember an interesting item of news that could be of common interest to one or more of your guests. Alternatively, suggest a suitable, reasonably light-hearted subject, directing it back to a guest to carry on.

Including Children

If are totally against having children at your party I advise you to write on the invitation that you are unable to accommodate children. If you are inviting them, it is best to arrange some form of entertainment – perhaps a face painter, clown or magician. Alternatively, organize some form of child minding. I am strongly of the opinion that no special arrangements should be made for children's food. Just serve the same as you do for the adults only on a smaller scale. Also, be warned – people often tell me that their teenage children can help serve the food or do extra tasks, but in 18 years' party giving I have rarely found young teenagers to be really willing to help. If you are inviting teenagers, make sure that they have some friends to socialize with – they will probably use another room.

REMEMBERING WHO

I CONFESS THAT I AM NOT VERY GOOD AT REMEMBERING NAMES. I CAN TRY SEVERAL DIFFERENT NAMES AND STILL NOT HAPPEN UPON THE RIGHT ONE. MY TRICK IS TO SAY, SIMPLY, 'IT IS RATHER NOISY IN HERE AND I DID NOT QUITE CATCH YOUR NAME.'

Replying to Invitations

Invitations should be replied to as soon as you have checked your commitments. Do not put off replying until the host has to telephone you.

SAYING 'THANK YOU'

A HOST PUTS LOTS OF TIME INTO CREATING A MEMORABLE PARTY, SO SHOW YOUR APPRECIATION BY WRITING A 'THANK YOU' NOTE WITHIN THREE DAYS.

Drunken Guests

Dealing with drunken guests is probably one of a host's most difficult tasks. We know that some people have a tendency to drink just a little too much and your duty to your guests is to ensure that the intoxicated person is not a nuisance. Make sure that the person is not driving home – order them a taxi or perhaps offer a bed for the night. Try to be discreet when handling the problem – this is easier in a large crowd than at a smaller party.

The Smoking Dilemma

You can expect some of your guests to smoke and it may be impolite to tell them not to. Most smokers will ask if they can smoke so, if you feel very strongly, request that they smoke in the garden or on the terrace. If you allow them to smoke in the house, open a window, offer plenty of ashtrays and change them frequently. Scented candles help to neutralize the smell.

How Do I Ask My Guests to Leave?

For a dinner party, serve coffee in a separate area or room to encourage guests to move around. Reduce the amount of drink served and, if some people are still there at 3am, offer to start booking taxis. If all else fails say good night and go to bed! Even the hardiest party animal should take the hint. Our experience is that as soon as the bar closes guests depart very quickly, so my advice is, if you want guests to leave, stop offering drinks. (The reverse applies too – a steady supply of alcohol will ensure your party continues through to the small hours!)

food & drink

For a party, drinks require as much planning as the menu. Like the food, they need to be carefully thought out to echo the mood of the party. Think about how you will present them, whether you will need garnishes, what sort of glasses will be most appropriate and who is going to serve them.

the party spirit

Large Parties

Make sure that the bar is positioned in a convenient area that is easily accessible and will not become congested with guests. Protect the floor around it with a waterproof floor covering, taping it down to prevent anyone tripping over a corner or edge. Choose a table that is at least 2 metres (6 feet) long and 1 metre (3 feet) high. Cover it with a cloth to the ground as it is useful to be able to store spare glassware and ice bins under the table. If you are using an electric blender at the table for making cocktails, make sure that there is a supply of current to that area of the bar. Tape down the flex of the blender to prevent any accidents. If you do not want to hire glassware for a large number of guests, consider plastic glasses. These are now available in many wonderful shapes and colours, and most can be used many times.

Small and Informal Gatherings

Enliven the room by making the drinks table or bar look attractive. Cover the table or serving top with a pretty or exotic-looking cloth, and scout around your home to find an unusual and decorative container for the ice. Arrange the glasses in matching rows, each glass complementing the other. If serving fruit juices or fruit cocktails, pour them into jugs or jars and place a ladle next to them. It is a good idea to tie labels around the handles or lids, to

remember which is which, and to allow guests to serve themselves at any time. For an informal party, I like to use fun glasses with wonderful garnishes, such as stems tied with ribbons, ivy or raffia. If there are just a small number of guests, make fruit or herb ice cubes by adding pieces of fresh fruit or herb sprigs to the water in each compartment of the ice tray before freezing. These decorative ice cubes look particularly lovely in glasses of mineral water. For a summer party outdoors, half-fill a large terracotta pot or wooden barrel with ice and use to chill and serve bottled or canned beers. Place the beers on the ice and cover with more ice, leaving a few beers on top – guests will be able to help themselves.

What Drinks to Serve

Appropriate drinks to serve will depend on the style of party, with occasions varying from a formal champagne or cocktail reception to a more casual party with a choice of wines and soft drinks, a barbecue with beers and a bring-a-bottle party. It really depends on what you feel would work well for you. For example, you could serve pitchers of Bloody Marys and home made fruit coolers at a brunch party with great success. When budgeting, a good rule of thumb is to allow half the cost of the food as the budget for the drinks. The drinks you choose to serve should be within the budget you have allowed for.

Setting Up a Bar

Blender
Bottle opener
Cloth for mopping up spills
Cocktail shaker
Corkscrew (a good one)
Crushed ice
Cutting board and knife
Drink napkins to wrap around glasses
Ice bucket or bowl (one for ice cubes
    and one for crushed ice)
Ice cubes
Ice tongs, or spoon
Jugs, glass and metal
Long spoon
Olives
Slices or twists of lemon, lime and
    orange
Stirrers
Strainer
Straws
Tin opener

Cooling Drinks

To cool champagne, wines, beers and soft drinks, find a large waterproof container – such as a dustbin, a smart galvanized container, a plastic toy box, a large cool box or a half-wooden barrel. When using ice bins like these in the home, place inside a large rubbish bag to protect the floor from condensation. Put in enough ice to cover the bottom of the container, place the bottles in the ice bin and cover with ice. If you do not have enough ice fill the container

with cold water. Once the bottles are submerged they will quickly chill. For larger parties, I would suggest you use separate ice bins for champagne, wines, beers and soft drinks. To make serving guests quicker and easier, loosen the foil on champagne bottles and remove and replace the corks in white wine bottles. Place the drinks in the ice at least 2 hours before guests arrive.

For a dinner party, place the drinks that require chilling in the refrigerator 2 days before the party and turn the refrigerator to almost the coldest setting. Make your ice cubes at the same time, using trays or bags. You may find that once you have started the food preparations for the party that your refrigerator is not quite big enough to hold all the drink and the food. In the winter this is not a problem – drinks can easily be kept cold outside, but in the summer you may have to be a little more inventive. Fill a sink with cold water and ice for the drinks or be ruthless in removing items from the refrigerator that either are not needed for your party or will not deteriorate at room temperature. Remember the food hygiene rules however (see A Good Cook's Kitchen Guide page 79).

Quantity of Ice Required

For a cocktail party of 50 guests, the amount of ice required for cooling drinks and using in glasses is 4 x 13.6kg (30lb) bags. You can divide or multiply this number to assess quantities required for different numbers of guests. If the weather is very hot, add a further 2 bags.

Glamorous Glassware

There is a wonderful range of glassware available today, both to buy and for hire, ranging from classic to fun and even garish. The style you choose will depend on your taste and the type of party you are giving. It may well be worth hiring glassware as many hire companies have exciting ranges. The advantage of this, too, is that you can send back dirty glasses for a small extra charge.

Quantity of Glassware Required

When serving champagne, wine or cocktails at large drinks parties and buffets, allow for 2 glasses per person. Some of your guests will then go on to soft drinks so, in addition, allow for 2 glasses per person for soft drinks.

Quantity of Drink Required

FOR A COCKTAIL PARTY (2 HOURS)

Wine or champagne Allow half a bottle per person (to provide 2½ glasses each)
Cocktails Allow 3 glasses per person
Soft drinks, mineral water allow half a litre per person

FOR PRE-DINNER DRINKS

Wine or champagne Allow a third of a bottle per person (to provide 1½ glasses each)

FOR A DINNER PARTY

White wine Allow a third of a bottle per person
Red wine Allow half a bottle per person
Mineral water Allow a litre per person

I have chosen the cocktails and fresh-fruit drinks on the following pages for their enduring popularity – when we create a party with a cocktail bar, these are the most requested. You will also find that they are relatively easy to make up in jugs for large numbers.

In the recipes, I use freshly blended fruit juices. These will not give the bitter after-taste that prepared juices can, and the colours are much more vibrant. Most of the cocktails can be prepared in advance, then stored in the refrigerator or on ice. Pour the prepared cocktails into jugs or containers and label with hand-written stickers. Why not also make fun garnishes and look for interesting stirrers and straws to add to the party spirit?

coolest cocktails

Bellini

This delicious summer drink is made with fresh, ripe peaches, which give it its delightful colour. To be really authentic use white peaches. MAKES 10

12 ripe peaches, for 750ml
   (1½ pints) juice
1 bottle chilled semi-sweet, good sparkling
   white wine, or Prosecco

To remove the skins from the ripe peaches, first pour enough water to cover the peaches into a large pan and bring to the boil. Lower the heat, place the peaches in the water and count to 10. Remove them with a slotted spoon and place in a bowl of ice-cold water. Drain, then peel off the skins with a sharp knife. Cut the peaches in half, remove the stone and slice. Place the peach slices in a blender or food processor, and blend to a smooth purée. Strain over a bowl. Pour into a jug, then cover and refrigerate. Chill the sparkling wine for 1 day before serving. To serve, stir the peach juice and pour into a large jug. Add the sparkling white wine and stir until blended. Pour into elegant glasses.

Bloody Mary

This one is my recipe of several available, and definitely worth trying! MAKES A LARGE JUG

300ml (just under ½ pint) plain, pepper, chilli
   or lemon-flavoured vodka, placed in the
   freezer
500ml (1 pint) tomato juice
100ml (4fl oz) Clamato juice
juice of 4 limes
5g (¼ oz) celery salt
freshly ground black pepper to taste
pinch of sea salt & pinch of sugar
10 drops of West Indian pepper sauce, or
   20 drops of jalapeno Tabasco sauce
2 tbsp Worcestershire sauce
2 tsp freshly grated horseradish
ice cubes
long celery sticks & lime wedges to garnish

Mix together all the ingredients in a jug. Fill a tall glass with ice cubes, pour in the Bloody Mary, and garnish with a celery stick and a wedge of lime. If you prefer a hotter Bloody Mary, add more pepper sauce. To make a Virgin Bloody Mary, mix as above but omit the vodka.

BEST TOMATO JUICE

MAKE YOUR OWN TOMATO JUICE BY BLENDING FRESH TOMATOES IN A BLENDER, OR BUY A GOOD BRAND, TO ENSURE A REALLY GOOD BLOODY MARY THAT HITS THE SPOT INTENDED.

Winter Whisky Warmer

We made this delicious drink for a cocktail party on a freezing January night. It proved very popular, particularly as guests arrived in from the cold – what better way to warm up! MAKES 8

peel of 1 orange & 1 lemon
5 x 5cm (2.5in) cinnamon sticks
½ litre (about 1 pint) good Scotch whisky
100ml (4fl oz) lime juice
2 tbsp brown sugar
cinnamon sticks, to garnish

Peel the orange and lemon, place in an airtight container and refrigerate. Break the cinnamon sticks into small pieces. Place a stainless steel saucepan over a low heat and pour in the whisky. Add the lime juice, sugar, orange and lemon peels, and cinnamon sticks, and stir until the sugar has dissolved and the punch is warm. Do not bring to the boil as you will lose the alcohol. Pour into the punch bowl. Ladle the Warmer into a glass and garnish with a cinnamon stick.

PRESERVING PEELINGS

IF CONVENIENT, YOU CAN PEEL THE ORANGE AND LEMON 2 DAYS IN ADVANCE AND STORE THE PEEL IN AN AIRTIGHT CONTAINER IN THE REFRIGERATOR.

Bellini

West Indian Rum Punch

My friend, Steve Camacho, makes the best rum punch I have ever tasted. It takes time to mature but it is well worth the wait! MAKES 12

600ml (1¼ pints) light brown rum, such as
    Mount Gay or Cavalier
200ml (7fl oz) freshly squeezed lime juice
    (about 12 limes)
400ml (14fl oz) sugar syrup made with
    Demerara sugar or any light brown sugar
    (see page 74)
freshly grated nutmeg
Angostura bitters
ice cubes
lime, to garnish

Mix the essential first 3 ingredients in a large jug, then add the nutmeg. Cover and refrigerate for 36 hours. Add the bitters to the punch and stir. Fill the glasses with ice and pour in the punch. Garnish with a slice of lime. Now put your feet up and enjoy!

CARIBBEAN COCKTAILS

RUM IS A STAPLE INGREDIENT IN THE COCKTAILS OF THE CARIBBEAN AND EACH ISLAND HAS ITS OWN METHOD FOR MAKING A PUNCH. THESE VARY BUT THE GENERAL RULE OF MEASUREMENTS IS 1 OF SOUR, 2 OF SWEET, 3 OF STRONG AND 4 OF WEAK (A GLASS TOPPED UP WITH ICE).

Champagne Cocktail

I love the French term *eau de vie* (water of life) for fruit-distilled alcohol. All variations combine well with champagne to make unusual champagne cocktails. Experiment, using Kirsch, Poire William, Mirabelle or Fraise. 1 BOTTLE OF CHAMPAGNE MAKES 5 GLASSES

small sugar lump
Eau de Vie de Framboise
chilled champagne

Place a sugar lump in a tall, elegant champagne flute, then cover with the Eau de Vie, top up with champagne and serve.

West Indian Rum Punch

DAMPING DOWN

ABOUT 30 MINUTES BEFORE IT IS REQUIRED POUR A LITTLE CHAMPAGNE INTO THE GLASS. THEN WHEN YOU POUR THE CHAMPAGNE (OR OTHER SPARKLING DRINK), IT WILL NOT OVERFLOW THE GLASS.

Pina Colada

The most famous of all cocktails, made well it should be smooth and easy to drink – sometimes too easy! If possible, use fresh pineapple. Have fun serving the drinks in non-traditional 'glasses'. MAKES 16

800ml (just under 1 pint) rum, preferably a
    white rum such as Bacardi
1.6 litres (2¾ pints) fresh pineapple juice
750ml (1¼ pints`) coconut cream
crushed ice
toasted coconut curls, to garnish (see
    page 126)

Place all the ingredients in a blender, blend for about 10 seconds, add a handful of crushed ice, then blend for 5 seconds more. Pour into glasses or containers such as hollowed out baby pineapples or coconuts; garnish with coconut curls and serve with straws.

Watermelon Margarita

A drink that looks wonderfully decorative, and is delicious made with either tequila or vodka. For a refreshing soft drink, you can omit the tequila. MAKES 20

1 3.5kg (7lb 6oz) ripe, seedless
   watermelon, rind removed & cut into
   pieces, for 2 litres (3 pints) juice
10 juicy limes
salt
crushed ice, or ice cubes
2 tbsp ginger cordial
750ml (1½ pints) tequila or vodka
wedges of watermelon or slices of lime,
   to garnish

If you cannot find seedless watermelon, remove the seeds before blending. (Unfortunately there is no easy way to do this. I advise slicing the watermelon into manageable triangles and then, with the point of a sharp knife, picking out as many as you can. You could also gently 'shave' the most 'pip-dense' areas – this can unlodge quite a few. Place the pieces of watermelon in a blender or food processor, and blend well. Pour into a jug. Cut the limes in half and squeeze out the juice, strain, then add to the watermelon juice. Refrigerate. Salt the rim of the glasses, then half-fill with crushed ice or ice cubes. Add the ginger cordial and tequila to the juice, stir, and pour into the glasses. Garnish with a wedge of watermelon or a slice of lime. The watermelon margarita can be mixed and placed in the refrigerator, or on ice, about 2 hours before serving.

TO SALT THE RIM OF THE GLASS

THIS IS THE REV. FRANK MERCURIO'S FOOLPROOF METHOD. POUR LIME OR LEMON JUICE ONTO A PLATE, THEN COVER WITH AN UNFOLDED TEA TOWEL. SPRINKLE ENOUGH FINE SALT OVER A SECOND PLATE TO COVER IT. MOISTEN THE RIM OF EACH GLASS ON THE TEA TOWEL, THEN DIP AND TWIST BRIEFLY IN THE SALT.

Strawberry Daiquiri

Strawberry Daiquiri

The first frozen Daiquiri was created in Cuba early this century. Always use fresh strawberries for this drink, and serve in large cocktail glasses with a straw to slurp it up. If you want to garnish it, a slice of strawberry and and some fresh mint, look and taste wonderful. MAKES 7

150ml (5½fl oz) light rum
50ml (2oz) strawberry liqueur
2 dssp fresh lime juice
12 large strawberries
5 handfuls of crushed ice
strawberries & mint to garnish

Place the rum, liqueur, lime juice and strawberries in a blender and blend for about 10 seconds, then add the crushed ice and blend for a further 4 seconds. Pour into glasses, garnish and serve with straws. Alternatively, blend all the ingredients but omit the crushed ice, then pour into a jug or container. Be careful not to overblend the strawberries as you want to retain a certain amount of texture in the drink. Store in the refrigerator, or on ice, for a least 2 hours before serving. Stir well, then fill glasses with crushed ice and pour in the drink. Garnish with strawberries and mint and add straws.

Watermelon Margarita

Classic Margarita

One of the simplest and most refreshing of all cocktails, it is no wonder that the Classic Margarita is one of the all-time favourites. MAKES 25

fine salt for the rims of glasses
1 litre (1¾ pints) tequila
½ litre (18fl oz) triple sec
1 litre (1¾ pints) fresh lime juice
ice cubes
lime wedges, to garnish

FROZEN MARGARITA

FOR A FROZEN MARGARITA, BLEND ALL THE INGREDIENTS WITH CRUSHED ICE IN A BLENDER. THE RESULT IS SIMPLY THE MOST PERFECT COCKTAIL FOR A SUMMER'S DAY — SALT IN THIS CASE IS NOT NECESSARY.

Salt the rims of the glasses (see page 70). Pour the tequila, triple sec and lime juice into a jug or container and stir. Place in the refrigerator, or on ice, at least 2 hours before serving. To serve, fill medium-sized glasses with ice cubes, pour in the drink and garnish with wedges of lime.

Mai Tai

I first tasted this mouthwatering cocktail in Hawaii – its wonderfully exotic flavour will transport you to the tropics. It is also deceptively alcoholic – a fact the sweetness covers up. MAKES 6

200ml (7fl oz) dark rum
200ml (7fl oz) golden rum
100ml (3½fl oz) triple sec
100ml (3½fl oz) orange-flavoured liqueur
100ml (3½fl oz) almond-flavoured syrup
juice of 4 limes
1 dash of Grenadine
ice cubes
orange slices, to garnish

Pour all the ingredients into a shaker and shake for about 10 seconds, then strain into the glasses. Add ice cubes, stirrers and straws, then garnish with the orange slices.

Moscow Mule

A combination of lime and ginger beer makes this drink extremely refreshing, and it is one of my favourites. It is actually an excellent blend to drink without the alcohol – the ginger beer gives it that essential bite. MAKES 18

750ml (24fl oz) vodka
375ml (12fl oz) fresh lime juice
1.5 litres (just under 2 pints) Old Jamaican ginger beer
ice cubes
lime wedges to garnish

Mix the ingredients in a large container and pour into jugs. Serve in tall glasses filled with ice, add a stirrer and garnish with a wedge of lime. All the ingredients, apart from the ginger beer, can be mixed at least 2 hours before serving, then placed in the refrigerator or on ice.

Long Island Iced Tea

An innocent-sounding name for a delicious mixture of alcoholic drinks, this is one of the most frequently requested cocktails. Beware though – one glass is usually enough! MAKES 14

200ml (7fl oz) Bacardi or white rum
200ml (7fl oz) gin
200ml (7fl oz) vodka
200ml (7fl oz) Cointreau
200ml (7fl oz) tequila, preferably gold label
200ml (7fl oz) lime juice
1 litre (just under 2 pints) cola
ice cubes
lime wedges to garnish

Pour the rum, gin, vodka, Cointreau and tequila into a jug or container. Place in the refrigerator, or over ice, for at least 2 hours before you plan to serve the drink. Then, when ready, pour the lime juice and cola into the blend of alcohols and stir. Pour into tall glasses filled with ice cubes, then add stirrers and straws and garnish with lime.

Cosmopolitan

This popular drink looks most stylish served in classic cocktail glasses. Before serving, chill the glasses as well as the vodka in the freezer. MAKES 16

500ml (18oz) vodka
100ml (3½oz) Cointreau
100ml (3½oz) cranberry juice
100ml (3½oz) fresh lime juice
twists of lime, to garnish

Pour all the ingredients, except for the twists of lime, into a jug or container and stir well. Place in the refrigerator, or on ice, at least 2 hours before serving. To serve, pour into iced cocktail glasses and add a delicate twist of lime into each glass.

Terry's Dry Martini

A classic cocktail, the Dry Martini is always in great demand. The best are made by first chilling the gin and glasses in the freezer. Stir or shake to mix – as demonstrated by James Bond – or pour directly into chilled glasses. Garnish with a twist of lemon. If you prefer your Dry Martini made with vodka, choose a good Polish brand. MAKES 10

900ml (30fl oz) gin
1 tsp dry vermouth
10 twists of lemon, to garnish

Pour the gin into a jug, then add the vermouth. Stir and place in the freezer at least 2 hours before serving. Pour into classic chilled cocktail glasses and finish with a twist of lemon.

VERMOUTH VARIATION

FOR JUST A HINT OF VERMOUTH IN YOUR MARTINI, MAKE IT IN A COCKTAIL SHAKER. SHAKE ICE AND VERMOUTH TOGETHER WELL THEN STRAIN OUT THE VERMOUTH, PLACING A SLOTTED SPOON OVER THE TOP OF THE SHAKER. NOW ADD THE GIN TO THE SHAKER, SHAKE VIGOROUSLY AND POUR THE FLAVOURED GIN INTO CHILLED GLASSES.

Singapore Sling

The origins of this famous cocktail lie in Raffles Hotel, Singapore. Its bright orange colour is testament to the fact that it was originally intended as a woman's drink. Today, however, it is very definitely a drink enjoyed by all. MAKES 12

200ml (7fl oz) gin
200ml (7fl oz) cherry brandy
100ml (3½fl oz) cointreau
100ml (3½fl oz) lemon or lime juice
600ml (1 pint) fresh orange juice
600ml (1 pint) fresh pineapple juice
ice cubes
pineapple slices and cherries, to garnish

Place all the ingredients in a shaker and shake for about 10 seconds. Strain into tall glasses filled with ice cubes. Add stirrers and straws, and garnish with pineapple slices and cherries. Alternatively, place all the ingredients in a container, omitting the ice, and stir. Cover and place in the refrigerator.

BRAZILIAN NIGHTS

FOR THE AUTHENTIC BRAZILIAN EXPERIENCE (SEE RIGHT), SEARCH OUT REAL BRAZILIAN RUM — IT HAS A UNIQUELY PIQUANT FLAVOUR — AND SERVE YOUR CAIPIRINHA VERY COLD ON A VERY HOT NIGHT. THEN PARTY UNTIL DAWN!

Caipirinha

A Brazilian speciality, this cocktail is my editor's favourite and is easy to make. Since it must be mixed in the glass, the quantities given are for an individual drink. MAKES 1

1 fresh lime, skin well washed, then cut into
   small segments
1½ tsp caster sugar
50ml (2fl oz) Brazilian rum

Place the lime segments and sugar in an old-fashioned glass. Crush the lime with a spoon to release the juice and stir to dissolve the sugar. Fill the glass with ice, add the rum and stir.

fresh fruit drinks

Sugar Syrup

Most of these fruit drinks, and some of the cocktails, require sugar syrup – you can, if necessary, use a low-calorie sugar substitute. MAKES 1 LITRE (1¾ PINTS)

1 litre (1¾ pints) water
1kg (2¼lb) caster sugar

Place the water and sugar in a saucepan and bring to the boil. Reduce the heat and stir until all the sugar is dissolved, then remove from the heat and allow to cool. Pour into a clean container, cover and refrigerate. Sugar syrup will last for a long time chilled.

Watermelon & Lime Cooler

Mexico is known for its fruit coolers – this one reminds me of Mexico's jewel-like colours. MAKES 12

2 litres (3½ pints) watermelon juice
250ml (9fl oz) fresh lime juice
100ml (3½fl oz) sugar syrup
ice cubes
lime wedge to garnish
melon & lime slices & of mint to garnish

Pour the watermelon juice into a jug or large container, add the lime juice and sugar syrup, then stir well. Fill the glasses with ice, pour in the coolade. Garnish with mint and a slice of melon.

Raspberry & Redcurrant Frappé

Melon, Apple & Lime Coolade

This fresh combination of flavours makes a truly mouthwatering drink. MAKES 6

2 ripe green melons, sliced, seeds & skin removed, cut into small cubes
300ml (½ pint) fresh apple juice, a sharp variety
2 tbsp lime and ginger cordial
ice cubes
melon & lime slices & sprigs of mint to garnish

Place the melon in a blender and process until smooth, then pass through a sieve. Pour the melon juice into a large jug, add the apple juice and the lime and ginger cordial, then stir well. Cover and refrigerate. Fill glasses with ice and pour in the coolade. Garnish with a melon or lime slice, and a sprig of mint.

Raspberry & Redcurrant Frappé

When raspberries and redcurrants are plentiful, this makes a very refreshing soft drink. MAKES 6

sugar syrup to taste
2kg (4lb 8oz) raspberries, fresh or frozen
600g (1lb 5oz) redcurrants with stalks removed
ice cubes
300ml (½ pint) mineral water
sprigs of raspberries, redcurrants, mint, basil or lemon-balm to garnish

Make the sugar syrup and chill. Place the raspberries in a blender and blend until smooth. Pour this purée into a fine sieve, then use a ladle to press the juice through it until only the seeds remain; repeat with the redcurrants, blending in the same way. Pour into a jug and refrigerate. Fill glasses with ice. Add the mineral water and sugar syrup to the frappé and garnish with fruit or herbs.

Banana & Coconut Sunset

I first tried this soft, creamy drink in the Caribbean, sitting by the sea watching the sun go down and nibbling toasted coconut curls. (They seemed so perfect for the drink that I added them to my recipe.) For me, the splash of grenadine at the top represents the sun setting through the clouds. MAKES 12

6 ripe bananas
1.2 litres (2¼ pints) fresh pineapple juice.
500ml (18 fl oz) coconut milk
ice cubes
splash of grenadine
toasted coconut curls (see page 126)

Process the bananas, pineapple juice and coconut milk in a blender until smooth. Pour into a tall glass filled with ice, pour a little grenadine on top and sprinkle with coconut curls.

FREEZING FRUIT

YOU CAN MAKE THE FRUIT PURÉES WHILE FRESH FRUIT IS IN SEASON AND FREEZE FOR LATER, BUT DO NOT REFREEZE IF USING FROZEN FRUITS.

Banana & Coconut Sunset

Mango & Passion Fruit Cooler

For me, the mango is a favourite fruit. I had an aunt who used to say that the only way to eat a ripe mango is sitting in the bath, or in the sea. It can be quite messy, but there is no need for anyone to sit in the bath or sea to enjoy this drink. Sweet and luxurious, it captures beautifully the taste of the tropics. MAKES 6

4 ripe mangoes, skinned & the flesh cut
  away from the stone
16 ripe passion fruits, flesh scraped away
from the husks & strained to remove the
  seeds
300ml (½ pint) mineral water
sugar syrup to taste
crushed ice or ice cubes
mango slices to garnish

Blend the mango flesh and strain the juice into a jug. Then blend the passion fruit, and strain into the jug of mango juice. Add mineral water and sugar syrup to taste; stir well. Cover and refrigerate. Pour into glasses filled with ice and garnish each with a mango slice.

Paw Paw & Pineapple Cooler

This is a very refreshing drink – if the pineapple juice is a little sharp, add some sugar syrup. MAKES 7

2 paw paws, each weighing about 450g
  (1lb), skinned, deseeded & chopped
  (makes about ½ litre/1 pint)
½ litre (1 pint) fresh pineapple juice
200ml (7fl oz) mineral water
ice cubes
pineapple slices, to garnish

Process the paw paw in a blender until smooth, then pass through a sieve and pour into a jug. Add the pineapple juice and water; stir well. Cover and refrigerate. Fill the glasses with ice, pour in the fruit cooler, and garnish with the pineapple slices on the sides of the glasses.

FRESH FRUIT DRINKS

WITH THE EXCEPTION OF THE BANANA & COCONUT SUNSET, WHICH SHOULD NOT BE MADE MORE THAN 2 HOURS AHEAD, ALL THESE DRINKS CAN BE PREPARED A DAY IN ADVANCE AND THEN CHILLED.

Mango & Passion Fruit Cooler

When you know how many guests to expect and have read the section on Menu Planning (page 32), you need to address the cooking and preparation of the food in a practical manner. Think about the people invited. Are they young or old? Will there be children? Are there special dietary requirements or dislikes?

practical cooking

It's All in the Preparation

All the menus in this book are planned to give you time to be a host as well as the chef. Most can be prepared in advance, with only a little assembling required before serving. Follow the timing guides and you will be able to entertain with great confidence. The guides give the maximum time in advance you can prepare each element of the meal – watch out for marinading however, because this ideally does need to be done at the time specified and not on the day. (If you are very rushed, most marinades will produce a good enough flavour after 2 hours.)

Golden Rules

Give yourself time to read through the recipes before preparing them to familiarize yourself with what is required. I would not advise you to cook any meal for a party that you have not tried before. Friends and family will be more than happy for you to practise on them, and may also be good critics. If your timing begins to slip a little on the day do not worry, just carry on; if your guests see that you are anxious it will make them feel uncomfortable whereas no-one minds food served a little later than expected in a relaxed atmosphere.

Food Quantities

The numbers each recipe or menu serves have been worked out on the basis of the average numbers at each sort of party – therefore the dinner and supper menus serve 10 guests while each cocktail food recipe makes enough for 30. With twice or half the number of guests, doubling or halving the recipes will work. Any more or less and you should refer to the chart on food quantities (page 79). When arranging food for buffets using a variety of dishes you may not be confident as to whether there will be the right amount. In this case, train yourself to imagine an amount of 20 smallish portions – you will soon become expert at it.

MAKING THE MOST OF THE MENUS

THE MENUS ARE DESIGNED TO GIVE A BALANCE OF FLAVOURS AND TEXTURES SO IT IS BEST NOT TO MIX AND MATCH. IF THERE IS ONE INGREDIENT THAT YOU HATE YOU CAN OF COURSE REPLACE IT.

Ovens – Timings and Temperatures

The oven times given are only approximate because every oven behaves differently. Check that the food is properly cooked before removing it from the oven. For cakes, this can be done by pressing the top lightly or inserting a fine larding needle. Press meat or fish with your fingers – it will feel firm when cooked. Always allow meat to rest in a warm place before carving – for at least 5 minutes for a small amount and for up to 15 minutes for a large joint. This allows the flesh to retain its juices. Some recipes also suggest refreshing vegetables in cold water to stop them cooking so that they retain their colour.

Kitchen Equipment

On page 170 there is a list of what I consider the ideal equipment for a party kitchen. Obviously you will not have everything on the list, but some of the recipes will require you to use a few special utensils such as an ice cream maker or a deep-fat fryer. Do not always feel you have to rush out and buy these – it may well be that a friend can lend you the item you need.

Plate Sizes

I recommend that the size of plates used for every course – first and dessert as well as main – should be a dinner size. Trying to arrange food on smaller plates will make the presentation over-crowded and messy. Always warm plates before using them to serve hot food, although they should not be so hot that the food continues to cook and the sauce starts to separate; you want to be able to handle the plates comfortably.

A HANDY HINT

I KEEP DISPOSABLE GLOVES IN MY KITCHEN AND FIND THEM VERY USEFUL FOR MESSY JOBS SUCH AS HANDLING FOOD THAT STAINS, OR STRONG-SMELLING INGREDIENTS SUCH AS CHILLIES, GARLIC AND ONIONS TO KEEP THE ODOURS FROM YOUR HANDS.

Be Vegetarian Friendly

If one or more of your guests is vegetarian, whatever sort of party you are having, they must not go hungry. The buffets and cocktail food section all include vegetarian dishes and most of the dinner menus in this book can easily be adapted for vegetarians: fill the cabbage parcels on 128 with beans or lentils rather than duck confit; marinade vegetables rather than lamb or chicken in the Moroccan Buffet; and if serving the Mediterranean Dinner (page 133), you could make the risotto with a vegetable stock, garnish it with fresh herbs and offer that as the vegetarian main course. Be sensitive too to the less obvious 'meat' products used in cooking: avoid chicken stock and animal fats – use vegetable-based oils instead and check before adding gelatine. Some people do not eat red meat but will eat chicken and fish, while others may not eat any fish, meat or dairy products. The Vegetarian Dinner on page 142 is completely free of meat and dairy products to allow you to cater for vegetarians and vegans alike – in fact it's delicious enough for all to enjoy.

Well-Stocked Kitchen

Plan a well-stocked storecupboard and freezer so that you can always cater for unexpected visitors. The foods should be interesting and easy to prepare when it comes to cooking an impromptu meal. For example, there is a wonderful range of dried pastas and bottled sauces on the market today and Parmesan, if stored as I recommend, will keep for a long time. Other excellent staples include potato crisps and crackers, ready-made tart shells, tins of Italian beans for salads, risotto rice, vegetable stock cubes, jars of marinaded baby artichokes, olives and sundried tomatoes, and tins of tuna in brine and anchovies. Always have a supply of eggs in the refrigerator, too, as a plate of scrambled eggs makes a perfect late-night snack. Whole salamis and slices of ham will keep well if stored correctly. In the freezer, keep some interesting bread, soups that freeze well, Parmesan choux puffs and ice creams. Corn and wheat tortillas are good stand-bys as well, making tasty snacks when filled with salad, sausage and cheese. Always keep a bottle of wine, beers and soft drinks in the refrigerator so that chilled drinks are readily on hand.

A Good Cook's Kitchen Guide

• Always cover food left to cool with a cloth, pierced foil or mesh food cloche
• Keep jars with lids; once washed, they are useful for storing dressings, flavoured oils or soaking dried fruit
• Make sure that all containers are clean and dry before use
• After a party, dispose of food that has been on a table and in the heat for a long time
• Never put food that is still warm in the refrigerator as this raises its internal temperature and bacteria may start to breed
• Cover food in the refrigerator with either a lid, cling film or foil
• Wrap cheese for the refrigerator in greaseproof paper and muslin before placing it in a plastic bag or box
• Wrap a cooked ham, such as honey roast, for the refrigerator in greaseproof paper and muslin before placing in a container to prevent it from sweating
• Store salad leaves for up to a week in airtight boxes lined with tea towels, wiping the inside of the lid daily to remove any moisture
• Keep all surfaces clean and tidy, and only bring out utensils necessary for the meal you are preparing at the time

A Note on the Recipes

• Work in either metric or imperial when measuring and never mix the two.
• Amounts for chopped herbs are given in an average-sized tea cup measurement (approximately 8fl oz)
• Tablespoon and teaspoon measures are level unless otherwise stated – a set of measuring spoons is invaluable
• Onions, shallots and garlic are all medium size unless specified
• Eggs are large size; buy organic ones,

for their flavour and colour
• All the vegetables are peeled raw weight unless otherwise stated
• Immune-impaired people, children, the elderly and pregnant women should avoid eating lightly cooked or raw eggs and unpasteurised cheese.

Food Quantities for Large Parties

The following is a guide to estimating amounts of food required for 1 portion. The raw weights given for fish and meat allow for shrinkage.

MEAT, CHICKEN, DUCK AND GAME

Lamb, beef, veal and pork 225g (8oz) per person for roasting; 140g (5oz) meat per person for stews and casseroles; 115g (4oz) meat per person for a buffet, if serving fish and poultry
Grilled ribs 3 per person
Roasted whole duck serves 2
Roasted large chicken serves 4
Braised or roasted whole pheasant serves 2
Grouse, pigeon and snipe 1 bird per person
Quail 2 per person

FISH AND SEAFOOD

Fish 220g (7oz) filleted weight per person for a main course; 115g (4oz) fish per person for a buffet; 85–115g (3–4oz) per person for a buffet, if also serving meat and poultry
Large lobster half per person
Small lobster whole per person
Scallops 2 large for a first course; 4 large cut in half for a main course
Large shrimps 3 per person for grilling

VEGETABLES AND SALAD

Vegetables (prepared) 115g (4oz) per person if served with another vegetable
Salad leaves (washed and picked) 60g (2oz) per person for a first course or buffet; 30g (1oz) for a main course.

POTATOES, RICE, PASTA AND GRAINS

Potatoes (unpeeled) 180g (6oz) per person
Potatoes (washed and scrubbed new) 115g (4oz) per person
Risotto rice 45g (1½oz) per person for

a first course; 85g (3oz) per person for a main course
Rice (all other types) 30g (1oz) per person with a main course or in a salad
Dried beans, lentils or grains 60g (2oz) per person to accompany a main course or in a salad
Pasta and noodles 85g (3oz) per person for first course; 140g (5oz) per person for single main course
Pasta and noodles 30g (1oz) per person to with a main course and 2 vegetables

DAIRY PRODUCTS

Cheese 115g (4oz) per person served as a separate course; 60g (2oz) cheese per person for a buffet
Butter 30g (1oz) per person for bread and biscuits with cheese
Cream or milk 60ml (2fl oz) per person for coffee or tea
Cream (pouring) 85ml (3fl oz) per person for desserts
Ice cream 50ml (2fl oz) per person to accompany a dessert; 140ml (5fl oz) for a single dessert
Eggs 2 per person for omelettes and scrambled eggs

BREADS, DESSERTS AND FRESH FRUIT

Small rolls 2 per person
Large rolls 1½ per person
Bread 2 slices per person
Mousses, parfaits and brûlées 115g (4oz) per person
Fresh fruit (prepared) 115g (4oz) For a buffet a 30cm (12in) tart gives 10 portions

SAUCES AND DRESSING

Sauce 60ml (2fl oz) per person for a main course
Mayonnaise 30ml (1fl oz) per person
Salad dressing 30ml (1fl oz) per pers

Key to Recipes

To prepare the recipes in advance, follow this key to when to do each step.

| 1 hour | | 1 week | |
| 1 day | | 1 month | 1m |

Cocktail parties are the most flexible and inexpensive way of entertaining a large crowd, be they friends, family or business colleagues. By the nature of the party, guests can circulate freely, stay as long as two hours or for only half an hour. For the host, a cocktail party is a very good way of returning hospitality.

for a cocktail party

The drinks served can be as grand and sophisticated as champagne or cocktails from a cocktail bar, or simply wines and beers. Make sure you also have a good supply of soft drinks and mineral water. As a host, you should offer your guests their first drink. Make the drinks table – or bar – accessible so that later on guests can help themselves. If you have help, offer a good range of drinks from serving trays so, as guests enter, they immediately have a selection to choose from. (See page 64 for more on the Party Spirit.)

Serving Canapés in Style

There are many ways to present canapés on serving trays. We serve ours on a myriad of trays and dishes, from gloriously coloured Vietnamese lacquer trays to simple Shaker-style trays or steamer baskets lined with banana leaves. Canapés look best arranged in lines, which offers a good selection and makes a colourful and tempting display. Alternatively, some of our canapés are offered on spoons, forks, or poured into shot glasses. Arranging your canapés in a different style can become a talking point with your guests. Do not try to be too clever, however. Simple elegance is best and most dramatic.

Tempting Table Snacks

Some 'nibbles' can be left on tables so that guests can help themselves. I like to fill bowls with Parmesan Choux Sticks, Parmesan Tuiles and Vegetable Crisps (see recipes on page 92). Another idea is to make 'birds' nests' from thin pasta and fill them with quails' eggs, then make an accompanying Chinese salt dip to hand out in a broken hen's egg. Arranging baby vegetables on a bed of herbs in baskets, Shaker-style boxes, glass tanks or trays is also popular. These should be refilled whenever necessary throughout the party – if you have staff, make sure they know this.

Professional Tips

• **Check that you have enough serving dishes – they do not need to match**

• **Canapés should be a single mouthful. Start with a combination of cold canapés, then serve hot ones**

• **Offer a supply of finger napkins ready for sticky fingers**

• **Avoid over-garnishing – it is very off-putting**

• **Avoid serving food on fabrics, unless they will be changed each time you replenish your trays with food**

HOW MANY CANAPES?

For a 1–1½-hour cocktail party Allow 8–9 canapes per person. For a 2–2½-hour party allow 10–12 pieces per person.

hot canapés

Salmon Fish Cakes with Spicy Tomato Dip

This is irresistible comfort food to add warmth to a party. MAKES 30

Spicy Tomato Dip
1 red chilli, deseeded & chopped
unscented vegetable oil
3 shallots, finely sliced
2 garlic cloves, finely chopped
3 plum tomatoes
2 tsp tomato purée
300ml (½ pint) vegetable stock
1 tsp white wine vinegar
2 tsp caster sugar
salt & freshly ground black pepper

Fish Cakes
500g (1lb 1oz) salmon fillet, bones removed
  & cut lengthways into 5cm (2in) wide strips
500g (1lb 1oz) potatoes, peeled & quartered
½ tea cup dill, chopped
2 shallots, finely diced
2 tbsp tomato ketchup
1 tbsp anchovy essence
1 tbsp Worcestershire sauce
salt & freshly ground black pepper

Fish Cake Coating
100g (3½oz) plain flour
2 eggs, whisked
100g (3½oz) fine breadcrumbs
60g (2oz) white sesame seeds

SPECIAL EQUIPMENT **deep-fat fryer**

(3d) To prepare the dip
Sauté the chilli, shallot and garlic in a little oil until soft, then add the tomatoes and tomato purée and cook for a further 2 minutes. Add the stock, vinegar and sugar and continue cooking for 10–12 minutes. Allow to cool, pour into a blender and blend until smooth. Pass through a fine sieve, season and pour into an airtight container. Refrigerate until needed.

(1d) To prepare the cakes
Bring a pan of salted water to the boil, then lower the heat and simmer. Poach the salmon strips in the water for 3–4 minutes. Drain and leave to cool. Place potatoes in a pan of cold water, bring to the boil and simmer until soft, then pass through a potato ricer or a fine sieve into a bowl. Flake the salmon into the potato, add the dill, shallot, tomato ketchup, anchovy essence and Worcestershire sauce. Season and mix well. Line a 1.5cm (½in) deep, 30 x 22cm (12 x 8½in) tray with baking paper and mould the mixture into the tray. Cover with more baking paper, then roll the top with a rolling pin until the mixture is level. Cover and chill.

(8h) To coat the cakes
Cut out the fish cakes using a 3.5cm (1¼in) round cutter and place on a tray. In 3 separate bowls, place the flour, the eggs, and the breadcrumbs mixed with sesame seeds. Coat 1 cake with each ingredient in order and repeat for the rest. Return all the fish cakes to the tray, cover and refrigerate.

To assemble
Preheat oven to 100°C/220°F/gas ¼ and a deep-fat fryer to 180°C/350°F. Heat the dip slowly in a saucepan. Once the oil is hot, place a few cakes at a time in the fryer to cook until golden brown. Place on a tray lined with kitchen paper and keep warm in the oven until ready to serve. Pour the sauce into a dipping bowl and push the fish cakes on to forks. Serve.

DUMPLING PREPARATION
THE PRAWN DUMPLINGS (RIGHT) CAN BE MADE 2 WEEKS IN ADVANCE AND FROZEN. THEN JUST DEFROST, STEAM AND SERVE.

Salmon Fish Cakes with Spicy Tomato Dip

Cheese Soufflé Tartlets

A party-food classic. MAKES 30

Pastry Bases

3 sheets filo pastry, 46 x 30cm (18 x 12in)
30g (1oz) unsalted butter, melted

Soufflés

300ml (½ pint) milk
30g (1oz) unsalted butter
30g (1oz) plain flour
60g (2oz) mature cheddar, grated
30g (1oz) Parmesan, grated
¼ tsp cayenne pepper
2 tsp English mustard
salt & freshly ground black pepper
2 eggs, separated
paprika, to dust

(2d) To make the tartlets

Preheat the oven to 190°C/375°F/gas 5.
Brush a sheet of filo pastry with
melted butter, place a second sheet
over the first, brush with butter, then
top with a third sheet and repeat. Cut
out 30 discs with a 5cm (2in) round
cutter. Lay the discs butter side down
in little tartlet moulds, press the pastry
into the corners. Half-fill with baking
beans. Bake for 8–9 minutes, or until
golden. Allow to cool, remove the
beans, then remove the tartlets from
the moulds. Store in a cool place.

(8h) To prepare the base

Bring the milk to the boil, then barely
simmer. In a pan, melt the butter, then
add the flour and mix to a smooth
paste. Add the milk slowly, a little at a
time, mixing until smooth. Cook over a
low heat, stirring, for 4–5 minutes.
Add both cheeses, cayenne and
mustard, and mix until the cheese has
melted. Remove from heat and check
seasoning. Pour into a bowl and cover
with greaseproof paper. Cool and chill.

(½h) To finish and serve the soufflés

Preheat the oven to 190°C/375°F/gas 5
Lay the tartlets on a baking tray. Mix
the egg yolks into the soufflé base. In
an electric mixer, whisk the egg whites
until they form firm peaks. Fold into

the soufflé mix, then pipe or spoon
into the tartlets. Bake in the oven for
4–5 minutes, then transfer to a serving
tray and dust with paprika. Serve.

Prawn Dumplings

These and the Chicken Dumplings
(right) were developed by our Thai
chef, Yani. MAKES 30

350g (12½oz) fresh prawns, peeled
  (preferably tiger prawns)
3 garlic cloves, finely chopped
¼ tea cup coriander roots, washed & finely
  chopped
30g (1oz) bamboo shoots, finely chopped
30g (1oz) water chestnuts, finely chopped
1 tbsp light soy sauce
1 tbsp soya bean sauce
1 tbsp caster sugar
1 tbsp potato flour
1 egg white
1 tbsp light sesame oil
salt & freshly ground black pepper
30 x 8.5cm (3½in) white dumpling wrappers
½ red pepper cut into small diamonds

(8h) To make the filling

Mince the prawns in a food processor
and transfer to a mixing bowl. Add the
remaining ingredients, season and mix
well. Cover and refrigerate.

(6h) To fill the dumplings

Lay the dumpling wrappers on a cool
surface. Place 1 teaspoon of the filling
in the centre of each wrap. Moisten the
edges of the wrappers with water.
Pinch each wrapper into 8, then make
into rounds with a little of the filling
showing. Top with red pepper. Place on
a tray, cover and refrigerate.

To cook and serve the dumplings

Half-fill a pan with water, bring to the
boil, then reduce to a simmer. Brush a
steamer basket that fits the pan with a
little oil. Put in the dumplings, then
cover and steam for 4–5 minutes.
Remove from the heat and transfer to a
clean steamer lined with a banana leaf
or bamboo sushi mat.

Chicken Dumplings

Eternally popular! MAKES 30

450g (1lb) minced chicken breast
3 garlic cloves, puréed
¼ tea cup coriander root, finely chopped
1 tbsp potato flour
4 spring onions, washed, & finely chopped
1 head of bok choy, washed, & finely chopped
30g (1oz) shiitake mushrooms
3 tbsp light soy sauce
1 tbsp soya bean sauce
¼ tsp white pepper
1 egg yolk
1 tbsp caster sugar
salt
5 x 20.5 x 18cm (8 x 7in) nori sheets
30 picked coriander leaves, to garnish

Dipping Sauce

150ml (¼ pint) light soy sauce
150ml (¼ pint) water
1 tbsp caster sugar
1 tbsp rice wine vinegar

(2d) To make the filling

Mix all the main ingredients in a large
bowl, cover and refrigerate.

(2d) To make the sauce

Combine the ingredients for the sauce
in a pan and bring to the boil. Remove
from the heat when the sugar has
dissolved. Cool, and refrigerate.

(8h) To fill the dumplings

Transfer the filling into a piping bag fixed
with a 2.5cm (1in) nozzle. Lay a sheet of
nori on a sushi mat, then carefully pipe a
line of mixture along the nearest edge.
Brush the opposite edge with water, then,
using the mat, roll up gently into a
cylinder. Cover tightly in cling film. Repeat
for all the nori, then freeze for 1 hour.
Remove, take off cling film, trim the ends
and cut into 2.5cm (1in) rounds. Cover
and chill.

To cook and serve the dumplings

Cook following the instructions for
cooking Prawn Dumplings, then garnish
with coriander, pour the sauce into a
bowl and serve with finger napkins.

cold canapés

Buckwheat Blinis with Smoked Salmon Curls

You can finish these with a little caviar for a touch of sheer luxury. MAKES 30

450g (1lb) long, sliced smoked salmon
450ml (¾ pint) milk
15g (½oz) fresh or dried yeast
pinch of sugar
100g (3½oz) plain flour
200g (7oz) buckwheat flour
4 eggs, separated
15g (½oz) unsalted butter, melted
salt & freshly ground black pepper
unscented oil for cooking the blinis
150g (5½oz) crème fraîche
60g (2oz) caviar (optional)
chives, to garnish

1d — To prepare the curls
Cut the salmon into 10 x 2.5cm (4 x 1in) pieces, allowing 1 per portion. Line a tray with greaseproof paper. Take one end of each salmon slice between your thumb and index finger and wrap around delicately to create a rose effect. Lay all the 'roses' on a tray, cover with plastic wrap and place in the refrigerator.

8h — To make the blinis
Heat the milk in a pan over a low heat until warm, then pour into a jug. Stir in the yeast and sugar. Sieve the flours into a large metal bowl, add the egg yolks, then whisk in the warm milk until smooth. Cover with a clean, damp tea towel and leave to prove in a warm place for about 1 hour. Do not allow the batter to rise for any longer then this, otherwise the blinis may taste over-proved. After proving, stir in the melted butter and season. In a clean bowl, whisk the egg whites until firm and fold into the blini mixture. Heat a little oil in a sauté or frying pan. Pour in enough batter to cover the base of the pan – about 7mm (¼in) thick.

When golden brown on one side, turn and repeat for other side. Slide on to a dry cloth to cool, and continue until all the batter is cooked. When cool, cut into rounds with a 3.5cm (1½in) cutter. Store in a cool place.

4h — To assemble
Place the blinis on a tray. Pipe crème fraîche in the centre of the blinis and place the salmon rose on top. Snip the chives roughly, and garnish each blini with a couple of snips. Cover with cling film and refrigerate until needed. If using caviar, top the salmon just before serving and garnish with chives.

Thai Beef Salad

My friend, Alison, had the idea for this in Antigua while we were enjoying a glass of her husband Steve's rum punch (page 69). MAKES 30

Dressing
2 tbsp Thai fish sauce (nam pla)
2 tbsp lime juice
1 tbsp sugar
1 small red chilli, deseeded & finely diced
1 garlic clove, finely diced
salt & freshly ground black pepper

320g (11½oz) sirloin of beef
300ml (½ pint) light soy sauce
2 medium cucumbers
unscented vegetable oil
90g (3oz) carrots, finely diced
1 large red onion, finely diced
2 plum tomatoes, peeled, deseeded & finely diced
2 stems of lemon grass finely sliced
2 lime leaves, finely chopped
salt & freshly ground black pepper

1d — To prepare the dressing
Mix the fish sauce, lime juice, sugar, chilli and garlic in a bowl. Season, pour into a small jar, seal and refrigerate.

1d — To marinade the beef
Coat the beef liberally with soy sauce. Refrigerate in an airtight container.

1d — To prepare the cups
Cut the cucumber into 1.5cm (½in) slices. With a 3.5cm (1¼in) fluted cutter cut into the centre of each slice. Scoop out the middle with a small melon scoop. Invert the cups and lay on a tray lined with a clean cloth, cover with cling film and refrigerate.

8h — To cook the beef
Preheat the oven to 180°C/375°F/gas 6. Heat a little oil in a pan. Seal the beef until golden brown on all sides, then transfer to the oven. Cook for about 10 minutes or until medium rare. Remove, allow to cool and cut into small dice. Refrigerate in an airtight container.

1h — To assemble
Turn the cucumber cups hollow side up. Place the beef and the vegetables in a bowl, add the lemon grass, lime leaves and dressing. Mix and check the seasoning. With a teaspoon, fill the cups with the beef salad.

Tomato & Mozzarella Shortbreads

These delicious savoury biscuits can be served on their own or with pre-dinner drinks. MAKES 30

Shortbread
115g (4oz) plain flour, sifted
100g (3½oz) unsalted butter, cubed
85g (3oz) Parmesan, grated
pinch of salt
pinch of cayenne pepper
flour, to dust

Topping
250g (9oz) mozzarella, cut from a block
6 cherry tomatoes
1 tbsp Pesto Sauce (see page 168)

③ᵈ To prepare the shortbreads

Preheat the oven to 170°C/375°F/gas 5. Using the paddle blade in an electric mixer, beat the flour and butter on a slow speed to the consistency of breadcrumbs. Stop the mixer, add the Parmesan, salt and cayenne pepper, then continue on a slow speed until the mixture begins to combine. On a floured board, pat the mixture into a round, cover with cling film and refrigerate for at least 1 hour. Line a baking tray with greaseproof paper, dust a cool surface with flour and roll out the pastry to about 5mm (¼in) thick. Cut out the discs with a 3.5cm (1½in) cutter, place on the baking tray and return to the refrigerator for about ½ hour. Transfer to the oven and bake for 10 minutes, or until golden brown. Remove and allow to cool. Layer with greaseproof paper and place in an airtight container.

①ᵈ To prepare the mozzarella

Using a sharp knife, slice the mozzarella into 2mm (⅛in) slices, dipping the knife into hot water after each slice. Cut into 30 rounds with a 3.5cm (1½in) cutter. Lay on a flat tray, cover with cling film and refrigerate.

⑥ʰ To prepare the tomatoes

Slice the cherry tomatoes into 30 rounds. Remove the mozzarella from the refrigerator, place a tomato round on top of each slice and cover with cling film. Return to the refrigerator.

To assemble

Place the shortbreads on a tray. Using a palette knife, position the discs of mozzarella and tomato in the centre of each biscuit, top with pesto and serve.

CELEBRATIONS

CUT THESE INTO ANY SHAPE YOU FANCY, PERHAPS TO COMPLEMENT A THEME – HEARTS FOR VALENTINE'S DAY OR STARS FOR CHRISTMAS.

Back to front: Thai Beef Salad, Buckwheat Blinis with Smoked Salmon Curls, Crostini with Asparagus & Wild Mushrooms, Tomato & Mozzarella Shortbreads

Crostini with Asparagus & Wild Mushrooms

For sophisticated party snacks, these tastily topped crostini cannot be beaten. MAKES 30

1 thin French stick (ficelle)
olive oil
salt & freshly ground black pepper
1 small shallot, finely diced
2 tsp white wine vinegar
½ tsp sugar
60 spears of asparagus (preferably Thai)
60g (2oz) trompette de mort or other wild mushrooms, washed & cut into small pieces
6 tbsp mascarpone
30 small shavings of Parmesan

①ᵈ To prepare the crostini

Preheat the oven to 200°C/400°F/gas 6. Cut the bread about 7mm (¼in) thick, on an angle. Brush with olive oil and season. Lay on a baking tray and bake for about 4–5 minutes, or until golden.

Remove from the oven and cool. Layer with greaseproof paper and place in an airtight container.

②ᵈ To prepare the dressing

Place the shallot, 2 tablespoons of olive oil, vinegar and sugar in a bowl. Mix well, season, pour into a clean jar or bottle and refrigerate.

①ᵈ To prepare the asparagus

Cut the asparagus into 3cm (1¼in) spears and blanch in salted boiling water for about 30 seconds, then drain and refresh. Store in an airtight container and refrigerate.

To assemble

Lay the crostini on a tray. Toss the raw mushrooms into the dressing and season; repeat for the asparagus. Pipe a little mascarpone in the centre of the crostini. Place 2 spears of asparagus on top and garnish with the mushrooms and Parmesan shavings. Serve.

spoons

Quails' Eggs with Caviar

For sheer indulgence, this recipe cannot be beaten. MAKES 30

15 quails' eggs, hard boiled, peeled & stored
  in water in the refrigerator
125g (4½oz) Sevruga caviar
60 x 3cm (1in) snipped chives

To assemble
Lay 30 horn spoons or teaspoons on a tray. Remove the eggs from the refrigerator, drain and dry them with a clean tea towel. Use a sharp knife to cut the eggs in half lengthways, cutting a thin slice off the base of each so that it sits straight on the spoons. Top the eggs with a little caviar and garnish with the chives.

Spiced Indian Crab

You can serve this on spoons and it is also makes an excellent sandwich filling. MAKES 30

1 tbsp unscented vegetable oil
1 medium onion, finely chopped
2 garlic cloves, finely chopped
3 tsp medium-hot curry powder
½ tsp brown mustard seeds
1 tsp ground cumin
½ tsp chilli powder
2 tbsp chicken stock
450g (1lb) picked white crab meat, shelled
¼ tea cup coriander leaves, washed and dried
2 lemons, juiced
salt & freshly ground black pepper
4 tbsp yoghurt
30 coriander leaves, picked, washed & dried

(4d) To prepare the paste
Heat the oil in a saucepan, add the onion and garlic and cook until soft, without browning. Add the spices and cook for a further 2–3 minutes, then pour in the stock and cook on a low heat for 10 minutes. Transfer to an airtight container. Cool and refrigerate.

(1d) To finish the paste
In a bowl mix the crab meat, coriander and lemon juice into the spice mixture. Season with salt and pepper, place in an airtight container and chill.

To assemble
Lay teaspoons on a tray. Use a spare teaspoon to mould the crab paste on to each teaspoon. To serve, top each with a little yoghurt and a coriander leaf.

Chinese Duck with Plum Sauce

These neat parcels are a delicious treat certain to impress. MAKES 30

Marinade
4 tbsp light soy sauce
2 tbsp dry sherry
1 tbsp yellow bean paste
1 tbsp caster sugar
2 star anise
1 tsp 5-spice powder
2 thin slices of fresh ginger
300ml (½ pint) chicken stock

1 large duck breast
unscented vegetable oil for cooking
¼ cucumber, deseeded & julienned
2 spring onions, julienned
4 tbsp plum sauce

(4d) **To prepare the marinade**
Place all the marinade ingredients in a saucepan and bring to the boil. Lower the heat and simmer for 10 minutes. Allow to cool then pour into a container. Cover and refrigerate.

(2d) **To cook the duck**
Place the marinade in a large pan, bring to the boil and lower the heat. Meanwhile, sauté and seal the duck breast in a little oil until golden brown on all sides; add to the marinade, bring this back to the boil and simmer for 1 minute. Remove from heat and cool. Place the duck breast in a container, pour on the marinade, cover and chill.

(3h) **To roll the sliced duck**
Cut the duck widthways into 2mm- (⅛in-) thick slices. Place a few pieces of cucumber and spring onion in the centre of each duck slice, roll up the slice and place on a tray. Cover with cling film and refrigerate.

To serve
Lay the teaspoons on a tray, place a duck roll in the centre of each and coat with a little plum sauce. Serve.

Chinese Duck with Plum Sauce; Spiced Indian Crab

Gazpacho Soup Sip

Corn Chowder Soup Sips

You can fill a flask with this soup and serve it for a warming treat at a winter picnic.MAKES 30

3 fresh corncobs
1 litre (1¾ pints) milk
600ml (1 pint) chicken stock
1 tbsp sugar
60g (2oz) butter
60g (2oz) plain flour
1 bunch of spring onions, washed and sliced into rounds
cayenne pepper
salt & freshly ground black pepper
300ml (½ pint) double cream
snipped chives, to garnish

(1d) To make the soup

Remove the husks from the cobs, cut each of them into 3 portions and place in a medium-sized saucepan. Add the milk, chicken stock and sugar, bring to the boil, then simmer for about 1 hour. Heat the butter until melted in a pan, then add the flour to make a roux; set aside. Remove the cobs from the milk, cut the kernels from them and place in a bowl. Return the roux to a medium heat, add the milk slowly and mix until smooth. Lower the heat and cook for about 10 minutes, then add the spring onions, corn kernels and cayenne pepper, and season. Cook for a further 10 minutes, then add the double cream and remove from the heat. Allow to cool, then pour into a blender and blend until smooth. Pass through a sieve into a container, cover and chill.

To assemble

Pour the soup into a pan and bring to the boil. Transfer to a jug, then pour into shot glasses. Garnish with snipped chives and serve.

CHANGING THE CHOWDER

YOU CAN USE THIS METHOD TO MAKE SUBSTANTIAL CHOWDERS OF ALL VARIETIES — TRY SUBSTITUTING THE CORNCOBS WITH SEAFOOD, CHEDDAR CHEESE AND SAGE, CHICKEN OR MIXED VEGETABLES.

soup sips

Gazpacho Soup Sips

Our head chef, Richard Cubbin, brought this recipe from Spain. Unlike other recipes for gazpacho it omits the bread and I think this makes it all the more delicious. MAKES 30

3 shallots, chopped
3 garlic cloves, chopped
½ cucumber, peeled, deseeded & chopped
1 red pepper, deseeded & chopped
1 yellow pepper, deseeded & chopped
3 plum tomatoes, chopped
600ml (1 pint) tomato juice, preferably a thin variety
250ml (⅓ pint) white wine
2 tbsp olive oil
salt & freshly ground black pepper

(1d) To make the soup

Place the shallot, garlic, cucumber, pepper and tomato in a food processor and blend for about 10 seconds until finely chopped, not puréed. Pour into a bowl and stir in the tomato juice, white wine, olive oil and season. Cover and refrigerate.

To assemble

Pour into shot glasses and serve.

PERFECT ALL-YEAR ROUND

THESE LITTLE SOUPS CAN BE SERVED IN SHOT GLASSES AS GUESTS ARRIVE. THE HOT SOUPS ARE PARTICULARLY WELCOME ON CHILLY NIGHTS AND THE COLD ARE VERY REFRESHING. YOU CAN ALSO MAKE LARGER AMOUNTS TO SERVE AT LUNCH OR DINNER.

Green Pea Soup Sips

Try this soup very cold for a summer lunch. MAKES 30

3 shallots, finely chopped
2 garlic cloves, finely chopped
unscented vegetable oil
2 litres (3½ pints) vegetable stock
900g (2lb) frozen peas
½ tea cup of fresh mint leaves
300ml (½ pint) double cream
1 small bag of ice cubes
salt & freshly ground black pepper
3 tomatoes, skinned, deseeded & finely
  chopped, to garnish

(1d) To make the soup

Half fill a sink with cold water. Sauté the shallots and garlic in a little oil for about 2 minutes, without browning. Add the stock, bring to the boil, then add the peas and cook for 5 minutes or until are soft. Remove from the heat and add the mint and cream. Place the ice cubes in the sink of water, and put the pan in the sink. This will prevent the soup from cooking and retain the colour of the peas. When cold, season, blend until smooth and pass through a fine sieve into a container. Chill.

To assemble

Pour a little soup into the shot glasses, garnish with the chopped tomato.

Tomato & Lemon Grass Soup Sips

This soup captures the light fresh tastes of eastern cuisine. MAKES 30

unscented vegetable oil
3 shallots, finely chopped
2 garlic cloves, finely chopped
5 stems of lemon grass, finely chopped
30g (1oz) ginger, peeled & finely chopped
10 plum tomatoes, skinned & deseeded
1 tbsp tomato purée
2 litres (3½ pints) vegetable stock
1 tbsp sugar
1 tsp tom yum (Thai curry) paste
1 stem of lemon grass, thinly sliced, to
  garnish
30 coriander leaves, to garnish

(1m) To make the soup

Heat a little oil in a pan. Add the shallot, garlic, lemongrass and ginger, cook until soft; add the tomatoes, tomato purée and sugar and cook for 2 more minutes. Then add the tom yum paste and stock and simmer over a low heat for 1 hour, pass through a fine sieve into a container, cool and freeze.

To assemble

Pour the defrosted soup into a pan, bring to the boil, then transfer to a jug. Pour into shot glasses, garnish with the lemon grass and coriander and serve.

Green Pea Soup Sip

wraps

Goats' Cheese & Rocket Wraps

A deliciously mouthwatering combination. MAKES 30

200g (7oz) sour cream
3 spinach tortilla, 30cm (12in) round
30g (1oz) rocket, picked & washed
5 tbs Red Onion Jam (see page 168)
200g (7oz) long log of goats' cheese, cut into
   15 x 1.5cm (½in) pieces
salt & freshly ground black pepper

(1d) **To make the wraps**
Spread the sour cream evenly over the tortillas. Cover the first quarter of the wrap with rocket and onion jam, then top with goats' cheese and season. Roll up the wraps, seal with cling film to stop them drying out, and chill.

To serve the wraps
Cut the wraps at an angle and serve.

Parma Ham & Avocado Wraps

Made with ripe avocado and good-quality Parma ham, this is quite sensational. MAKES 30

200g (7oz) sour cream
3 tomato tortillas in 30cm (12in) rounds
90g (7oz) sliced Parma ham
60g (2oz) picked & washed spinach
1 avocado, peeled, stoned & cut into strips
salt & freshly ground black pepper
juice of 1 lemon

(6h) **To prepare the wraps**
Spread the sour cream over the tortillas, followed by the sliced ham, the spinach and the avocado strips. Season, then sprinkle lemon juice over the avocado. Roll up the wraps and seal with cling film.

To serve
Cut the wraps at an angle and serve.

Rice Paper Wraps with a Spicy Soy Dip

These oriental-style wraps look very elegant when served. Makes 30

Filling

150g (5½oz) tuna, the tail end
60g (2oz) mangetout, julienned
60g (2oz) carrot, julienned
60g (2oz) daikon radish, julienned
1 punnet of mustard & cress, trimmed from the base
1 tbsp sweet soy sauce
juice and zest of 2 limes
1 tbsp sushi vinegar

8 sheets of Vietnamese rice paper, 21cm (8½in) round
black sesame seeds for garnish

Spicy Soy Dip

2 tbsp light soy sauce
1 tbsp sugar
1 tbsp sushi vinegar
1 tsp ginger, peeled & finely chopped
1 garlic clove, finely chopped
2 tsp sweet chilli sauce
salt & freshly ground black pepper

TUNA ALTERNATIVES

IF YOU DO NOT LIKE TUNA, FRESH SALMON OR COOKED TIGER PRAWNS CAN BE USED INSTEAD.

(1d) To prepare the filling and dip

Line a tray with parchment paper. Slice the tuna into wafer-thin discs, place on the tray, cover with cling film and refrigerate. On a separate tray, lay out the vegetables and cress, cover with cling film and refrigerate. For the marinade, combine the sweet soy sauce, zest and juice of limes, and sushi vinegar in a bowl. Pour into a container and refrigerate. Mix together all the ingredients for the spiced soy dip, pour into a container and chill.

(8h) To make the wraps

Soak the rice paper in a bowl of cold water for 3–4 minutes until soft. Remove from the water and cut on the diagonal into triangle quarters, laying these on a tea towel so that all the points are facing the same way; season. Dip the tuna in the marinade and place on the rice-paper triangles at the opposite side to the points. Place 3 pieces of each vegetable on the tuna and top with cress. Roll up the rice paper, then place each wrap on a tray lined with a cloth. Cover the wraps with cling film to prevent them drying out. Refrigerate until needed.

Rice Paper Wraps with Spicy Soy Dip

To serve

Place the wraps on a tray and sprinkle liberally with sesame seeds. Transfer the dip into a small bowl and serve.

WRAP IT UP

I DISCOVERED WRAPS AS ON A RECENT TRIP TO SAN FRANCISCO, AND HAVE ADAPTED THEM FOR CANAPÉS. MADE LARGER THEY ARE FABULOUS FOR PICNICS.

easy snacks

Parmesan Choux Sticks

Eat with a glass of wine. MAKES 30

Egg Wash
2 eggs
water
pinch of salt

pinch of cayenne pepper
350g (12½oz) Parmesan, grated
450ml (¾ pint) water
15g (½oz) salt
15g (½oz) caster sugar
200g (7oz) unsalted butter, cubed
400g (14oz) plain four, sieved
10 eggs

WHEN FRIENDS DROP BY
CHOUX STICKS FREEZE WELL AFTER BAKING.
FOR A READY-MADE COCKTAIL SNACK, COOK
STRAIGHT FROM FROZEN IN A PREHEATED
OVEN FOR 10 MINUTES.

Parmesan Choux Sticks

To prepare the egg wash
Whisk together all the ingredients.
Cover and keep in a cool place.

(8h) To prepare the sticks
Preheat the oven to 180°C/350°F/gas 4
Mark straight piping guidelines in
pencil on the reverse side of
greaseproof paper. Line a baking tray
with a separate sheet of greaseproof
paper. Mix the cayenne pepper into the
Parmesan, and place in a bowl. In a
saucepan, mix the water, salt, sugar
and butter, and bring to the boil. Add
the flour and beat vigorously until the
mixture comes away from the sides of
the pan. Transfer to an electric mixer
with a paddle beater and beat on a
slow speed until the mixture cools. Add
the eggs 1 at a time. When they are all
incorporated, add 250g (9oz) of the
Parmesan and cayenne mixture; mix
well. Put a 12mm (½in) nozzle on a
piping bag, fill the bag with ⅔ of the
mixture and twist the end. Pipe along
the length of the greaseproof paper
lining the baking tray. Continue,
leaving a 2.5cm (1in) gap between
each row. Brush the top of each stick
with the egg wash and sprinkle with
the remaining Parmesan and cayenne.

To cook the sticks after making
Preheat the oven to 180°C/350°F/gas 4.
Place in the oven and cook for 10
minutes, then turn the sticks and cook
for a further 15–20 minutes, or until
the sticks are golden brown and will
stand up when held. Leave to cool and
place in an airtight container lined
with kitchen paper.

CRISP AND CRUNCHY
IF, WHEN YOU ARE READY TO SERVE THEM,
THE VEGETABLE CRISPS (RIGHT) ARE A
LITTLE SOGGY, PREHEAT THE OVEN TO
140°C/275°F/GAS 1, SPREAD THE CRISPS
ON A BAKING TRAY AND COOK FOR A FEW
MINUTES UNTIL CRISP.

Vegetable Crisps

To ring the changes, toss these in
herbs and spices. SERVES 30

unscented vegetable oil for frying
6 green plantains
900g (2lb) long parsnips
900g (2lb) white sweet potatoes
900g (2lb) orange sweet potatoes
900g (2lb) salsify, washed and peeled
3 medium uncooked beetroot
sea salt flakes

SPECIAL EQUIPMENT deep-fat fryer

(8h) To make the vegetable crisps
Preheat the deep-fat fryer to
160°C/325°F. Slice the vegetables
lengthways as thinly as possible. Make
sure that each slice remains intact and
is uniform in thickness. Place the
slices on a tray, then deep fry in small
batches until golden brown and crisp.
Drain on kitchen paper and sprinkle
with sea salt. Cool and store covered.

Parmesan Tuiles

Make these snacks in different
shapes and sizes. MAKES 30

300g (11oz) Parmesan, very finely grated

(8h) To make the tuiles
Preheat the oven to 190°C/375°F/gas 5.
Line a tray with greaseproof paper or,
better still, a silicon mat. Sprinkle
Parmesan evenly inside several ring
cutters. Remove the cutter and bake
for 4 minutes. The tuiles are ready
when slightly bubbly and golden.
Remove from the oven and use a
palette knife to transfer the discs onto
a wire cooling rack. Allow to cool and
store layered in greaseproof paper in
an airtight container.

Vegetable Crisps

Buffet parties, like cocktail parties, are usually planned for entertaining a large number of guests in an informal atmosphere for special occasions such as a 21st birthday party, a christening, or a New Year's Eve party. They are also ideal for brunch occasions such as before important sporting finals.

for a buffet party

Buffet parties offer a great opportunity to be expressive in the way that you combine flavours, textures and colours, and lend themselves to themes. We have served fantastic buffets with Indian, Moroccan, Chinese, Thai, Italian, French, American, West Indian and Japanese themes, for example, and there are many more possibilities. One option is to serve canapés followed by beautiful desserts and a cheese buffet. You can be expansive and serve lots of dishes, or decide that simplicity is best and serve only a few. For formal buffets, set an arrangement of a few small tables with fine china and silver. If you are organizing a stand-up buffet, eaten with a fork or chopsticks, you can ensure that guests move around and mingle by serving the dessert in another area or room.

Arranging Tables

Plan ahead, deciding where to place the bar and buffet table so that they are not too near each other, which will create a bottleneck. Calculate how your space and whether you will need to use other rooms or areas – in summer, the garden can become another room. If possible, position the food tables near to the kitchen so that you do not have to carry hot dishes too far. For formal, seated buffets, a first course can be placed on the tables just before guests are seated. The main course should be a self-service buffet, but then serve a plated dessert. While adding a touch of formality to an occasion this also allows guests to move around and chat to each other.

Estimating Food Quantities

Most people tend to over-cater for a buffet. This is fine, as you can always eat what is left the next day (see page 79 for a guide to food quantities). Plan your menu, allowing for each guest to have a little of everything – most of the recipes on the following pages will give 20 portions. From the menus, choose about 6 items for a small gathering and 8 for a larger party, plus desserts and coffee.

Professional Tips

• Arrange food and place china, cutlery and napkins at both ends of each table
• Give a separate table over to desserts
• Invite guests to serve themselves in small groups
• Present hot food in small dishes that can be replenished frequently
• Always offer guests the opportunity for 'seconds'
• At any sort of buffet, there will be a considerable amount of movement from the guests so ensure there is enough space around the chairs and tables
• Set up a separate table for coffee and tea – guests can help themselves when they wish

CLEARLY BEAUTIFUL

IF GUESTS ARE STANDING UP TO EAT, SERVE FOOD THAT IS NOT MESSY OR EASY TO SPILL – AVOID THIN SOUPS, OR CASSEROLES OR DESSERTS WITH THIN SAUCES.

street food buffet

Apart from the clam chowder, this menu is designed to be eaten with your fingers, and is therefore ideal for eating while moving around. Perfect for teenage social gatherings and for street parties, the recipes are easy to prepare and offer plenty of interesting flavours, colours and textures.

Manhattan Clam Chowder

Serve this soup from big galvanized containers, ladling it into either disposable cups or hard wearing bowls. The clam shells are a vibrant decoration. SERVES 20

unscented vegetable oil
5 medium onions, peeled cut into large dice
8 garlic cloves, finely chopped
1 head of celery, washed, peeled & diced
120g (4oz) lardons of smoked bacon

4.5kg (10lb) fresh clams, washed and rinsed of sand and grit
600ml (1 pint) dry white wine
1.8 litres (3 pints) thick tomato juice
3.6 litres (6 pints) fish stock
2 tsp Tabasco sauce
2 bay leaves
salt & freshly ground black pepper
5 corncobs, cooked & kernels removed
1kg (2lb 2oz) potatoes, diced & cooked
12 plum tomatoes, peeled, deseeded & diced
1 tbsp caster sugar
½ tea cup flat-leaf parsley, washed, dried & chopped, to garnish

Manhattan Clam Chowder, Pan Bagnat

(1d) **To make the soup**
Heat a little oil in a saucepan that is large enough to cook the clams. Add the onion, garlic, celery and bacon, then sauté until soft. Turn up the heat and add the clams and white wine. Cover with a lid and cook for about 4–5 minutes until the clams open. Remove the clams from the shells, discarding any that have not opened; reserve 12 for garnishing. Allow to cool, cover and refrigerate. Return the pan to the heat with the cooking liquid. Add the tomato juice, fish stock, Tabasco and bay leaves and bring to the boil; simmer for 20 minutes. Season, remove from the heat and allow to cool then place in an airtight container in the refrigerator.

To serve
Bring the soup to the boil, then add the sweetcorn, potatoes, clams, tomatoes and sugar. Check the seasoning, pour into a bowl, sprinkle with parsley and garnish with the clams in their shells.

Pan Bagnat

These sandwiches are ideal for a large group and bring back memories of eating on the beach. SERVES 20

2 x 200g (7oz) corn-fed chicken supremes
unscented vegetable oil
4 large ciabatta loaves
6 tbsp pesto (see page 168)
150ml (¼ pint) extra-virgin olive oil
salt & freshly ground black pepper
8 shallots, finely sliced
10 plum tomatoes, sliced
200g (7oz) baby spinach leaves, washed & dried
4 tbsp balsamic vinegar

(1d) **To prepare the pan bagnat**
Preheat the oven to 180°C/350°F/gas 4. Heat a chargrill pan. Brush the chicken with a little oil, season and cook until good bar marks are visible. Transfer to a metal tray and cook in the oven for about 10 minutes. Allow to cool, then cut into slices about 6mm (¼in) thick

and cover. Cut the loaves in half lengthways, spread each half with pesto, brush with oil and season. To assemble the filling, place a layer of chicken followed by the shallot, tomato and spinach; season between each layer and drizzle on the vinegar. Put on the tops of the loaves and wrap each bagnat in cling film. Press with cans or weights for 24 hours in the refrigerator.

To serve
Remove from refrigerator 1 hour before needed, slice into individual servings and arrange in rough piles on large plates.

Chopped Steak with Chunky Tomato Sauce

This tasty alternative to a traditional hamburger cannot be beaten. The sauce works well with sausage and mash too. SERVES 20

MADE TO ORDER
THESE STEAKS DO REQUIRE A BIT OF LAST-MINUTE ATTENTION, SO BE PREPARED.

Chunky Tomato Sauce
unscented vegetable oil
8 shallots, finely sliced
6 garlic cloves, finely diced
900ml (1½ pints) tomato juice
1 tbsp white wine vinegar
4 tbsp caster sugar
5 plum tomatoes, skinned, deseeded, diced
salt & freshly ground black pepper
1 tsp West Indian pepper sauce (optional)

Chopped Steak
unscented vegetable oil
3 onions, finely diced
8 garlic cloves, finely diced
3.6kg (7½lb) rump of beef, coarsely minced
5 tbsp tomato purée
5 tbsp Worcestershire sauce
1 tsp Tabasco sauce
5 egg yolks
2 tea cups flat-leaf parsley, washed, dried & chopped
salt & freshly ground black pepper

20 sesame-seed buns

Garnish
20 slices of beef tomato
2 cos lettuce heads, washed, dried & shredded into large pieces
20 slices of Spanish onion

(2d) To make the sauce
Heat a little oil in a saucepan. Add the shallot and garlic, sauté until soft, then add the tomato juice, vinegar and sugar; simmer for about 20 minutes. Add the tomatoes and season. Allow to cool, cover and place in the refrigerator.

(1d) To prepare the steak
Line a tray with greaseproof paper. Heat a little oil in a sauté pan and cook the onion and garlic until soft, without browning; allow to cool. Place the remaining ingredients, including the cooled onion and garlic, in a large mixing bowl and mix well; season. Mould the mixture into 20 x 180g (6oz) steaks and place on a metal tray, layering with greaseproof paper. Cover with cling film and refrigerate.

(½h) To grill the steak Heat a grill, barbecue or chargrill pan. Brush the steaks with a little oil and grill for 5 minutes on each side or until medium done. Keep warm.

To serve
Pour the tomato sauce into a bowl, then add the pepper sauce if using; stir. Half the buns, grill and serve with the steak, tomato sauce and garnishes.

Quesadillas with Tomatillo Salsa

Quesadillas are delicious with this salsa; serve with a green salad for supper. SERVES 20

Tomatillo Salsa
1.5kg (3lb 8oz) tomatillos, husks removed
1 onion, finely chopped
½ tea cup coriander, finely chopped
4 Serrano chillies, chopped
a few drops of lime juice
a few drops of nut oil

salt & freshly ground black pepper
a few avocado slices or crumbly, white cheese such as feta (optional)

Quesadillas
unscented vegetable oil
10 spring onions, washed & finely sliced
3 garlic cloves, finely chopped
800g (1¾lb) refried beans
salt & freshly ground black pepper
½ tea cup coriander, washed, dried & chopped
8 x 25cm (10in) round flour tortillas
250g (9 oz) Monterey Jack cheese, grated
8 plum tomatoes, skinned, deseeded & diced
100g (3½oz) jalapenos, chopped (optional)
2 egg whites, beaten
sour cream, to garnish

(8h) To prepare the salsa
Grind the tomatillos in a mortar and pestle then transfer to a bowl. Add the remaining ingredients, season and stir well. Cover and place in the refrigerator.

(2h) To make the quesadillas
Heat a little oil in a sauté pan, then add the onion and garlic and sauté until soft. Add the beans and cook for about 5 minutes; stir, season and then stir in the coriander. Allow to cool. Place 4 tortillas on a work surface and spread with the beans. Sprinkle on the cheese, then top with the tomatoes and jalapenos and season. Brush the edges with the egg whites, place the remaining tortillas on top; seal and place on a metal tray. Cover and refrigerate.

To serve
Preheat the oven to 180°C/350°F/gas 4. Warm up the quesadillas for about 10 minutes, then cut into triangles and serve with bowls of sour cream and the tomatillo salsa.

SPECTACULAR SALSA
REMEMBER THAT FOR TACOS AND QUESADILLAS IT IS BEST TO SERVE SALSA VERDE RAW OR MIXED WITH AVOCADO TO MAKE A GUACAMOLE MIXTURE. COOKED SALSA IS FOR ENCHILADAS OR FOR BRAISING MEAT OR CHICKEN.

Chicken Satay Sticks

It is worth taking the time to make these. SERVES 20

Chicken Marinade
3 heaped tbsp coriander seeds
3 heaped tbsp cumin powder
4 whole star anise
2 tbsp mild curry powder
1 tbsp ground turmeric
3 mild red chillies, deseeded & chopped
½ tea cup coriander leaves, stalks & roots, washed, dried & chopped
3 tbsp palm sugar
150ml (¼ pint) chilli sauce
150ml (¼ pint) light soy sauce
450ml (¾ pint) coconut milk
4 garlic cloves, finely chopped
15g (½oz) fresh ginger, chopped
5 x 200g (7oz) chicken supremes, skin removed & cut into 4cm (1½in) pieces
unscented vegetable oil
salt & freshly ground black pepper

Peanut Dipping Sauce
2 tbsp smooth peanut butter
60g (2oz) unsalted roasted peanuts, chopped

(3d) **To make the marinade and sauce**
Dry fry the spices for 2–3 minutes in a sauté pan, without browning. Remove from heat and allow to cool. Grind in a food processor and place in a bowl. Add the remaining marinade ingredients and mix well. Pour 150ml (¼ pint) of this marinade into a separate bowl, mix with the peanut butter and peanuts, cover and chill. Coat the chicken with the rest of the marinade. Cover and refrigerate.

(8h) **To skewer the satay**
Soak the wooden satay skewers in water for at least 30 minutes. This prevents the sticks from burning during cooking. Place 2 pieces of chicken on each stick, cover and return to the refrigerator.

(30m) **To cook the satay**
Preheat a barbecue, grill pan or grill. Brush the chicken lightly with oil, season and grill on each side until golden and firm to the touch. Pour the dipping sauce into a pan and heat.

To serve
Line bamboo steamers or trays with banana leaves, arrange the satay, pour the sauce into a serving bowl and serve. The satay can be served hot or cold.

Marinated Tiger Prawns

This is a great favourite of mine – the sauce can also be served with grilled sea bass or tuna. SERVES 20

Mango Dipping Sauce
2 ripe mangoes, peeled & flesh removed
1 red chilli, deseeded & finely chopped
¼ tea cup coriander, washed, dried & chopped
¼ tea cup mint, washed, dried & chopped
2 garlic cloves, finely chopped
juice of 3 limes
salt & freshly ground black pepper

Prawn Marinade
5 tbsp thin, light honey
2 tbsp red Thai curry paste
30g (1oz) galangal, finely chopped
juice & zest of 3 limes
60 tiger prawns, shells left on
unscented vegetable oil
salt & freshly ground black pepper

(1d) **To make the sauce**
Blend the mango flesh in a food processor until smooth. Remove and place in a bowl with the remaining ingredients; season and stir. Cover and place in the refrigerator.

(6h) **To marinade the prawns**
Mix together all the marinade ingredients in a bowl, then add the prawns. Cover and refrigerate.

(½h) **To skewer and cook the prawns**
Soak the sticks as for the satay. Preheat a grill pan, barbecue or grill. Skewer the prawns and brush with a little oil; season and grill on both sides until firm to the touch. Keep warm.

To serve the prawns
Pour the dipping sauce into a bowl, arrange the skewers on a serving dish with the sauce and serve.

Focaccia Bruschetta

Experiment with other interesting breads or invent your own toppings. This recipe is enough for 10 of each topping. MAKES 20

Flavoured Oil & Bread
150ml (¼ pint) olive oil
2 garlic cloves, sliced
5 sprigs of thyme
20 slices of focaccia, cut into 10cm- (4in-) long pieces

Mozzarella & Red Pepper Topping
3 garlic cloves
2 shallots, finely sliced
olive oil
2 tbsp white wine vinegar
4 tbsp Demerara sugar
4 red peppers, skinned, deseeded, veins removed & cut into strips
2 plum tomatoes, skinned, deseeded & diced
salt & freshly ground black pepper
4 buffalo mozzarella, cut into 20 slices
2 tsp rosemary, roughly chopped
10 coppa or Parma ham slices
10 basil leaves, to garnish

Mushroom, Tomato & Rocket Topping
250g (9oz) flat mushrooms, cut into 20 slices
olive oil for grilling
salt & freshly ground black pepper
1 tbsp extra-virgin olive oil
1 tbsp aged balsamic vinegar
2 shallots, finely sliced
2 garlic cloves, finely chopped
20 baby plum tomatoes
1 teaspoon sugar
30g (1oz) rocket, picked, washed & dried
shavings of Parmesan

(2d) **To flavour the oil**
In a pan warm the oil and the garlic for about 5 minutes. Remove from heat and allow to cool. Pour into a jar with a lid, add the thyme and store in a cool place.

(2d) **To make the red pepper topping**
Finely chop 2 of the garlic cloves. Sauté the shallot and garlic in a little olive oil for about 5 minutes without browning. Add the vinegar and sugar and reduce until syrupy. Add the peppers and

tomatoes, season and cook for 5 more minutes. Allow to cool then refrigerate in an airtight container. Place the mozzarella in an airtight container. Finely slice the remaining garlic clove, and mix with the rosemary and 3 tablespoons of olive oil, season and pour over the cheese. Cover and refrigerate.

(1h) To prepare the mushroom topping

Preheat a grill pan. Brush the mushrooms with olive oil and season. Grill for 2 minutes on each side or until bar marks are visible; allow to cool. Pour the olive oil and balsamic vinegar into a bowl, add the shallot and garlic, season, add the mushrooms and toss well. Cover and chill. In a sauté pan, in a little olive oil cook the tomatoes with the sugar until soft. Remove from the heat and cool. Cover and refrigerate.

(8h) To grill the focaccia

Preheat the oven to 180°C/350°F/gas 4. Heat a grill pan and brush the focaccia lightly with flavoured oil. Season and grill on both sides until bar marks are visible. Bake in the oven for 3–4 minutes. Allow to cool and store in an airtight container in a cool place.

To assemble

Lay out the bruschetta on a dish. On 10 of the breads arrange 2 mushroom slices, 2 tomatoes and a rocket leaf; top with a shaving of Parmesan. Top the other bruschetta with the mozzarella, ham and red pepper chutney; garnish with basil leaves and serve.

Marinated Tiger Prawns, Focaccia Bruschetta (Mozarella & Red Pepper Topping, Mushroom, Tomato & Rocket Topping)

moroccan buffet

We are very lucky to have Moroccan chef Djery, and, apart from the rosewater cream which one of our pastry chefs developed these are his family's recipes. Other typical desserts include fresh fruits and sweet pastries purchased from a specialist baker. The only thing you should ever drink is of course mint tea so Djery's recipe is an essential.

Moroccan Lamb

This popular buffet dish looks great in a traditional tagine. SERVES 20

Harissa Sauce
60g (2oz) hot red chilli, chopped
4 garlic cloves, chopped
4 tsp cumin seeds, roasted
½ tsp coriander seeds, roasted
salt & freshly ground black pepper
4 red peppers, roasted, skins & seeds removed
2 tbsp olive oil
lemon juice to taste

Lamb Marinade
olive oil to cover
3.7kg (8lb) middle neck of lamb fillet, cubed
2 tbsp ground turmeric
6 tbsp ground cumin
1 tea cup coriander, chopped
4 medium onions, finely sliced
150ml (¼ pint) extra-virgin olive oil
8 garlic cloves, chopped
4 cinnamon sticks
salt & freshly ground black pepper
3.5 litres (6 pints) chicken stock
200g (7oz) dried prunes
3 tbsp soft brown sugar
picked coriander, to garnish

(1w) To make the harissa sauce
Grind or blend the dry ingredients in a mortar or food processor until smooth, then add the peppers, olive oil

Chicken with Lemon & Olives,
Carrot & Orange Salad (see following page)

and lemon juice and blend for a further 10 seconds. Transfer the paste to a sterilized jar and cover with a layer of olive oil. Seal and refrigerate.

(1d) To marinade the lamb
Put the lamb in an airtight container. Place the dry spices, coriander, onion, olive oil, garlic, cinnamon sticks, salt and black pepper in a bowl and mix. Rub the mixture into the meat until it is completely coated. Cover with cling film and marinade for 24 hours.

(1d) To cook the lamb
Heat a little olive oil in a large pan. When it starts to smoke, add the lamb (in batches if necessary) and cook until browned (about 8 minutes). Add the stock, prunes and sugar; cover. Cook on a low heat for about 45 minutes or until the lamb is tender. Remove the meat from the pan with a slotted spoon, place in an airtight container and put aside. Turn up the heat to reduce the remaining sauce by half. It is ready when shiny and it can coat the back of a spoon. Pour the sauce over the lamb and allow to cool. Cover and refrigerate.

To assemble
Preheat the oven to 130°C/250°F/gas 2. Warm the tagine or serving bowl. In a large pan, bring the lamb to the boil then reduce the heat to low. Check the seasoning and transfer the lamb to the tagine or bowl. Garnish with coriander.

Chicken with Lemon & Olives

This is great for serving chicken to a large group, especially since it is so easy to prepare. SERVES 20

Chicken Marinade

20 skinless chicken breasts
2 tsp saffron strands
2 tbsp ground cumin
4 garlic cloves, chopped
½ tea cup chopped coriander
150 ml (¼ pint) olive oil
4 large onions, finely diced
3 litres (5 pints) chicken stock
2 lemons
450g (1lb) pitted green olives
salt & freshly ground black pepper
2 tbsp shelled, unsalted pistachio nuts
picked coriander or mint, to garnish

(2d) **To marinade the chicken**
Cut the chicken into 4cm (1½in) cubes, or leave whole; place in a bowl. Add the saffron, cumin, garlic, coriander and olive oil. Cover and place in the refrigerator for 24 hours.

(1h) **To cook the chicken**
Heat a little olive oil in a large saucepan. When it starts to smoke, add the chicken and onions and cook until lightly golden. Add the chicken stock, bring to the boil then simmer for about 10 minutes. Remove the chicken from the sauce using a slotted spoon and place in an airtight container. Increase the heat and reduce the sauce by about half. Pour over the chicken and leave to cool. When cold, cover and place in the refrigerator. Peel and slice the lemons, about 4mm (⅛in) thick. Place in an airtight container and refrigerate.

To assemble
Preheat the oven to 130°C/250°F/gas 2. Heat the serving dish. Place the chicken in a large saucepan and bring to the boil. Add the green olives and sliced lemons; reduce to a low heat and check the seasoning. Transfer into the serving dish and scatter on the pistachio nuts. Garnish with picked coriander or mint.

Chermoula Marinaded Seabass

Djery recommends that daurade or large red mullet are excellent alternatives to seabass. SERVES 20

Seabass Marinade

450ml (¾ pint) extra-virgin olive oil
4 medium onions, peeled & finely chopped
6 garlic cloves, finely chopped
2 tbsp ground cumin
2 tsp paprika
1 tsp cayenne pepper
juice of 4 lemons
2 large seabass (total weight of 3.6kg/8lb), whole, scaled & fins removed
salt & freshly ground black pepper
300ml (½ pint) water

Garnish

1 tea cup coriander, washed, dried & chopped
1 tea cup flat-leaf parsely, washed, dried & chopped
15 plum tomatoes, skinned, deseeded & diced

(8h) **To prepare the marinade**
Heat a large sauté pan and, when hot, add the olive oil, onion, garlic, spices and lemon juice. Sauté for about 3–5 minutes, without browning. Remove from the heat, place in a bowl and leave to cool. Place the fish on a baking tin that will fit in the oven. Make 6 slashes on each side; season with salt and freshly ground black pepper. When the marinade is cold, rub it into the fish on both sides. Cover and place in the refrigerator for at least 6 hours.

(1h) **To cook the seabass**
Remove the fish from the refrigerator at least 20 minutes before baking. Preheat the oven to 190°C/375°F/gas 5. Pour the water into the baking tin, place the fish in as well, cover tightly with foil and bake for between 45 minutes and 1 hour. Remove and keep warm.

To serve
Remove the foil and place the fish on a warm serving platter. Scatter on the herbs and tomatoes and serve.

Carrot & Orange Salad

A refreshing foil to the highly flavoured main dishes. SERVES 20

1.8kg (4lb) carrots, coarsely grated
8 large oranges, preferably Valencia, peeled, segmented & pips removed
zest of 2 oranges
250g (9oz) large raisins

Dressing

2 tsp ground cumin
1 tsp ground cinnamon
1 tsp caster sugar
juice of 2 lemons
2 tbsp orange flower water (optional)
300ml (½ pint) olive oil
salt & freshly ground black pepper
1½ tea cups flat-leaf parsley, washed, dried & chopped
2 tbsp toasted sesame seeds

(8h) **To prepare the salad**
Place the carrots, oranges, orange zest and raisins in an airtight container; cover and refrigerate.

(8h) **To prepare the dressing**
Place the cumin, cinnamon and caster sugar in a bowl. Add the lemon juice and orange flower water; mix. Pour in the oil and mix. Season and pour into a jar with a lid. Store in a cool place.

To assemble
Remove the salad from the refrigerator. Pour the dressing over it, add the parsley, toasted sesame seeds and toss well. Check the seasoning and arrange in a salad bowl.

DJERY'S MINT TEA

TO MAKE 10 MOROCCAN GLASSES OF TEA, POUR 1.8 LITRES (3 PINTS) BOILING WATER INTO A TEAPOT CONTAINING 4 TEASPOONS JAPANESE GREEN TEA AND 2 TEA CUPS CHOPPED FRESH MINT. ADD SUGAR TO TASTE. POURING THE WATER FROM A GOOD HEIGHT HELPS TO OXYGENATE THE TEA. LEAVE TO STAND FOR 5 MINUTES THEN POUR INTO TEA GLASSES. HAND ROUND EXTRA SUGAR.

Couscous

If you are having vegetarians to dinner, this can make an interesting salad for a first course SERVES 20.

1.5 litres (2½ pints) vegetable stock
150ml (¼ pint) olive oil
900g (2lb) couscous
2 tea cups chopped coriander
2 tea cups chopped parsley
300g dried apricots, cut into three
juice of 4 limes
350g (12½oz) whole roasted almonds, skins removed
salt & freshly ground black pepper
picked coriander to garnish

(1d) To prepare the couscous
In a pan, bring the vegetable stock and olive oil to the boil. Place the couscous in a large bowl and pour in the boiling vegetable stock and olive oil. Cover with cling film for 10 minutes; remove the cling film and break up the grains with your hands. When completely separate, re-cover and then refrigerate when cold.

(6h) To prepare the herbs and fruit
Place the herbs, apricots, lime juice and two thirds of the almonds in an airtight container; mix. Cover and chill.

To assemble
Preheat the oven to 130°C/250°F/gas 2. Heat the serving bowl. Warm the couscous in a microwave for about 4 minutes. Alternatively, place the couscous in a fine sieve over a pan of simmering water. When hot, transfer to the serving bowl and add the prepared herbs, apricots, lime juice and almonds. Season and mix well. Garnish with coriander and remaining almonds.

USING GOLD LEAF

USE ONLY 22 CARAT GOLD LEAF TO DECORATE THE MOROCCAN ROSEWATER CREAM (RIGHT). THE BEST METHOD IS TO PICK THE LEAF UP WITH A GILDERS BRUSH MADE FROM SQUIRREL HAIR AND LET IT FLUTTER ONTO THE DESSERT (CHECKING FIRST THAT YOUR ROOM IS DRAUGHT-FREE!)

Rosewater Cream

Rosewater Cream

Make this delicious cream in individual moulds or in 1 x 1.9 litre (3¼ pint) mould as here. SERVES 20

9 gelatine leaves
1.2 litres (2 pints) full-fat milk
3 vanilla pods, split
10 egg yolks
180g (6oz) caster sugar
9 tsp rosewater
2 tsp lemon juice
600ml (1 pint) double cream

Garnish
edible gold leaf (optional)
rose petals
pistachio nuts, shelled & unsalted

(2d) To make the cream
Cover the gelatine with cold water and put to one side. Pour the milk into a heavy-bottomed saucepan. Scrape out the vanilla seeds from the pods, then add the seeds and pods to the milk and bring to the boil. In an electric mixer, whisk the egg yolks and sugar until smooth. Turn down the speed and pour the boiling milk in a steady stream onto the egg mixture; whisk until smooth. Pour the mixture back into the pan, add the rosewater and lemon juice and return to the heat. Continue to whisk until the mixture coats the back of a spoon. Remove from the heat. Drain the gelatine, squeeze out the excess water and stir into the hot mixture. Pass through a fine sieve into a large bowl; allow to cool then whisk until the cream just holds its shape. When the rosewater cream is cold, fold in the cream; pour into the mould and place on a tray. Cover and refrigerate.

To assemble
Fill a large bowl or sink with hot water and dip the mould into the water to about 1.5mm (½in) from the top. Remove when the mould feels warm and place the serving platter on top; turn over quickly. Leave for about 2 minutes then remove the mould. Decorate the top with gold leaf if using and scatter on the rose petals and nuts. Serve with Moroccan pastries or fresh fruit.

east-west buffet

The people I work with all, like me, love oriental food. Our executive chef, Steve Bailey, has a particular flair and this is the menu that he has developed over the years. Take time to search out the unusual ingredients – nowadays the majority can be found in supermarkets and most towns have a good ethnic shop for the rest. Chilled dry white wines and Asian lagers are the perfect drinks to serve.

Warm Beef Salad with Orange Dressing

This recipe epitomizes East meets West cuisine. It is easy to prepare, too – just remember to marinade the beef for at least a day. SERVES 20

Beef Marinade
300ml (½ pint) light soy sauce
300ml (½ pint) mushroom soy sauce
2 tbsp cornflour
5 tbsp light brown sugar
4 tbsp chilli oil
4 red chillis, deseeded & finely chopped
2.5kg (5lb 8oz) rump steak, any fat removed, cut into finger-size pieces.

Orange Dressing
1 tbsp caster sugar
juice & zest of 3 small (ideally blood) oranges
juice & zest of 1 lemon
3 tbsp peanut oil
2 tbsp chilli oil
½ tsp cayenne pepper
4 garlic cloves, chopped
150ml (¼ pint) aged balsamic vinegar
4 tbsp light soy sauce

Salad
300g (11oz) baby spinach, picked, washed & dried
450g (1lb) mixed salad leaves, washed, dried & torn into small pieces
10 spring onions, washed & finely sliced
2 tea cups mint leaves, washed & dried
1 tea cup snipped chives
½ tea cup coriander leaves, washed & dried
deep-fried rice sticks, to garnish (optional)

(1d) **To marinade the beef**
Place the marinade ingredients in a large bowl, mix well and add the beef. Cover and place in the refrigerator.

(1d) **To make the orange dressing**
Combine all the ingredients in a jar with a lid, shake well, cover and refrigerate.

To assemble the salad
Place the leafy salad ingredients in a serving bowl and put to one side. Drain the beef. Heat a little unscented oil in a large wok or sauté pan and add the beef a few handfuls at a time; sauté until medium done and place in a metal bowl. Dress the salad, add the beef and mix; garnish with the deep-fried rice sticks if using and serve.

TO DESEED CHILLIES
IT IS BEST TO WEAR DISPOSABLE GLOVES WHEN HANDLING CHILLIES. CUT THE CHILLI IN HALF LENGTHWAYS AND THEN EITHER (WEARING GLOVES) REMOVE THE SEEDS WITH THE POINT OF THE KNIFE; OR REMOVE THE SEEDS UNDER RUNNING WATER. IF YOU ARE NOT USING GLOVES DO NOT RUB YOUR EYES OR MOUTH — THEY WILL BURN!

Massaman Chicken

Serve this with a bowl of steamed jasmine rice. SERVES 20

Chicken Marinade
1 tbsp cornflour
6 tbsp Massaman curry paste dissolved in 2 tbsp boiling water
8 garlic cloves, finely chopped
3 red chillies, deseeded & finely chopped
1 tea cup coriander leaves & roots, washed & chopped
20 x 200g (7oz) chicken supremes, skinned, wing bone removed, in 4cm (1½in) cubes

Curried Sauce
unscented oil
6 medium onions, diced
3 tbsp tamarind pulp
3 tbsp palm sugar
150ml (¼ pint) Thai fish sauce
4.8 litres (7 pints) coconut milk
450ml (1 pint) reduced white chicken stock
1kg (2lb 2oz) cooked sweet potato, cut into large dice

Garnish
1 tea cup coriander leaves, washed & dried
2 medium chillies, cut into strips
60g (2oz) toasted, unsalted cashew nuts

(2d) **To marinade the chicken**
In a large bowl, mix together all the ingredients for the marinade, add the chicken and coat well. Cover and chill.

(1d) **To make the curried sauce**
Cook the onions in a little oil until soft but not coloured. Add the chicken to the pan and sauté for about 5 minutes. Add the remaining curry ingredients, omitting the potatoes, and bring to the boil. Simmer for 30 minutes, then remove from the heat and leave to cool. Cover and chill.

To serve
Bring to a simmer slowly, add the potatoes, stir and leave for 5 minutes. Pour into a warmed bowl and garnish with coriander, chilli strips and nuts.

Front to back: *Warm Beef Salad, Massaman Chicken*

Pickled Cucumber & Pawpaw Salad

The sweet and spicy Thai-inspired combination is irresistibly uplifting. SERVES 20.

Salad

4 cucumbers, cut in half lengthways, deseeded & sliced

4 ripe pawpaw, peeled, deseeded & cut into thin wedges

2 red onions, finely sliced

1 tea cup coriander leaves, washed & dried

Pickling liquid

900ml (1½ pints) rice wine vinegar

300g (11oz) caster sugar

300ml (½ pint) water

3 garlic cloves, finely chopped

2 red chillies, deseeded & cut into fine strips

½ tsp turmeric

salt & freshly ground black pepper

(8h) To prepare the salad

Place the cucumber, pawpaw and onions in an airtight container. Mix the pickling ingredients in a stainless steel saucepan, bring to the boil, season, then simmer for about 5 minutes. Leave to cool slightly. Pour over the salad ingredients and leave to cool; cover and place in the refrigerator.

To serve

Drain the salad, check the seasoning and mix in the coriander. Arrange in a serving bowl.

Front to back: *Spicy Hot and Sour Prawns, Pickled Cucumber & Pawpaw Salad*

Spicy, Hot & Sour Prawns

As other recipes, these are easy to do. They are perfect for a picnic eaten straight from the container with chopsticks. SERVES 20.

Prawn Marinade

1 tea cup coriander, washed, dried & chopped

6 garlic cloves, finely chopped

4 small hot red chillies, deseeded & finely chopped

5 stems of lemon grass, finely sliced

10 spring onions, finely sliced

60g (2oz) peeled fresh ginger, finely chopped

1kg (2lb 2oz) shelled tiger prawns

Hot & Sour Dressing

juice of 5 limes

150ml (¼ pint) Thai fish sauce

150ml (¼ pint) light soy sauce

2 tsp caster sugar

5 choy sum (about 500g/1lb 1oz)

lemon grass to garnish

(1d) To marinade the prawns

Place the coriander, garlic, chillies, lemon grass, spring onions and ginger in a large bowl, then mix well. Add the prawns and mix. Cover and place in the refrigerator.

(1d) To make the dressing

In a bowl, mix the lime juice, fish sauce, soy sauce and sugar, stirring until the sugar is dissolved. Pour into a jar with a good lid and store in the refrigerator.

(8h) To cook the prawns and choy sum

Heat a little oil in a wok or sauté pan. Sauté the prawns, a handful at a time, and place in a bowl. Wilt the choy sum in the wok or sauté pan and place in the bowl with the prawns. Cover and chill.

To serve

Remove the prawns from the refrigerator at least 30 minutes before serving. Pour the dressing over the prawns and choy sum; toss well. Arrange on serving dishes and garnish with lemon grass.

Spicy Red Mullet on a Bed of Asian Greens

Red mullet is a very under-rated fish which, when cooked properly, is very tasty. Buy this fish ready-filleted, checking that all the bones have been removed. Do not over-cook, otherwise the fish will be very dry. SERVES 20

Asian Greens
peanut oil
3 garlic cloves, finely sliced
60g (2oz) pickled ginger, finely shredded
10 baby bok choy, washed, dried & leaves
    separated
150ml (¼ pint) sweet soy sauce
salt & freshly ground black pepper

Topping for the Red Mullet
5 shallots, finely diced
3 Kaffir lime leaves finely shredded
3 red chillies, deseeded, cut into fine strips
30g (1oz) fresh ginger, cut into fine strips
4 garlic cloves, finely chopped
½ tea cup coriander, washed, dried & chopped
4 tbsp Thai fish sauce
juice of 2 limes
salt & freshly ground black pepper
800g (1lb 8oz) red mullet fillets, pin boned,
    cut into 20 pieces (if unavailable, replace
    with red snapper)

(8h) To cook the greens
Heat a little peanut oil in a wok or sauté pan, then add the garlic and pickled ginger and cook for about 1 minute. Add the greens and soy sauce, cooking until the greens are wilted, then remove and season. Allow to cool, cover and place in the refrigerator.

(2h) To cook the red mullet
Preheat the to oven 180°F/350°F/gas 4. Line a metal oven tray with greaseproof paper. Mix all the ingredients for the topping (apart from the fish) in a bowl. Place the fish on the tray, spoon the mixture over the fillets and bake in the oven for about 5–6 minutes. Remove from the oven and leave to cool. Pour the cooking juices into a container, cover and place in the refrigerator.

To serve
Remove the red mullet from the refrigerator at least 30 minutes before serving. Line a wooden board with banana leaves. Pour a little of the red mullet cooking juices into the greens and mix. Place the greens on the banana leaves, top with the red mullet and serve.

Baby Pork Ribs

There is something very convivial about eating food without a knife and fork so encourage it with these pork ribs, but supply lots of napkins for sticky fingers. SERVES 20

6 garlic cloves, finely chopped
300ml (½ pint) sweet soy sauce
150ml (¼ pint) soy sauce
3 tbsp sweet chilli sauce
1 tsp shrimp paste
1 tbsp cornflour
1 tea cup Thai basil leaves shredded
20 baby ribs about 2kg (4lb 8oz)
Thai basil leaves, to garnish

(1d) To marinade the ribs
Mix the main ingredients in a large bowl, adding the ribs at the end so they can be evenly coated. Cover and place in the refrigerator.

To cook the ribs
Preheat the oven to 180°C/350°F/gas 4. Place the ribs on a metal baking tray, pouring any remaining marinade over them. Cook for about 1 hour. If the ribs begin to dry out or start to burn, cover them with foil. Transfer to a serving tray and garnish with Thai basil.

UNUSUAL INGREDIENTS
IF YOU CANNOT FIND EXACTLY THE INGREDIENT YOU ARE LOOKING FOR IN THE SUPERMARKET THERE IS USUALLY SOMETHING YOU CAN REPLACE IT WITH. FOR EXAMPLE, THE SLIGHTLY PURPLISH THAI BASIL USED IN AUTHENTIC ASIAN COOKING CAN EASILY BE SUBSTITUTED WITH SPRIGS OF FRESH COMMON BASIL.

Two-bean Salad with Sesame Dressing

We try to use different vegetables for salads, but if you find that some are not easy to obtain then replace them with the suggested alternatives – the salad will taste just as good. As with any salad do not dress this until just before serving or it will lose its crunch. SERVES 20

Sesame Dressing
2 tbsp light sesame oil
2 tbsp caster sugar
2 tbsp rice wine vinegar
2 tbsp light soy sauce
2 tbsp toasted sesame seeds
freshly ground Szechwan pepper

Salad
500g(1lb 1oz) wing beans, sliced into 7.5cm
    (3in) slices (if unavailable, use whole, thin
    asparagus stems)
600g (1lb 6oz) long beans, cut into 10cm
    (4in) slices (if unavailable, use extra-fine,
    whole French beans)
300g (11oz) Chinese chives, cut into 7.5cm
    (3in) lengths (if unavailable, use spring
    onions)
chive flowers

(8h) To make the dressing
Combine all the dressing ingredients in a jar with a lid, mix and store in a cool place.

(8h) To blanch the beans
Fill a large bowl or sink with iced water and bring a large saucepan of salted water to the boil. Blanch the wing beans and then the long beans each for a couple of minutes in the boiling water, refreshing each batch in the iced water. Drain and shake to dry. Mix the beans together then place in an airtight container lined with a tea towel. Put in the refrigerator.

To serve
Mix the beans and chives with the dressing in a large bowl; toss well and season. Arrange in a serving bowl and garnish with chive flowers.

brunch buffet

Weekends are brunch time, starting as early as 11.30am or as late as 2.00pm. What could be better than a lazy day spent reading the papers, relaxing with family and friends and enjoying this truly delicious selection of light meals and refreshing drinks? The menu has every essential for a classic brunch but when entertaining, I will also have lots of fresh fruit on hand – or perhaps you could make a fruit salad.

BRUNCH-TIME DRINKS
BELLINI (PAGE 68)
BLOODY MARY (PAGE 68)
MELON, APPLE & LIME COOLADE (PAGE 74)
PAW PAW & PINEAPPLE COOLER (PAGE 75)
FRESHLY SQEEZED BLOOD ORANGE JUICE
GALLONS OF FRESH COFFEE

New York Waffles with a Selection of Toppings

These waffles bring back happy memories of brunch in New York City 30 years ago. SERVES 20

Spiced Apple Topping
120g (4oz) unsalted butter
4 cinnamon sticks
3 vanilla pods, spilt
1½ tsp freshly ground nutmeg
10 large Cox's apples, peeled, cored & sliced
150g (5½oz) golden sultanas, soaked in rum or brandy for 24 hours
zest of 1 lemon
zest of 1 orange
60g (2oz) Demerara sugar

Apricot, & Pumpkin Seed Topping
500g (1lb 1oz) dried apricots, sliced
¼ medium-sized pineapple, peeled, hard core removed, cut into small slices
15g (½oz) fresh ginger, peeled & sliced
100g (3½oz) blanched almond slithers
Demerara sugar to taste

Garnish
500g (1lb1oz) crème fraîche
150g (5oz) toasted pumpkin seeds
sprigs of mint
560ml (1 pint) good-quality maple syrup
250g (9oz) unsalted butter

Waffle Mixture
300ml (½ pint) full-fat milk
60g (2oz) unsalted butter, melted
2 egg yolks
250g (9oz) plain flour
3 tsp baking powder
pinch of salt
4 egg whites

SPECIAL EQUIPMENT **waffle iron or sandwich maker**

(1d) To make the apple topping
Melt the butter in a pan, when hot add the cinnamon, vanilla and nutmeg; stir. Add the apple slices, sultanas and citrus zest, and simmer until soft; do not cover. Add the sugar, stir well and remove from the heat. Cool, then remove the vanilla pods and cinnamon sticks. Cover and refrigerate.

BEST APPLE SAUCE
DO NOT ALLOW THE APPLES TO OVER-COOK OTHERWISE THEY WILL BE LIKE APPLE SAUCE. THE AIM IS TO PRODUCE A CHUNKY TOPPING.

New York Waffles with a Selection of Toppings

(1d) To make the apricot topping

Bring a pan of water to the boil. Place the apricots in a bowl and pour in the boiling water to cover the fruit. Leave for about 1 hour. Pour the apricots and water into a large saucepan, bring to the boil and simmer for about 1 hour or until the apricots are almost turning to a pulp (during the poaching you may need to add more water). Add the pineapple, ginger and almonds; continue to cook for a further 15 minutes or until the pineapple is just soft. If you wish to add sugar to taste, remove from the heat and stir in the sugar. Allow to cool, cover and place in the refrigerator.

(1h) To prepare the batter

In a large bowl, add the milk, butter and egg yolks; mix until smooth. Sift the flour with the baking powder into a separate bowl. Add the milk mixture to the flour slowly and mix until smooth; add salt. Cover and refrigerate.

To cook the waffles

Preheat the oven to 140°C/275°F/gas 1. Heat the waffle iron. Whisk the egg whites until stiff and fold into the batter. Pour some batter onto the iron and cook until golden. Repeat for the rest of the mixture. Keep warm in the oven.

To serve

Place the toppings and crème fraiche in serving bowls, sprinkle pumpkin seeds on the apricot topping, offer leftover seeds on the side and garnish with fresh mint. Pour the maple syrup into a bottle with a pourer and put the butter on a serving dish. Pile up the waffles and let everyone help themselves.

SMOKED SALMON SPECIAL

AS WELL AS SERVING THE WAFFLES, YOU MAY ALSO LIKE TO TOAST SOME HALVED BAGELS FOR DELUXE SMOKED SALMON SANDWICHES. WHIP UP CREAM CHEESE AND CHIVES, SPREAD THICKLY ON THE BAGELS, THEN JUST ADD A GENEROUS SLICE OF SMOKED SALMON, A SQUIRT OF LIME AND A TWIST OF BLACK PEPPER. THE PERFECT SANDWICH!

Hot Salt Beef & Pickles

Salt beef with creamed carrots and split peas is also a wonderful winter supper dish. SERVES 20

3.5kg (7lb 8oz) silverside of salt beef
3 large carrots, cut into chunks
2 large onions halved & each studded with
  6 cloves
3 garlic cloves, crushed
2 bay leaves
10 sprigs of thyme
6 whole black peppercorns
selection of mustards
6 medium pickled cucumber
2 loaves of New York rye bread

(1d) **To soak the beef**
Place the beef in a large airtight container, cover with water and store in the refrigerator.

(4h) **To cook the beef**
Remove the beef from the container and place in a large saucepan, cover with cold water and add the vegetables, herbs and peppercorns. Place on the heat, bring to the boil and simmer for about 3–3½ hours. Remove from the heat, but leave in the water.

To serve
Place a selection of mustards and pickled cucumber in serving dishes. Slice the bread and arrange in boxes or baskets. Drain the beef, place it on a large wooden board and carve into thin slices to serve with bread and garnishes.

Blueberry Muffins

These delicious muffins are courtesy of Annie Waite, head chef at Nicole's in London. MAKES 10

100g (3½oz) unsalted butter, melted
plain flour to dust
150g (5½oz) unsalted butter
150g (5½oz) caster sugar
3 eggs
200g (7oz) sifted wholemeal flour
1 tsp baking powder

1 tbsp mixed spice
85ml (3fl oz) milk
300g (11oz) fresh blueberries

(1d) **To make the blueberry muffins**
Brush the inside of the moulds with the butter; dust with flour and set aside. Preheat the oven to 190°C/375°F/gas 5. In an electric mixer, cream the butter and sugar until light and fluffy, then add the eggs one at a time, beating well. Remove the bowl from the mixer to fold in the flour, baking powder and mixed spices, Mix well, then pour in the milk and mix again; gently fold in the blueberries. Spoon the mixture into the moulds and bake for about 25–30 minutes until golden brown and springy to touch. Leave the muffins to cool, remove from the moulds and place in an airtight container in a cool place.

To serve
Preheat the oven to 160°C/325°F/gas 3. Place the muffins on an ovenproof tray and warm for about 6 minutes before arranging in a bowl or basket lined with a napkin to serve.

Savoury Muffins

The basic mixture is enough for 10 muffins then just choose which of the flavours you want to add. Why not double the basic mixture and make 10 of each? MAKES 10

Basic Savoury Muffin Mixture
60g (2 oz) unsalted butter, melted
plain flour
100g (3½oz) fine cornmeal
140g (5oz) plain flour
1½ tsp salt
1½ tsp ground white pepper
4 eggs
140g (5oz) unsalted butter, melted
200g (7oz) sour cream
1 tea cup finely grated Parmesan cheese
1½ tsp baking powder

Goats' Cheese & Basil Muffins
250g (9oz) goats' cheese
12 basil leaves, shredded

Cheddar & Mustard Muffins
1 tbsp grain mustard
100g (3¼oz) grated mature cheddar

(1d) **To make the goats' cheese muffins**
Preheat the oven to 190°C/375°F/gas 5. Brush the inside of the moulds with the butter, dust with flour and set aside. Place all the ingredients for the basic savoury mixture in a large mixing bowl and mix until well combined. Crumble in the goats' cheese and add the basil. Spoon the mixture into the tins and bake for about 20–25 minutes or until golden. Allow to cool, then place in an airtight container in a cool place.

(1d) **To make the cheddar muffins**
Preheat the oven to 190°C/375°F/gas 5. Brush the inside of the moulds with the butter, dust with flour and set aside. Mix the mustard with all the ingredients for the basic savoury mixture in a large mixing bowl. Spoon the mixture into the tins, sprinkle with the cheese and bake for about 20–25 minutes or until golden. Allow to cool, then place in an airtight container in a cool place.

To serve
Preheat the oven to 160°C/325°F/gas3. Place the muffins on an ovenproof tray and warm for about 6 minutes, then arrange them in a bowl or basket lined with a napkin to serve.

MUFFIN MOULDS
IF YOU DON'T HAVE A MUFFIN TIN YOU CAN BUY PAPER CASES FROM KITCHEN SHOPS. IF USING ANOTHER MOULD ADJUST THE COOKING TIME ACCORDINGLY.

Hash Brown Potatoes

Hash browns with grilled bacon and eggs was one of the first breakfasts I ever ate in Florida. SERVES 20

unscented vegetable oil
2 medium onions, finely diced
200g (7oz) Parma ham, finely diced
2kg (4lb 4oz) potatoes, parboiled
sea salt & freshly ground black pepper

(6h) To prepare the hash browns

Heat a little oil in a sauté pan, then add the onions and cook for about 4–5 minutes. Add the ham and cook for a further 2 minutes without colouring; set aside. Grate the potatoes coarsely and place in a bowl, then add the onions and ham; season and mix well. Roll out the potato mixture and cut into 20 x 9cm (3½in) squares. Heat a little oil in a sauté pan and fry the squares, a few at a time, until golden brown on both sides. Place on an ovenproof tray to cool, then cover and refrigerate.

To serve

Preheat the oven to 200°C/400°F/gas 6. Cook for about 10–12 minutes until crisp. Transfer to a warm serving platter.

Huevos Rancheros

My friends, Gab and Lynn, have cooked these scrumptious eggs for me on many occasions. MAKES 10

Mexican Sauce

900g (2lb) tomatillos, husks removed
1 large onion, finely chopped
3 garlic cloves, chopped
unscented vegetable oil
4 Serrano chillies or green chillies
juice of 2 limes
1 tsp nut oil
salt & freshly ground black pepper
½ tea cup of picked & chopped coriander

Refried Beans

unscented vegetable oil
1 bunch of spring onions, washed & sliced
4 garlic cloves, finely chopped (optional)
1kg (2lb 2oz) refried beans
salt & ground black pepper
½ tea cup chopped coriander
juice of 2 limes

20 corn tortillas, 15cm (6in) in diameter
20 eggs

TIMING

ALLOCATE YOURSELF ENOUGH TIME TO COOK THE TORTILLAS AND EGGS BEFORE SERVING.

Huevos Rancheros

(1d) To prepare the Mexican sauce

Heat a grill pan. Place the tomatillos on the hot grill to singe the skin then chop in a food processor for about 10 seconds. Sauté the onion and garlic in a little oil until transparent, without browning. Add the tomatillos and chilli, bring to the boil, reduce the heat and cook for about 5 minutes. Remove from the heat, pour into a container. Add the lime juice, nut oil, then season and leave to cool. When cold, stir in the coriander. Cover and place in the refrigerator.

(½h) To prepare the beans

Sauté the onion and garlic in oil until soft. Add the beans and cook for about 5 minutes; stir and season. Add the coriander and lime juice, stir and cool.

(½h) To cook the tortillas

Heat a little oil in a frying pan and fry the tortillas on each side for about 10–15 seconds – holding them down with a pair of tongs makes this easier. Remove and keep warm. Heat a little oil in a sauté pan and fry the eggs; transfer them onto kitchen paper to keep warm.

To serve

Place the tortillas in a basket lined with a napkin. Place the refried beans and Mexican green sauce in bowls and serve with the eggs. The best way to eat Huevos Rancheros is to spread the tortilla with beans, place the egg on top and drizzle on the sauce. If the occasion calls for it, offer iced Mexican beers and frozen margaritas to accompany the dish.

desserts buffet

Creating a spectacular dessert buffet in a separate room or area lifts a buffet party out of the ordinary, giving guests a real sense of occasion. Fill tall glass vases with mousses, fruits and sauces and use Moroccan tea glasses to hold vanilla brûlée creams topped with melted sugar. For an impressive effect, serve chocolate, lemon or fruit tarts and meringues layered with fruits and cream on glass cake stands.

Three-Chocolate Mousse with Chocolate Shapes

Three-Chocolate Mousse with Chocolate Shapes

This recipe for a triple-layered chocolate mousse makes about 4 litres (7 pints) in total. Serve it in glass vases so you can appreciate the swirls of the different mousses. To decorate the dessert, have fun creating your own abstract marbled patterns with the tempered chocolate. SERVES 20

Sugar Syrup
1kg (2lb 2oz) caster sugar
750ml (1¼ pint) water

Bitter Chocolate Mousse
275g (9oz) extra-bitter chocolate, chopped into small pieces
8 egg yolks
600ml (1pint) double cream

White Chocolate Mousse
2 leaves of gelatine
350g (12oz) white chocolate, broken into small pieces
8 egg yolks
600ml (1 pints) double cream

Milk Chocolate Mousse
275g (9oz) milk chocolate, chopped into small pieces
8 egg yolks
600ml (1 pint) double cream

Chocolate Shapes
200g (7oz) extra-bitter chocolate, 70% cocoa, chopped into small pieces
150g (5oz) white chocolate, chopped into small pieces
cocoa powder to dust

(1d) **To make the sugar syrup**
Place the sugar and water in a large pan and leave for about 5 minutes. Bring to the boil, then turn down the heat and whisk; leave to simmer for 5 minutes. Divide into 3 x 250ml (9fl oz) amounts.

(1d) **To make the bitter chocolate mousse**
Place the chocolate in a bowl that will fit over a saucepan. Fill the saucepan almost halfway with water and bring to

the boil; reduce the heat to simmer. Place the bowl over the heat and melt the chocolate, stirring occasionally until smooth. Reheat the sugar syrup. In an electric mixer, whisk the egg yolks until doubled in volume. With the mixer on a slow speed, pour the hot sugar syrup in a steady stream into the egg mixture. Continue whisking until the mixture is cold and thick. Whisk the cream until it just holds its shape and put to one side. Once all the chocolate has melted, remove it from the heat and fold into the egg mixture. Mix until smooth, then fold in the cream. Pour the mousse into the base of the vases or containers, taking care not to dirty the sides.

BLOWING AWAY AIR BUBBLES

IF YOU SEE ANY AIR BUBBLES AS YOU POUR THE MOUSSE INTO THE VASE, KNOCK THEM OUT BY STIRRING GENTLY WITH THE HANDLE OF A WOODEN SPOON.

To make the white chocolate mousse,

Cover the gelatine in cold water and leave to soak. Place the chocolate in a bowl that will fit over a saucepan. Fill the saucepan almost halfway with water and bring to the boil, then reduce the heat to simmer. Place the bowl over the heat and melt the chocolate, stirring occasionally until smooth. Heat the sugar syrup. Whisk the egg yolks in an electric mixer until doubled in volume. With the mixer on a slow speed, pour the hot sugar syrup in a steady stream into the egg mixture. Continue whisking until the mixture is cold and thick. Drain the gelatine and squeeze out any excess water. Melt the gelatine over a low heat, stirring continuously and taking care not to let it boil. Pass through a fine sieve, pour into the egg mixture and whisk for about 30 seconds. Whisk the double cream until it just holds its shape, then put to one side. Fold the chocolate into the egg mixture, then fold in the cream. Pour into the vases and leave to set.

To make the milk chocolate mousse

Make just as the bitter chocolate mousse and pour into the vase.

(1d) **To make the chocolate shapes**
To make the chocolate malleable enough to create shapes from you will need to temper it. By following this method you will also be able to make cylinders, long cigarettes, or any shapes you wish for this dessert or any other. The important part is making sure that the correct temperature is achieved. Line 2 trays with the acetate or non-stick parchment paper. Choose 2 mixing bowls that will hold the chocolate and fit over 2 saucepans. Half-fill the saucepans with water, bring to the boil, then reduce the heat to simmer. Put ⅔ of the bitter chocolate in the first bowl and place over one saucepan. Put all the white chocolate in the second bowl and place over the other saucepan. Stir continuously and use a thermometer to take the temperature of the chocolates – it should be no higher than 45°C (113°F). Remove the pans from the heat and add the remaining bitter chocolate, stirring continuously until all the chocolate is melted. Take the temperature of the chocolates again – it should be 31°C (88°F). If it is lower, return to the heat until the correct temperature is obtained. This makes the chocolate much easier to use. When both types of chocolate are the desired temperature, use a spoon or spatula to make spiral patterns with each chocolate at at time on sheets of acetate paper or on non-stick parchment paper. With a large palette knife, spread the chocolate until it covers the whole sheet then place in the refrigerator. Once set, peel off the paper and break the chocolate into the desired shapes.

To serve

Dust the tops of the mousses with cocoa powder, arrange the chocolate shapes on top and serve.

MULTIPLE MOUSSES

FOR VARIATION, ALTERNATE WHICH ORDER YOU LAYER THE DARK, WHITE AND MILK CHOCOLATE MOUSSES IN EACH OF THE VASES. OR, IF YOU HAVE A BIG ENOUGH CONTAINER, MAKE ONE HUGE MOUSSE.

Brioche & Butter Pudding

The puddings can be assembled the day before but are best cooked and eaten on the day of the party. Serve warm in delicate (180ml/6 fl oz) Chinese tea cups. MAKES 10

8 baby brioches
600ml (1 pint) double cream
5 eggs
100g (3½oz) caster sugar
125g (4oz) unsalted butter, softened
1 tsp grated nutmeg
100g (3½oz) sultanas, soaked in rum or brandy for 24 hours or more
2 oranges, zested
2 lemons, zested
icing sugar, to dust
sprigs of mint to garnish

(4h) **To prepare the pudding**
Slice the brioche into 30 slices (allowing 3 slices per tea cup) and place in an airtight container. Bring the cream to the boil and whisk the eggs and sugar in an electric mixer until pale. When the cream boils, remove from the heat and pour into the egg mixture in a steady stream, whisking until combined; pass the custard mix through a fine sieve, then allow to cool, cover and refrigerate.

(1-2h) **To assemble the puddings**
Preheat the oven to 160°C/325°F/gas 3. Warm the custard. Butter the brioche and sprinkle each slice with the nutmeg; place one piece in the base of each cup. Add a few sultanas, sprinkle with the citrus zest and pour on enough custard to cover the brioche. Repeat the process for 2 more slices in each cup, finishing with the custard. Leave to soak for ½ hour, then top up with custard.

To cook and serve the puddings

Put the puddings into a deep roasting tin, then pour in boiling water to halfway up the moulds. Do this while the pan is in the oven so that you do not have to carry it too far. Cook for about 15–20 minutes until the puddings are almost set. Serve dusted with icing sugar and garnish with mint.

Glazed Lemon Tart

This recipe is simply delicious and very easy to make.
MAKES 2 x 26CM (10IN) TARTS

Pastry Case
450g (1lb) unsalted butter
180g (6oz) icing sugar
5 egg yolks
650g (1½lb) plain flour
60ml (2fl oz) water

Lemon Filling
450ml (¾ pint) double cream
24 eggs
900g (2lb) caster sugar
juice & zest of 8 lemons
icing sugar
bunches of redcurrants, to garnish

SPECIAL EQUIPMENT blow torch

(1d) **To make the pastry**
For the pastry case, beat the butter and icing sugar in an electric mixer until pale. Add the egg yolks one at a time, whisking well and making sure that each yolk is mixed in before adding the next one. If the mixture begins to curdle, add ½ tablespoon flour. When all the egg yolks are mixed in, add ½ the flour and, when this is incorporated, add the water and mix. Add the remaining flour and mix until the dough just comes together. Transfer to a cold work surface. Divide the dough in 2, wrap in cling film and leave to rest in the refrigerator for at least 2 hours. Now make the filling.

(1d) **To make the filling**
In a pan, bring the cream to the boil. Meanwhile in an electric mixer, whisk the eggs and sugar until smooth; add the lemon juice and whisk. Remove the cream from the heat and pour into the egg mixture in a steady steam. Whisk until smooth, then pass through a fine sieve into a jug; add the lemon zest.

(1d) **To bake the tarts**
Preheat the oven to 170°C/325°F/gas 3. Remove the pastry from the refrigerator. On a floured board, roll the pastry into a circle about 36cm (14in) in diameter by 3mm (⅛in) thick. Line the case carefully and trim the pastry. Make sure that the pastry does not have any holes in it, otherwise the filling will leak out. Line the pastry case with cling film and fill with ceramic baking beans. Bake for about 20 minutes until the edges are golden. Remove from the oven and lift out the cling film and beans. Return to the oven and bake for about 30–35 minutes until golden brown. Now reduce the oven heat to 110°C/225°F/gas ¼. Pour the mixture into the pastry cases and return to the oven. Cook for about 1 hour and 15 minutes or until the mixture is set. Remove and allow to cool. Place in airtight containers in a cool place.

To serve
Dust the top of the tarts liberally with icing sugar and, with a blow torch, glaze the sugar to obtain a light caramel. Garnish with redcurrants and serve.

Brûlée Cream

To vary the flavour add orange zest or mocha, or infuse the cream with cinnamon or cardamom. MAKES 10

6 vanilla pods
1.2 litres (2 pints) double cream
16 egg yolks
100g (3½oz) caster sugar
120g (4 oz) Demerara sugar

SPECIAL EQUIPMENT blow torch

(1d) **To make the brûlees**
Split the vanilla pods lengthways, scrape out the seeds and add the pods to the cream. Bring the cream to the boil over medium heat. In an electric mixer, whisk together the egg yolks and caster sugar. Pour the egg mixture in a steady stream into the cream as it boils; whisk until combined. Remove the vanilla pods. Bring a pan of water to the boil and remove from the heat. Pour the mixture into a flat-bottomed bowl that will fit over the pan. Place the pan over the heat and return to the boil, then turn down the heat to a simmer and whisk continuously until the mixture coats the back of a spoon (about 20–30 minutes). Remove the bowl from the heat and pass the mixture through a fine sieve. Pour into the tea glasses and allow to cool. Cover and refrigerate.

FRUIT SURPRISE
AS A VARIATION, LINE THE TEA GLASSES WITH APRICOTS OR RASPBERRIES BEFORE POURING IN THE BRÛLÉE MIXTURE.

To serve
About 30 minutes before serving, sprinkle the tops of the brulées with Demerara sugar and burn lightly with a blow torch to caramelise. Alternatively, decorate with Macadamia Nut Brittle (page 169).

Summer Fruits with Raspberry Sauce

The sauce can be made with any soft fruit. The amounts are enough for a 3-litre (4½pint) vase. I take a punnet to be about 250g (9oz). SERVES 20

Soft Fruits
4 punnets of strawberries, hulled, washed & dried
4 punnets of raspberries
4 punnets of blackberries
4 punnets of blueberries
2 punnets of redcurrants
2 punnets of tayberries or loganberries
2 punnets of whitecurrants
2 punnets of golden raspberries
2 punnets of wild strawberries
mint & edible flowers, to garnish

Raspberry Sauce
1kg (2lb 2oz) raspberries (fresh or frozen)
500g (1lb1oz) icing sugar
juice of 1 lemon

(1d) **To make the sauce**
Purée the berries for the sauce, icing sugar and lemon juice until smooth, then sieve finely. Pour into an airtight container and store in the refrigerator.

To serve

Layer the berries in a vase, garnishing with mint and flowers. Pour the sauce into a small jug. If serving with biscuits these can be placed on glass cake stands and dusted with icing sugar.

Passion Fruit Pyramid

This dessert can also be made with soft summer fruits. SERVES 20

Meringue
12 egg whites
500g (1lb 2oz) caster sugar

Passion Fruit Cream
30 whole passion fruit, halved, juices & pips scooped out, sieved to yield 200ml (7fl oz) purée
250ml (9fl oz) water
800ml (1½ pints) double cream
250g (9oz) sugar
50g (3oz) cornflour
10 egg yolks
170g (6oz) unsalted butter, cut into cubes
3 passion fruit
8 mangos, peeled & sliced

Garnish
icing sugar
oven-dried mango slices (page 169), optional
6 passion fruit
edible flowers, fresh or crystallized

(1w) **To make the meringue**

Preheat the oven to 110°C/225°F/gas ¼. Taking 4 sheets of silicone paper, draw a 30.5cm (12in) circle on the first, on the second a 25.5cm (10in) circle, on the third a 20cm (8in) circle and on the fourth a 15cm (6in) circle. Place these sheets on baking trays. Whisk the egg whites with 100g (3½oz) of the sugar until it forms stiff peaks. Continue to whisk, adding the sugar gradually. Once all the sugar is added, the egg whites should be stiff and glossy. Fill a piping bag with this mixture and pipe to fill each of the paper circles. Bake for about 10–12 hours until the meringue is dry and hard to the touch, leave to cool then layer with non-stick paper and store in airtight containers.

(1d) **To make the fruit cream**

In a heavy-based pan, bring the passion fruit purée, the water, 50ml (2fl oz) cream and the sugar to the boil, stirring continuously. Mix the cornflour with a little cold water then add to the boiling mixture, stirring. Reduce the heat and cook for 5 minutes, stirring to prevent it from burning. Remove from heat and leave to cool for about 2 minutes. Beat in the egg yolks then the butter. Cover with non-stick paper and leave to cool. Cut the 3 passion fruit in half, squeeze out the juice and pips and add these to the mixture. Whisk the remaining cream until it holds its shape and fold into the passion fruit. Cover and chill.

Passion Fruit Pyramid

(2h) **To assemble**

Pipe a blob of cream in the centre of a glass cake stand to prevent the meringue from sliding around. Place the largest disc of meringue on the stand and spread with cream, leaving a 2.5cm (1in) rim of meringue. Top with a layer of mango, then the next meringue disc. Repeat the process twice to finish with the smallest disc of meringue.

To garnish

Dust with icing sugar and arrange remaining slices of fresh or oven-dried mango on the top, squeezing over the juice of the passion fruits. Decorate the sides with fresh or crystallized flowers.

Giving a dinner party at home is generally the most popular form of entertaining. Large or small, formal or informal, it is offering your guests the warmest welcome. Dinners I give tend to be simple affairs. I like to serve champagne and wine before dinner, with savoury biscuits if I've made them.

for a dinner party

Ten or 15 minutes after the last guests have arrived and have had time to collect their thoughts and a drink, I start seating everyone. It is generally best not to be too clever with your plans – for example, I hate being moved from my place for dessert. If you do not know many guests, by the time dessert is served you are relaxed and to be moved and have to start the process of getting to know the people around you again is a great dampener.

An Affair to Remember

Planning a menu is not only very important, but fun to do. I always like to serve food that is in season, from wonderful asparagus and fresh berries in the summer, to juicy apples and pears in the autumn. Giving a dinner is very rewarding; you can set the table in a dramatic way, arrange flowers and decorations, serve wonderful food and wines, and enjoy the evening in the knowledge that your guests will have a memorable time. Dinner parties can last from 2½ to 4 hours; as a host you will then be able to judge when to start moving guests to serve coffee. If there is space, move to an adjoining room or area – in summer, this could be a garden or terrace. This will move the guests around and prevent the party from carrying on too late into the night.

Panic-Free Parties

The following menus are designed to make giving dinners easy and panic-free – because nearly all the dishes can be prepared ahead of time. I would advise never to cook any recipe for guests that you have not attempted beforehand. Trying out dishes for the first time on close friends or family will give you confidence on the night. There is nothing worse than worrying – you should be relaxed to enjoy your party. Take plenty of time to plan the menu and enjoy preparing each dish. It is very satisfying when you see your guests' plates empty. If any of your guests are vegetarian, you will find that most of the menus are easy to adapt.

Professional Tips

• Do check your table linen (including the napkins) is clean
• Organize an area for storing dirty plates and glasses and make sure the dishwasher is empty before dinner
• Serve pre-dinner drinks but not for longer than 1 hour
• Allow 10 minutes for latecomers but then stick to your plan – they will understand
• Every once in a while you'll get a 'no-show' – bear this light-heartedly and no-one will mind
• Choose wines that complement the food – suggestions are given for each dinner

CLEAN AND TIDY

Do not give way to the temptation to wash up between courses – guests do not want to hear the clatter of plates while they are still eating.

Roasted Vegetable Terrine

spring dinner

This menu makes the most of the produce available at this time of year – lamb, asparagus, strawberries and rhubarb. All the courses are easy to prepare ahead of time, allowing you to relax and enjoy the company of your guests. SERVES 10

Roasted Vegetable Terrine

Vegetable Terrine

6 red bell peppers, deseeded & quartered
olive oil
2 large aubergines
6 large courgettes
340g (12oz) log of goats' cheese
salt & freshly ground black pepper
6 tbsp pesto (see page 168)
80g (3oz) Parmesan, grated

SPECIAL EQUIPMENT **electric carving knife**

Red Pepper Sauce

1 garlic clove, chopped
1 shallot, chopped
olive oil
2 red peppers, roasted, skinned, deseeded
& chopped (roast these at the same time
as the peppers for the terrine)
2 plum tomatoes, chopped
1 tsp tomato purée
300ml (½ pint) vegetable stock
salt & freshly ground black pepper

Glaze

250ml (⅓ pint) aged balsamic vinegar
WINE *Crisp Sancerre*

(2d) **To make the terrine**
Preheat the oven to 190°C/ 375°F/gas 5. Brush the red peppers with oil, salt them and bake for 15–20 minutes.

Allow to cool, remove skins and set aside. Slice all the vegetables as straight as possible into 7mm- (¼ in-) thick strips. Score the strips, salt them, and leave for ½ hour. Cut the goats' cheese into 7mm- (¼in-) thick slices. Dry the courgettes and aubergines. Heat a chargrill pan, brush the courgettes and aubergines with olive oil, season with pepper and grill until bar marks are visible. Transfer to a tray and set aside.

(2d) **To build the terrine**
Preheat the oven to 180°C/350°F/gas 5. Cut thick cardboard to fit the top of a terrine mould, 30cm (12in) long by 10cm (4in) wide, and cover with foil. Brush the mould with olive oil and line with greaseproof paper. Cover the base with red pepper and season. Layer in the following way: aubergine, courgette, goats' cheese, red pepper, then aubergine, courgette, goats' cheese, courgette, aubergine, finishing with the red pepper. Spread pesto and sprinkle Parmesan over each layer. Cover the terrine with foil and cook for 25 minutes. Allow to cool, then place the covered board on top and press with weights or cans. Refrigerate.

(2d) **To prepare the glaze**
Reduce the balsamic vinegar by half in a pan over medium heat. Leave to cool to a thick, syrupy consistency. Store in a squeezy bottle and refrigerate.

(1d) **To make the sauce**
Sauté the garlic and shallot in a little olive oil for 2 minutes. Add the peppers, tomatoes and tomato purée, and sauté for a further 2 minutes. Add stock and seasoning. Cover and simmer for 20 minutes. Cool, then liquidize and sieve. Pour into a squeezy bottle and chill.

To serve the terrine
Turn out the terrine onto a board. Mop up any juices. Slice the terrine with an electric carving knife into 2cm- (¾in-) wide portions. Place in the centre of the plates (up to 1 hour before serving), drizzle on the pesto, balsamic glaze and pepper sauce. Serve.

Lamb with Potato Cake & Thyme Sauce

Thyme Sauce
3 shallots, chopped
10 sprigs of thyme
unscented vegetable oil
1 glass red wine
1.8 litres (3 pints) reduced chicken stock

5 short loins of lamb
salt & freshly ground black pepper

Potato Cake
2 shallots, finely chopped
2 garlic cloves, finely chopped
unscented vegetable oil
500g (1lb 1oz) mixed wild mushrooms
2kg (4lb 4oz) Desiree potato, peeled
3 sprigs of thyme, chopped
15g (½oz) unsalted butter

3 carrots, cut into 2cm (1in) cubes
30 asparagus spears, peeled & cut into
　8cm (3in) lengths
WINE *Savigny-lès-Beaune or Californian Pinot Noir*

(2d) To prepare the sauce
Sauté the shallots and thyme in a little oil in a sauté pan until golden. Pour in the wine and reduce by half. Add stock, reducing to a syrupy consistency and allowing approximately 600ml (1 pint) for 10 portions. Strain the sauce and leave to cool. Cover and refrigerate.

(8h) To seal the lamb
Heat a little vegetable oil in a sauté pan. When the pan starts to smoke, add two loins and season. Seal on all sides until brown, then place on an oiled tray. Repeat for all the lamb. Cover and chill.

(6h) To make the potato cake
Preheat the oven to 190°C/375°F/gas 5. Sauté the shallots and garlic in a little oil in a and sweat until soft. Add the mushrooms, season and sauté for 3–4 minutes. Set aside in a colander. Julienne the potatoes, place in a bowl, season and mix in the thyme. Heat the butter with a little oil in an ovenproof sauté pan about 30 x 7cm (12 x 2¾in).

When hot, add half the potatoes, spreading them evenly. Cook for 5 minutes or until golden at the edges. Add the mushrooms, spreading them from the middle of the pan outwards to leave a gap of about 2.5cm (1in) from the rim. Put in the remaining potatoes, spreading them evenly. Brush with a little oil and place in the oven for 20 minutes. Remove from the oven and turn it over onto a plate. Slide the cake back into the pan, then return to the oven for 10 minutes, or until the other side is golden. Slide the potato cake on to a board, slice into portions (flattening off the rounded edges if serving as in the photograph) and place on a baking tray. Cool, cover with plastic wrap and chill.

(6h) To prepare the carrots
Sauté the carrots in a little oil until slightly brown, season and place on an ovenproof tray. Allow to cool, cover with plastic wrap and refrigerate.

To assemble
Preheat the oven to 200°C/400°F/gas 6. Bring the sauce to the boil, then simmer slowly, checking the seasoning. Place the potato cake portions and carrots in the oven for about 15 minutes. After 5 minutes, put in the lamb and cook for 8–10 minutes. Remove and rest, but keep warm. Bring a pan of salted water to the boil. Add the asparagus and cook for 3–4 minutes. Drain and season. Place a potato-cake portion (upright if desired) in the centre of each plate and lean asparagus next to it. Halve the short loins, then slice each half at an angle of 45°. Place next to the cake with the points in opposite directions. Drizzle sauce around the plate, scatter on carrot cubes and serve.

Lamb with Potato Cake & Thyme Sauce

Strawberry Tart with Rhubarb Ice Cream

Rhubarb Ice Cream

500g (1lb 1oz) rhubarb, peeled & cut into
  2.5cm (1in) lengths
3 cardamom pods
250g (9oz) caster sugar
600ml (1 pint) double cream
SPECIAL EQUIPMENT ice cream maker

Tart Base

200g (7oz) icing sugar for rolling the pastry
500g (1lb 1oz) block puff pastry
butter for greasing baking tray

Strawberry Sauce

1 punnet strawberries (about 250g/9oz)
60g (2oz) icing sugar
juice of 1 lemon

Topping

Diplomat Cream (see page 169)
Sugar Cobwebs (see page 169)
4 punnets strawberries, washed & dried

*WINE Sauternes or Australian Botrytis
Riesling*

To make the ice cream – 4 days ahead.
Tip the rhubarb into a saucepan and
cover with 2 tablespoons of water; add
the cardamom pods and sugar, then
cover, bring to the boil and simmer to a
purée for about 5–8 minutes. Pour into
a bowl and remove the cardamom. Allow
to cool, then stir in the cream. Pour into
an ice cream maker and churn for about
30 minutes. Remove, place in an
airtight container and freeze.

(4d) **To prepare the pastry**
Sprinkle a cold work surface with icing
sugar and roll out the puff pastry into
an oblong 33 x 23cm (13 x 9in). Dust
with icing sugar. Take the longest side
and roll up the pastry like a Swiss roll.
To seal the roll, dampen the edge with
water and press gently in place along its
length. Wrap the cylinder of pastry in
cling film. It can now be frozen.

Strawberry Tart with Rhubarb Ice Cream

(2d) **To make the sauce**
Put all the ingredients in a pan and
bring to the boil. Now simmer until the
berries are soft. Remove from the heat
and allow to cool. Blend until smooth,
then pass through a fine sieve. Pour into
a squeezy bottle and refrigerate.

(1d) **To prepare the pastry**
Preheat the oven to 200°C/400°F/gas 6.
Butter a baking tray. Remove the pastry
from the freezer if necessary and
sprinkle a cool work surface with icing
sugar. Cut the pastry into 2cm- (¾in-)
thick slices. Leave to defrost for 10
minutes. Sprinkle more icing sugar on
the work surface and roll the pastry out
very thinly. Cut out the discs with a
12.5cm- (5in-) round pastry cutter. If
the frozen pastry starts to crack around
the edges, leave to defrost a little
longer. Place the discs on the tray and
refrigerate for ½ hour. Place in the oven
for 10 minutes. Remove the tray, turn
the discs and bake for a further 5
minutes or until golden brown and
glazed. Cool on a wire rack. Place the
discs in an airtight container, layering
with greaseproof paper.

(8h) **To ball the ice cream**
Follow the instructions for balling Stem
Ginger Ice Cream on page 126.

(8h) **To prepare the topping**
Make the Diplomat Cream and Sugar
Cobwebs. Halve the strawberries, and
refrigerate in an airtight container.

To assemble
Fill a piping bag with the Diplomat
Cream and pipe a small blob of cream
onto the centre of each plate to prevent
the tart from sliding around. Place a
pastry disc on top. Pipe a large blob of
cream onto the tart and arrange the
strawberry halves around the cream.
Drizzle the sauce around the plate.
Place a ball of ice cream on top of the
tart, followed by a cobweb. Serve. (The
tarts can be assembled 2 hours in
advance, then kept in a cool place and
topped with an ice cream ball and a
cobweb just before serving.

summer menu

I used to grow vegetables on an allotment with my friend, Bruce. In summer, one of our great joys was collecting bunches of asparagus, herbs and artichokes, for a simple, fresh salad. To follow this, the seabass recipe is from holidays spent in Southwold, where I would grill fish fresh from the local fishermen for a delicious, healthy meal. SERVES 10

Asparagus & Artichoke Salad

350g (12½oz) mixed prepared salad leaves

Salsa Verde
2 tea cups picked parsley, washed & dried
½ tea cup marjoram, washed & dried
1 tbsp mini capers
5 tbsp olive oil
2 limes, zested & juiced
2 garlic cloves, finely chopped
2 shallots, finely chopped
2 tsp whole-grain mustard
1 tbsp caster sugar
salt & freshly ground black pepper

Asparagus & Artichoke
10 medium globe artichokes, cooked, with
   leaves & chokes removed to leave hearts
3 tbsp olive oil
salt & freshly ground black pepper
2 garlic cloves, crushed
5 sprigs fresh thyme
30 white asparagus spears, peeled & cut
   into 10cm (4in) lengths
30 green asparagus spears, peeled & cut
   into 10cm (4in) lengths
1 tea cup chives, cut into 4cm (1½in) lengths
WINE *Californian Sauvignon or Pouilly Fumé*

Asparagus & Artichoke Salad

(3d) **To prepare the salad leaves**
Salad leaves keep best if stored in an airtight container lined with a clean tea towel. Wash the leaves and dry well. Place in the container and refrigerate.

(3d) **To prepare the salsa verde**
Finely chop the herbs and place in a bowl. Add the remaining ingredients, season, mix well and refrigerate in an airtight container.

(1d) **To chargrill artichokes**
Trim the hearts around the artichoke base with a sharp knife, ensuring that none of the choke has been left on. Slice each in half crossways to give a total of 20 discs. Heat a chargrill pan. Brush the discs with olive oil, season and chargrill for about 45 seconds until the bar marks are defined. Turn the discs and repeat. Place the discs in an airtight container, drizzle with a little olive oil and cover with the garlic and thyme. When cool, cover and refrigerate.

ARTICHOKE PREPARATION
THE DELICIOUSLY MELT-IN-THE-MOUTH FLAVOUR OF GLOBE ARTICHOKES IS WORTH PURSUING. COOK FOR ABOUT 30–45 MINUTES IN BOILING WATER FLAVOURED WITH SHALLOTS, GARLIC, HERBS AND PEPPERCORNS. ADD LEMON JUICE TO STOP DISCOLOURATION AND POUR A LAYER OF OLIVE OIL ON TOP. WHEN READY, PULL OFF ALL THE LEAVES AND THEN PULL OFF THE HAIRY CENTRAL CHOKE OR REMOVE IT WITH A SPOON TO LEAVE THE FLESHY HEART.

Seabass with Sweet Potato Mash and Fennel

To chargrill asparagus
1d

Bring a pan of salted water to the boil. Blanch the asparagus for 1 minute, drain and refresh. Dry and brush with olive oil, season and chargrill until the bar marks are defined. Cool, then toss with a little olive oil. Cover and chill.

To assemble

Place a small handful of salad leaves in the centre of each plate, add an artichoke disc, then continue to build up layers with another small handful of leaves followed by 3 asparagus spears. Add a second artichoke disc, then the remaining salad leaves followed by 3 asparagus spears. Top with chives. Drizzle salsa verde around the plate. Serve with Parmesan Tuiles if desired (see page 92). (The salad can be assembled 20 minutes before serving.)

COOKING WITH WINE

WHEN WINE IS A MAIN COMPONENT OF A DISH AS IN THE RED WINE SAUCE (SEE RIGHT) MAKE SURE IT IS GOOD QUALITY.

Seabass with Sweet Potato Mash & Fennel

Red Wine Sauce
vegetable oil
4 shallots, chopped
1 glass red wine
1.8 litres (3 pints) reduced brown chicken stock

Sweet Potato Mash
1.35kg (3lb) orange sweet potatoes, cut into large chunks.
1kg (2lb 2oz) Desiree potatoes, cut into chunks
3 garlic cloves, finely chopped
150ml (¼ pint) olive oil
salt & ground white pepper

10 x 200g (7oz) fillets seabass, with skin & pin boned
20 baby fennel, roots trimmed, shoots cut at the top at an angle
200g (7oz) girolles mushrooms, cleaned, brushed & sautéed in a little unscented vegetable oil (optional)
400g (14oz) baby broad beans, blanched & shelled
freshly ground black pepper

WINE Australian Dry Riesling or Fleurie

To make the sauce
2d

Sauté the shallot in a little oil until golden brown. Pour in the red wine and reduce by half. Add the stock and reduce until the mixture has a smooth, velvet consistency. Pass through a sieve. Allow 600ml (1 pint) for 10 portions.

To prepare the sweet potato mash
6h

Simmer all the potatoes with the garlic in salted water until the potatoes are soft. Drain and pass through a potato ricer or sieve. In a bowl, add the olive oil and mix to a creamy consistency. Season with salt and white pepper. Cool and place in a container. Cover and chill.

To seal the seabass
6h

Heat a little oil until smoking in a sauté pan, lay the fish skin side down and season. Sauté until the edges are golden and the skin is crispy. Turn and sauté for 10 seconds more then place on a greased metal tray, skin side up. Allow to cool, cover and refrigerate.

To prepare the fennel
6h

Blanch the fennel in boiling salted water for 4–5 minutes, drain and refresh in iced water. Dry, then brush with oil and season. Heat a chargill pan and grill the fennel until bar marks are defined. Remove and allow to cool. Place on a greased metal tray. Cover and refrigerate.

To assemble

Preheat the oven to 200°C/400°F/gas 6. Bring the sauce to a simmer and season. Bring a pan of salted water to the boil. Stir the potato purée in a pan over low heat until bubbling. Season and keep warm. Place the fish and fennel in the oven for 7–8 minutes and on heat up the mushrooms if using. The seabass is ready when firm. Cook the beans in the boiling water for 1 minute, drain and set aside. Dip a spoon into a jug of hot water and scoop an oval of potato purée onto the centre of each plate. Place 2 pieces of fennel over the purée, then top with the seabass. Scatter on the broad beans and girolles, drizzle on the sauce and serve.

Champagne Berry Jelly with Summer Fruits

Take all punnets to be 250g(9oz).

Pistachio Biscotti
3 eggs
200g (7oz) caster sugar
450g (1lb) plain flour
½ tsp baking powder
320g (11½oz) shelled pistachio nuts

Champagne Jelly
unscented vegetable oil
1 punnet fraises des bois
1 punnet redcurrants
1 punnet white currants
1 punnet golden raspberries
1 punnet blueberries
1 punnet loganberries
10 leaves of gelatine
150g (5½oz) caster sugar
150ml (¼ pint) water
1 bottle (750ml/1¼ pints) pink champagne

Berry Compote
100g (3½oz) caster sugar
200ml (7fl oz) water
1 punnet blueberries
1 punnet fraises des bois
1 punnet redcurrants
1 punnet white currants
1 punnet golden raspberries
1 punnet loganberries
CHAMPAGNE *Pink Champagne*

(1w) **To prepare the biscotti dough**
In an electric mixer, beat the eggs and sugar until white. Add the flour, baking powder and nuts, mixing to a smooth dough. On a floured board, roll the mixture into a 10cm- (4in-) thick roll. Cover with cling film and freeze.

(2d) **To cook the biscotti**
Preheat the oven to 190°C/375°F/gas 5. Defrost the biscotti roll and place on a greased baking tray. Bake for 30 minutes or until golden brown. Remove and cool on a wire rack. Cut into 7mm (¼in) slices, angling these at 45°, and place on a tray. Return to the oven and bake for 5 minutes. Remove, allow to cool and place in an airtight container.

(1d) **To make the jelly**
Brush 10 tall jelly moulds (holding about 150ml/¼ pint) with a little unscented vegetable oil. To remove excess oil, turn the moulds upside down and place on kitchen paper. Pick over the fruit, wash and dry well. Place the gelatine leaves in a bowl and add cold water to cover; let the leaves soften. In a pan, bring the sugar and water to the boil. Reduce the heat and simmer for about 5 minutes to form a clear syrup. Remove from the heat. Squeeze out excess water from the gelatine then dissolve it in the syrup. Add the champagne, stir and strain through a fine sieve into a large jug. Place the jelly moulds on to a tray that will fit inside your refrigerator. Pour in enough jelly to coat the base of the moulds – about 7mm (¼in). Leave to set in the refrigerator. When set, remove from the refrigerator and half-fill the moulds with

Champagne Berry Jelly with Summer Fruits

fruit. Pour in enough jelly to cover three quarters of the fruit (any more and the fruit will float). Leave to set in the refrigerator then fill to the top with the remaining jelly to encase the fruit entirely. Leave to set in the refrigerator.

(1d) **To make the compote**
Place the sugar and blueberries in a stainless-steel pan, add the water and bring to the boil. Add the remaining fruit and bring back to the boil. Once boiling, remove from the heat immediately. Pour into a container and leave to cool. Cover and refrigerate.

To assemble
Dip the jelly moulds into warm water; remove and shake to loosen the jelly. Place a jelly in the centre of each plate and spoon round a little compote. (This can be done 2 hours in advance.) When ready to serve, add the biscotti.

autumn menu

In the autumn I love to serve squash soup inside baby pumpkins. The French black-legged Challans chicken has a melting texture which combines perfectly with the spring rolls, but you could use a good free-range variety. SERVES 10

Butternut Squash Soup

Soup Base
45g (1½oz) butter
2 tbsp vegetable oil
1.5kg (3lb 8oz) butternut squash, deseeded & diced
430g (15oz) carrots, chopped
5 shallots, chopped
4 garlic cloves, chopped
1.8 litres (3 pints) vegetable stock
10 baby pumpkins
600ml (1 pint) double cream

Chilli Cream
250ml (½ pint) double cream
2 large red chillies, deseeded & finely diced
2 tbsp coriander
salt & freshly ground black pepper

WINE Australian unoaked Chardonnay

(1d) **To make the soup**
Heat the butter and vegetable oil in a large pan. Add the squash, carrot, shallot and garlic, and sweat for 5 minutes. Pour in the stock, bring to the

Butternut Squash Soup

boil, then simmer for 1 hour. Cool, liquidize until smooth then store in an airtight container and chill.

(1d) **To prepare the pumpkins**
Cut a slice off the base of the pumpkins so that they will sit flat on the plates. Do not cut off too much – you do not want to make a hole in the base. Cut off the top to remove all the seeds. Cover in cling film and refrigerate.

(8h) **To make the chilli cream**
Whisk the double cream until it just holds its shape. Fold in the chopped chilli and coriander, then season. Place in an airtight container and refrigerate.

To assemble
Preheat the oven to 150°C/300°F/gas 2. Arrange leaves on the dinner plates if using (see below). Place the pumpkins on a tray to warm in the oven for about 20 minutes. Bring the soup to the boil, then add the double cream. Stir, check the seasoning, lower the heat and simmer. If serving with fresh bread, warm it in the oven, then wrap in a linen napkin. Wipe the insides of the warmed pumpkins with kitchen towel to remove any moisture. Place a pumpkin in the centre of each plate. Fill it with soup and top with chilli cream. Serve.

AUTUMN LEAVES
TO PRESENT THIS SOUP IN AN ORIGINAL AND BEAUTIFUL WAY, LINE THE PLATES WITH A SELECTION OF WASHED, DRIED LEAVES.

Black Challans Chicken with Spring Rolls

unscented vegetable oil
10 supremes of black Challans, trimmed with skin on, or free-range, corn-fed chicken
620g (1lb 4oz) carrots
10 baby bok choy
peanut oil
1 tbsp white sesame seeds
15g (½oz) ginger, chopped
salt & freshly ground black pepper
1.2 litres (2 pints) reduced chicken stock
150ml (¼ pint) sweet soy sauce

Spring Roll

1 tbsp flour

2 tbsp water

100g (3½oz) glass noodles

peanut oil

3 garlic cloves, puréed

400g (14oz) carrots, finely sliced

300g (11oz) Chinese cabbage, finely sliced

200g (7oz) shiitake mushrooms, sliced

400g (14oz) mangetout, finely sliced

5 tsp sugar

10 tbsp light soy sauce

salt & freshly ground black pepper

10 spring roll pastry sheets, each 25cm² (10in²)

SPECIAL EQUIPMENT **deep-fat fryer**

WINE Spanish Chardonnay or Chilean oaked Chardonnay

(8h) To seal the chicken

Heat a little oil in a sauté pan. When the pan starts to smoke, add the supremes of chicken, 2 at a time, skin side down, and season. Turn when golden brown to seal the other side. Place on a metal tray to cool, then cover and refrigerate.

(8h) To prepare the vegetables

Bring a pan of salted water to the boil. Cut the carrots so that they have 4 flat sides. Using a mandolin, slice each carrot into 3mm- (⅛in-) thick ribbons. Fill a bowl with iced water. Blanch the ribbons, a handful at a time, for about 1 minute, then refresh in the iced water. Dry, cover and put aside. Separate the bok choy leaves and wash. Heat a little peanut oil in a sauté pan. Add half the sesame seeds, the ginger and a handful of bok choy. Season and continue to sauté until the leaves wilt. Place in a large bowl. Repeat, using the remaining sesame seeds. Cool, mix with the carrot ribbons and divide into 10 portions on a greased metal tray. Sprinkle with water, seal with foil, then refrigeratel.

(8h) To prepare the chicken and sauce

In a pan, bring the (preferably brown) chicken stock to the boil then reduce to about 600ml (1 pint), which is enough for 10 portions. Add the sweet soy sauce and simmer for 5 minutes. Allow to cool, then cover and refrigerate.

Black Challans Chickens with Spring Rolls

(8h) To prepare the spring roll filling

Mix the flour and water into a smooth paste for the glue; cover. Bring a pan of salted water to the boil and blanch the noodles for 1 minute, or until soft, then drain. Cut into 2.5cm (1in) lengths and set aside. Heat a little peanut oil in a wok or sauté pan. Add the garlic, carrot, cabbage and shiitake mushrooms, and sauté for 2 minutes. Add the mangetout, sugar, soy sauce and noodles. Cook for 2 minutes more and season. Allow to cool, then cover and refrigerate.

(2h) To prepare the spring roll wrapping

Line a metal tray with a clean tea towel. Place a spring roll wrapper on a work surface to form a diamond shape. Put a heaped tablespoon of vegetable filling in the centre of the first third. Brush the corners with the glue. Fold the bottom corner over the filling (quite tightly so that it is 4cm/1½in round). Fold the sides into the centre, then roll up. Each roll should be 12.5cm (5in) long. When all the rolls are made up, place them on a tray, cover and chill..

To assemble

Preheat the oven to 200°C/400°F/gas 6; heat the deep-fat fryer to 190°C/375°F. In a pan, bring the sauce to the boil, lower the heat and simmer. Cook the spring rolls in the deep-fat fryer until golden. Drain on kitchen paper and keep warm until needed. Place the chicken, carrot and bok choy in the oven for about 10–12 minutes. The chicken is ready when it is firm to the touch. Remove from the oven and keep warm. Trim off the ends of the spring rolls and cut in half on an angle. On each plate, place 2 spring roll halves, bok choy and carrots. Slice each chicken supreme into 3 and place against the bok choy. Pour a little sauce around the plate. Serve.

COOKING REFRIGERATED FOOD

WHEN ROASTING ANY MEAT OR FISH, OR REHEATING VEGETABLES, ALWAYS REMOVE FROM THE REFRIGERATOR 15 MINUTES BEFORE COOKING. OTHERWISE THE INITIAL COOKING PROCESS WILL BE LESS EFFECTIVE.

Stem Ginger Ice Cream with Glazed Pineapple

Ice Cream
12 egg yolks
250g (9oz) caster sugar
600ml (1 pint) milk
600ml (1 pint) double cream
100g (3½oz) chopped stem ginger

SPECIAL EQUIPMENT **ice cream maker**

1 large coconut, for the coconut curls

Glazed Pineapple
2 large pineapples, peeled, cut into 10 x
   3cm (1¼in) rounds, cored, & cut into fingers
freshly ground black pepper
unscented vegetable oil
150g (5½oz) soft brown sugar
WINE Australian Botrytis Riesling

(7d) **To make the ice cream**
Place the eggs and sugar in an electric mixer, and whisk until pale and creamy. In a heavy-based saucepan, bring the milk and cream to the boil. Remove from the heat. On a slow speed, pour into the egg mixture in a steady stream, then scrape down the sides. Return the mixture to the pan and heat, stirring until the custard coats the back of the spoon. Do not allow the mixture to boil. Sieve into a bowl and add the stem ginger, then allow to cool. Pour into an ice cream maker and churn. Store the ice cream in a container and freeze.

(2d) **To prepare the coconut curls**
Preheat the oven to 160°C/325°F/gas 3. Break open the coconut and remove the flesh. (Reserve the milk since it makes a lovely cold drink.) Peel the flesh into long strips and place on a tray in the oven until golden. When cool they will be crispy. Store in an airtight container.

(8h) **To ball the ice cream**
Line a metal tray with non-stick paper and place in the freezer for 30 minutes. Fill a jug with hot water. Dip a scoop into the water then into the ice cream. Make a ball, place it on the tray and repeat for all the ice cream. Return the tray to the freezer.

Stem Ginger Ice Cream with Glazed Pineapple

PEELING PINEAPPLES
PLACE THE PINEAPPLE ON A BOARD AND CUT OFF ITS TOP AND BASE USING A SHARP KNIFE WITH A SERRATED EDGE. STAND THE PINEAPPLE UPRIGHT AND SLICE AROUND IT, ABOUT 6MM (¼IN) DEEP, TO REMOVE THE RIND AND EYES.

(8h) **To glaze the pineapple**
Place the pineapple fingers on a tray and grind black pepper over them. Heat a little oil in a sauté pan and, when it begins to smoke, add a few pineapple fingers. Sauté until golden, then turn. Repeat for all the pineapple, and place on a tray, leaving the juices in the pan.

Add the brown sugar to the pan juices and caramelize. If the sugar starts to become too dark, add a little water and continue to cook. Pour the caramelized sugar over the pineapple fingers. Allow to cool, then cover and refrigerate.

To assemble
Preheat the oven to 150°C/300°F/gas 2. Place the pineapple fingers in the preheated oven for about 6 minutes, then drain the juices into a jug. Place 4 fingers of pineapple in the centre of each plate. Top with ice cream and arrange the coconut curls. Drizzle a little juice on the plates, and serve.

winter menu

To brighten winter's long, grey days and dark nights, I always think that salmon gives a welcome splash of colour at the dinner table. Its fresh flavour seems particularly piquant in this season, and marinaded and mixed with smoked salmon it is always popular with guests. The exquisite chocolate tart (one of our most requested desserts) marries delightfully with the seasonal and unusual tamarillo or tree tomato. SERVES 10

Fresh Salmon Wrapped in Smoked Salmon

1kg (2lb 2oz) fresh salmon fillet, skin removed
2 shallots, finely diced
3 tbsp virgin olive oil
1 tbsp sea salt flakes
½ tsp ground black pepper
10 lime segments
10 orange segments
10 pink grapefruit segments
500g (1lb 1oz) long, sliced smoked salmon
1 bunch of chives
½ tea cup picked dill, washed & refrigerated

Whole-Grain Mustard Dressing

2 tsp whole-grain mustard
1 tbsp white wine vinegar
1 tsp caster sugar
1 tbsp virgin olive oil
salt & freshly ground black pepper
WINE Pink Sancerre or Chablis Grand Cru

(1d) **To marinade the salmon**
Cut the salmon into 2.5cm- (1in-) wide strips, then slice each strip as thinly as possible widthways. Place in a bowl. Add the shallot, olive oil, salt and black pepper, then mix thoroughly. Place in an airtight container and chill for 12 hours.

(1d) **To make the dressing**
Mix together all the ingredients and season. Pour into a jar and refrigerate.

(8h) **To prepare the fruits**
Cut the lime, orange and grapefruit segments into 7mm (¼in) pieces. Place in an airtight container and refrigerate.

(8h) **To prepare the smoked salmon**
Cut the smoked salmon into 10 strips, 25.5 x 5cm (10 x 2in). Layer in greaseproof paper and chill. Cut 20 of the chives into 15cm (6in) lengths, then snip the rest up for the garnish. Place in an airtight container and chill.

REMOVING SMALL BONES FROM FISH

A PAIR OF ARTERY FORCEPS (AVAILABLE FROM SURGICAL INSTRUMENT SHOPS OR GOOD CHEMISTS) ARE THE BEST UTENSILS FOR REMOVING THE SMALLEST BONES.

Fresh Salmon Wrapped in Smoked Salmon

To serve
30 minutes before ready to serve, mix half the citrus segments and dill with the salmon. Place a 7cm-wide x 3cm-deep (2¾ x 1¼in) ring mould in the centre of each plate (10 in all). Wrap a piece of smoked salmon around the inside of each mould, making sure it reaches the base of the mould and flaps over the top. Fill with marinaded salmon, then remove the mould. Place the long chives vertically in the centre. Drizzle over dressing and scatter on the remaining segments and chives. Serve.

Port Wine Duck with Cabbage Parcels

Duck Confit

3 duck legs, weighing 700g (1lb 8oz)
2 garlic cloves, crushed
5 sprigs of thyme
3 tbsp sea-salt flakes
6 peppercorns
1 litre (1¾ pints) goose or duck fat

Cabbage Parcels

2 medium savoy cabbages
30g (1oz) unsalted butter
2 medium onions, finely sliced
250ml (½ pint) white chicken stock
salt & freshly ground black pepper
unscented vegetable oil

Potato & Turnip Gratin

30g (1oz) unsalted butter
750ml (1¼ pints) double cream
3 garlic cloves, finely chopped
1.3kg (2lb 9oz) Desiree potatoes, very finely sliced
900g (2lb) turnips, very finely sliced
a generous pinch of grated nutmeg
salt & ground white pepper

10 female barbary duck breasts

Port Wine Sauce

4 shallots, chopped
olive oil
1 glass port
1.8 litres (3 pints) reduced brown chicken stock

WINE *Nuits St Georges or Chilean Cabernet*

 To prepare the confit
Place all the ingredients except for the fat in a large bowl and mix, covering the legs with the herbs and seasoning. Cover and refrigerate for 12 hours.

 To make the confit
Heat the fat in a large pan. Wash the marinade from the duck legs and dry. Add them to the fat and cook on a very low heat for about 2 hours, then place on a tray. Allow to cool, then remove the skin and shred the meat. Place in an airtight container and refrigerate.

 To prepare the parcels
Bring a pan of salted water to the boil. Select 5 leaves from each cabbage and blanch them, 2 at a time, in the pan of boiling water for 30 seconds, remove and refresh in iced water. Dry, place in an airtight container and chill. Remove

Port Wine Duck with Cabbage Parcels

the core of 1 cabbage and shred the leaves finely. Heat the butter in a pan and sauté the onions until soft. Add the stock and cabbage and cook for 8–10 minutes. Drain and allow to cool. Add to the duck confit, season and mix well.

 To make the parcels
Place the leaves on a cloth and season with salt and pepper. Put 1 tablespoon confit and cabbage in the centre of each leaf and fold up into a round. Wrap in a cloth and twist to form a tight ball. Put onto a buttered metal tray and sprinkle with water. Seal with foil and chill.

 To make the sauce
Sauté the shallot in olive oil until golden. Add the port and reduce by half. Pour in the stock and reduce to a velvety consistency (600ml/1 pint for 10 portions). Sieve, cool and chill.

 To seal the duck
Heat a little oil in a sauté pan. When the pan starts to smoke, add 2 duck breasts, skin side down, and season. When golden, turn and seal until the second side is golden. Place on a greased metal tray. Repeat for all the duck breasts. Cover and refrigerate.

 To prepare the gratin
Preheat the oven to 180°C/350°F/gas 4. Butter an ovenproof dish. In a pan, bring the cream to a simmer and add the garlic. Sprinkle the potatoes and turnips with salt and leave for 5 minutes, then squeeze to remove water and starch. Add the potato, turnip and nutmeg to the cream and return to the boil for 5 minutes. Stir, check seasoning, then pour into the ovenproof dish, smoothing the top. Cook in the oven for 1 hour, or until soft and golden. Allow to cool, then divide into 10 portions. Do not refrigerate, but store in a cool place.

To serve

Preheat the oven to 200°C/400°F/gas 6. Bring the sauce to the boil, season and lower the heat. Place the gratin in the oven. After about 10 minutes, add the cabbage parcels and duck, cooking for

10–12 minutes. Remove the gratin, cabbage parcels and duck. Cover the duck loosely with foil and leave to rest for 5 minutes before slicing into 3 portions. Place the gratin and cabbage in the centre of the plates. Arrange the duck against the cabbage and gratin, then pour on the sauce. Serve.

Bitter Chocolate Tart

Pastry
140g (5oz) unsalted butter
100g (3½oz) icing sugar
1 egg
250g (9oz) plain flour, sifted
30g (1oz) ground almonds
melted butter
flour for rolling the pastry

Tamarillos & Sauce
10 tamarillos
2 star anise
1 vanilla pod
3 cloves
750g (1lb 7oz) caster sugar
750ml (1¼ pints) red wine
250ml (⅓ pint) water

Chocolate Ganache
310g (11oz) bitter chocolate, about 70%
  broken into small pieces
675ml (just over 1 pint) double cream
13 egg yolks
110g (3¾ oz) caster sugar
cocoa powder, to dust
250g (9oz) crème fraîche, to garnish
WINE Nuits St Georges or Chilean Cabernet

(2d) To prepare the tart case
Preheat the oven to 180°C/350°F/gas 4
In a mixer, beat the butter and sugar until pale and creamy. On a slow speed, add the egg, then the flour and almonds. Transfer the mixture to a floured board and knead until smooth. Cover with cling film and refrigerate for 2 hours. Place a flan ring on a baking sheet and brush with melted butter. Dust a cool work surface with flour and roll out the pastry to a thickness of 7mm (¼in). Use the pastry sheet to line the flan ring, allowing 2.5cm (1in)

Bitter Chocolate Tart

overlap. Line the pastry with cling film, fill with ceramic beans and refrigerate for 1 hour. Transfer to the oven to bake for about 30 minutes until golden brown. Remove the beans and cling film and return to the oven for 30–35 minutes. Allow to cool and cut off the overlap. Store in an airtight container.

(2d) To poach the tamarillos
Clean the stalk of the tamarillos. Put the spices, sugar, wine and water into a large pan. Bring to the boil. Reduce the heat, then add the tamarillos and simmer for about 5 minutes. Allow to cool in the liquor then strain 300ml (½ pint) into a pan. Peel the tamarillos, place in an airtight container and pour the remaining liquor over them. Refrigerate. Bring the liquor to the boil and reduce by half. Allow to cool, place in a jar and keep this sauce refrigerated.

(8h) To make the ganache
Put the chocolate in a large bowl. In a pan, bring the cream to the boil. Whisk together the egg yolks and sugar until

pale and creamy. Pour the cream onto the chocolate and whisk smooth. Add the egg mixture gradually and whisk for 1 minute. Sieve into a jug.

(8h) To bake the tart
Preheat the oven to 120°C/250°F/gas 1 Place the tart case on a baking tray. Pour the chocolate mixture into it and bake for 45–50 minutes or until the tart is set. Remove and allow to cool. Store in an airtight container in a cool place.

(2h) To cut the tart and tamarillos
Cut the tart into slices then reassemble, leaving small gaps between each slice. Cover and store in a cool place. Drain the tamarillos and cut a small slice off the base of each fruit so that it stands up. Return to the container and chill.

To serve
Dust the top of the tart with cocoa powder. Place a slice in the centre of each plate with a tamarillo and a blob of crème fraîche next to it. Drizzle the sauce over the tamarillo and serve.

do-ahead dinner

This menu is easy to prepare ahead of time, and each delicious course is sure to impress your guests. The hot chocolate mousse, in particular, is always extremely popular. I once served it, still hot, for 400 guests in a tent in the middle of a field! SERVES 10

Mussel & Saffron Broth

Mussel & Saffron Broth

unscented vegetable oil
4 shallots, finely sliced
3 garlic cloves, finely chopped
1 medium-sized fennel bulb, finely sliced
2 large leeks, washed & finely sliced
4kg (9lb) fresh mussels in their shells
1 glass dry white wine
2.4 litres (4 pints) fish stock
2g saffron dissolved in 1 tbsp boiling water
300ml (½ pint) double cream
salt & freshly ground black pepper
10 plum tomatoes, skinned, deseeded & cut into large dice
½ tea cup flat-leaf parsley, chopped
Wine *Muscadet or a young, unoaked Chardonnay*

(5h) **To prepare the broth**
Scrub the mussels thoroughly to remove all barnacles and any trace of grit or sand. Remove the beard from the side of each mussel by pulling it sharply. Heat a little oil in a large pan and sauté the shallot, garlic, fennel and leek for 2 minutes. Turn up the heat, then add the mussels and white wine. Cover and, after 1 minute, shake the pan well, then continue cooking for a further 2–3 minutes. The mussels are cooked when the shells are open. Drain the mussels into a clean pan, keeping the cooking liquid and vegetables. Discard any unopened mussels, and reserve 60 mussels in their shells to garnish. Remove the remaining mussels from their shells. Place in a bowl, cool, cover and chill. Bring the liquid back to the boil, add the fish stock, saffron and cream and simmer for 5 minutes. Take off the heat and season. Allow to cool, place in an airtight container and chill.

To serve
Place the serving bowls in a warm oven. Remove the mussels from the refrigerator. Bring the broth to the boil slowly, then add the tomatoes and parsley. Remove from the heat and pour into a jug. Divide the mussels between the serving bowls and pour the broth over them. Decorate with the reserved mussels and serve.

Pheasant Supreme with Crispy Potato

Red Wine Sauce
unscented vegetable oil
3 shallots, roughly chopped
4 sprigs of thyme
1 glass red wine
2 tbsp quince jelly
1.8 litres (3 pints) reduced brown chicken
  stock

Pheasant & Vegetables
unscented vegetable oil
salt & freshly ground black pepper
10 pheasant supremes, thighbone trimmed
6–8 carrots, cut into at least 40 x 5cm-
  (2in-) long batons
4–6 leeks, cut into at least 40 x 2cm (¾in)
  slices
40 shallots, peeled
3 tbsp caster sugar

Crispy Potato
1kg (2lb 2oz) Desiree potatoes, julienned
10 rashers cooked back bacon, cut into
strips
salt & freshly ground black pepper
unscented vegetable oil
60g (2oz) unsalted butter
Wine Gevrey Chambertin

Pheasant Supreme with Crispy Potato

(2d) To make the sauce
Sauté the chopped shallot and thyme in a little oil until the shallot is soft and transparent. Add the wine and jelly and reduce by half. Pour in the stock and reduce to about 600ml (1 pint). Remove from heat and sieve finely. Cool. Place in an airtight container and refrigerate.

(8h) To seal the pheasant & vegetables
Heat a little oil in a large pan. Season the pheasant on both sides and place skin side down in the hot pan. Seal until golden, turn and repeat. Transfer to a tray. Cool, then cover and chill. Clean the pan, return it to the heat and pour in a little oil; season the leeks and carrots. Sauté them separately until golden; remove and place on a metal tray. Allow to cool, then cover and chill. Clean the pan again, return to the heat with a little oil and cook the shallots slowly until golden. Then season, add the sugar and continue cooking until caramelized and soft. Remove, place on a tray. Cool, then cover and chill.

(4h) To make the crispy potato
In a bowl, mix the potato and bacon strips and add seasoning. Heat a little oil in a pan. Add half the butter and place 5 small handfuls of potato in the pan. Using the back of a large spoon, press each the potato into 12cm (4¾ in) rounds. Cook until crisp and golden on both sides, then place on a tray. Repeat for all the potato. Cool, cover and chill.

To assemble
Preheat the oven to 200°C/400°F/gas 6 Bring the sauce to the boil, then reduce the heat and simmer. Season. Cook the pheasant, vegetables and potato cakes in the oven for 10 minutes. Remove the pheasant and let rest for 5 minutes covered with foil. Slice each supreme into 3. Pour the sauce into a jug. Place a potato cake on each plate with the pheasant on top. Scatter the vegetables over, drizzle on the sauce and serve.

WINE Australian Botrytis Riesling

(9h) To prepare the tea cups
Brush the insides with melted butter and coat with caster sugar. Refrigerate.

(8h) To make the mousses
Cut the chocolate and butter into 2.5cm (1in) pieces, then place in a metal bowl over a pan of barely simmering water to melt. Do not allow the chocolate to get too hot as this will make it difficult to combine with the other ingredients. In an electric mixer, whisk the egg whites on a high speed until foamy. Add the caster sugar gradually, continuing to whisk until the consistency is smooth, glossy and stiff. Remove the chocolate from the heat, add the egg yolks and mix thoroughly. Fold in the egg whites and add the sieved flour. Continue to fold until all the ingredients are well combined. Remove the cups from the refrigerator. Divide the extra chopped chocolate pieces between them. Spoon the mousse mixture into the cups until each is three-quarters full, then return to the refrigerator.

To cook the mousses
Preheat the oven to 160°C/325°F/gas 3. Boil a kettle of water. Put the mousses into a deep roasting tin, then pour boiling water into the tin to halfway up the moulds. I suggest that you do this while the roasting pan is in the oven, so that you do not have to carry it. Cook the mousses for about 20 minutes or until well risen above the edge of the moulds.

To serve
Carefully remove the tea cups from the water – remembering they will be hot. Place them on a clean tea towel to drain away any excess water. Dust with icing sugar and serve with a spoonful of clotted cream on the side.

A LIGHT TOUCH
TAKE CARE NOT TO BE HEAVY-HANDED WHEN FOLDING IN THE INGREDIENTS. YOU DO NOT WANT TO KNOCK TOO MUCH AIR OUT OF THE MIXTURE.

Hot Chocolate Mousse

Hot Chocolate Mousse

Serve in Chinese tea cups about 6 x 6cm/2½ x 2½in, or 180ml/6fl oz.

70% PROOF CHOCOLATE
ALTHOUGH SOME RECIPES WILL WORK WITH 50% COCOA CHOCOLATE YOU MUST SEEK OUT THE DARKEST YOU CAN FIND FOR THIS MOUSSE — OTHERWISE YOU WILL LOSE THE ESSENTIAL RICH FLAVOUR.

60g (2oz) butter, melted
70g (2½oz) caster sugar
250g (9oz) extra-bitter chocolate, (70% cocoa butter)
125g (4½oz) butter
8 eggs, separated
180g (6½oz) caster sugar
60g (2oz) plain flour, sieved
90g (3oz) extra-bitter chocolate, chopped into small pieces
icing sugar, to dust
250g (9oz) clotted cream

mediterranean dinner

This menu is an interesting variation on some classic Mediterranean dishes. The first course was developed by head chef Richard Cubbin, in the South of France. With the enviable task of shopping in the local market, he one day prepared this tart whose flavours marry delightfully – the richness of the goats' cheese enhanced by the sweetness of the figs. All the courses are easy to prepare, and you will be amply rewarded by the risotto! The tiramisu is best served in small glasses. SERVES 10

Goats' Cheese, Fig & Red Onion Jam Tart

Pastry Discs

plain flour for dusting

675g (1½lb) puff pastry

3 egg yolks

1 tbsp milk

pinch of salt

Topping

10 fresh figs

30g (1oz) caster sugar

225g (8oz) log of goats' cheese

10 tbsp Red Onion Jam (see page 168)

1 tea cup picked chervil, washed & dried

1 tea cup picked flat-leaf parsley, washed & dried

1 tea cup chives, snipped into 4cm (1½in) lengths, washed & dried

Red Wine Vinaigrette (see page 168)

salt & freshly ground black pepper

SPECIAL EQUIPMENT **blow torch**

WINE *Chilled Chinon*

(1d) **To prepare the pastry**

Dust a cool surface with flour and roll the pastry to a thickness of 3mm (⅛in). Cut from it 10 x 10cm (4in) discs and place on a floured baking tray. Prick the pastry discs with a fork and chill for about 1 hour to rest. Preheat oven to 200°C/400°F/gas 6. Beat together the egg yolks, milk and salt in a small mixing bowl. Brush the pastry with this

Goats' Cheese, Fig & Red Onion Jam Tart

glaze. Cook in the oven for 10 minutes or until golden. Remove; leave to cool. Layer in greaseproof paper and store in an airtight container in a cool place.

(4h) To prepare the topping
Cut each fig into 12 segments, place on a metal tray and dust with caster sugar. Caramelize the figs with a blow torch. Allow to cool, but do not refrigerate. Cut the goats' cheese crossways into 5 equal slices. Quarter each slice.

(1h) To assemble
Place the pastry discs on a metal tray and spread half the Onion Jam over them. Arrange the figs and goats' cheese alternately, then top with the remaining jam. Leave in a cool place.

To serve
Preheat the oven to 150°C/300°F/gas 2. Warm the tarts for 6–8 minutes. Toss the herbs in a bowl with 1 tablespoon of vinaigrette; season. Place a tart in the centre of each plate and drizzle on the vinaigrette. Top each with herb salad.

Loin of Veal with Lemon Risotto & Spinach

Mustard Sauce
3 shallots, finely diced
2 garlic cloves, finely chopped
unscented vegetable oil
1 glass white wine
900ml (1½ pints) reduced brown chicken stock
300ml (½ pint) double cream
1 tbsp Pommery mustard

Veal, Spinach & Mushrooms
unscented vegetable oil
10 x 200g (7oz) loin of veal portions
salt & freshly ground black pepper
500g (1lb 1oz) spinach, washed 3 times, drained, dried & placed in an airight container lined with a clean tea towel
30g (1oz) unsalted butter
200g (7oz) prepared oyster mushrooms

Lemon Risotto
2.4 litres (4 pints) vegetable stock
60g (2oz) unsalted butter
4 shallots, finely chopped

Loin of Veal with Lemon Risotto & Spinach

3 garlic cloves, finely chopped
5 sprigs of thyme, finely chopped
560g (1lb 4oz) Arborio rice
1 glass dry white wine
60g (2oz) unsalted butter
100g (3½oz) Parmesan cheese, grated
zest & juice of 4 lemons
¼ tea cup flat-leaf parsley, chopped
salt & freshly ground black pepper
WINE Chianti Classico Riserva

(1d) To prepare the sauce
Sauté the shallot and garlic in a little vegetable oil until soft, then add the white wine and reduce until syrupy. Add the chicken stock and double cream, then reduce by half. Allow 600ml (1 pint) for 10 portions. Pour into an airtight container. Cool, then refrigerate.

(6h) To seal the veal
Heat a little unscented oil in a large pan. When the oil begins to smoke, add the portions of veal a few at a time. Season, then sauté until golden brown on each side. Remove from the pan and place on a baking tray. Leave to cool, cover and refrigerate.

(6h) To prepare the spinach
Butter a metal tray. Blanch the spinach in boiling water for 10 seconds. Refresh, drain, then squeeze to remove excess water. Season in a large bowl then separate into 10 portions and set on a tray. Seal with tin foil and chill.

(6h) To sauté the mushrooms
Heat butter in a pan, and sauté the mushrooms until soft. Drain, place on a metal tray and allow to cool. Seal with tin foil and refrigerate.

(½h) To cook the risotto
Bring the vegetable stock to the boil, turn down the heat to simmer. In a large pan, melt the butter, add the shallot and cook for 2 minutes. Add the garlic and thyme, cook for a further 2 minutes without browning, then add the rice. Stir to make sure that the rice is coated with butter. Pour in the wine and, when it is absorbed, add a little stock, a ladleful at a time. When almost

absorbed, repeat until all the stock is used. If required, add extra boiling water. The rice should now be 'al dente' and creamy, not runny or dry. Stir, taking care not to break the grains. Add the butter and cheese, stir gently, then add the lemon zest and juice with the parsley. Stir, season and serve within 5 minutes. (See Perfect Creamy Risotto page 150.)

To assemble
Preheat the oven to 200°C/400°F/gas 6. Pour the sauce into a pan and bring to a simmer. Cook the veal for 10–12 minutes and the spinach and mushrooms for 2 minutes less. Leave the veal to rest for about 5 minutes before serving. Whisk the mustard into the sauce and check seasoning. Spoon the risotto into the centre of each plate, place the spinach, mushrooms and veal to the side. Drizzle on the sauce. Serve.

Ginger Tiramisu

Ginger Tiramisu

Genoise Sponge
10 large eggs, separated
500g (1lb 1oz) caster sugar
10 tbsp boiling water
350g (12½oz) plain flour
5 tsp baking powder
pinch of salt

Jasmine Tea Soaking Liquid
2 tbsp jasmine tea
300ml (½ pint) boiling water
1 tbsp caster sugar
120ml (4fl oz) ginger wine
1 tbsp syrup from the preserved (or stem) ginger
1 orange, rind finely grated

Mascarpone Cream
625g (1lb 4oz) mascarpone cheese
6 egg yolks
105g (3½oz) caster sugar
60ml (2fl oz) orange juice, strained
60ml (2fl oz) ginger wine
75g (2½oz) preserved (or stem) ginger, cut into small dice
6 egg whites
300ml (½ pint) double cream
***WINE** Californian Orange Muscat*

1d To make the sponge
Preheat the oven to 180°C/350°F/gas 4 Grease and line 2 x 28 x 35cm (11 x 14in) Swiss roll tins with baking parchment. Whisk the egg yolks and sugar in a mixer on a high speed until light and creamy. Add the boiling water slowly and continue to whisk for a further 5 minutes. In a bowl, whisk the egg whites until they form soft peaks. Sift together the flour, baking powder and salt. With a metal spoon gently fold in the egg yolks then the egg whites, ½ at a time until well incorporated. Divide the mixture between the 2 tins. Cook for 20 minutes or until golden brown and springy to the touch. Remove from the oven and cool on a wire rack. When cool, cut the sponge in half lengthways, then cut 30 discs from it using a cutter slightly smaller than the glasses. The discs should be about 7mm (¼in) thick.

1d To make the soaking liquid
Infuse the jasmine tea in the boiling water for about 30 minutes. Add the sugar, ginger wine, ginger syrup and orange zest, then put aside.

1d To make the mascarpone cream
Remove the mascarpone from the refrigerator ½ hour before you need to use it. Whisk the egg yolks in a mixer with 75g (2½oz) of sugar, until light in colour and a thick consistency. Add the mascarpone, orange juice, ginger wine and pieces of preserved (or stem) ginger. Whisk until creamy and smooth. Whisk the egg whites with the remaining sugar until they form stiff glossy peaks. Whip the double cream gently. With a large metal spoon, gently fold the egg whites, then the cream, into the mascarpone mixture. Mix in well, making sure that there are no lumps. Set aside.

8h To assemble
Place 1 disc in the base of each mould, brush with soaking liquid then put 1 tablespoon mascarpone mixture on top of each. Repeat for all the sponge discs, finishing with the mascarpone mixture on top. Level off the tops with a palette knife. Cover and refrigerate.

To serve
Dust ½ with cocoa and ½ with icing sugar.

effortless dinner

I like to plan menus that do not require too much time in the kitchen, allowing you more time to spend with your guests. This menu is a perfect example of this practice. If preferred, the cherries for the clafoutis can be replaced with fresh or dried apricots, or plums. I like to serve it in individual oval dishes. SERVES 10

Tian of Crab

Dressing

2 tbsp white wine vinegar

1 tsp of caster sugar

4 tbsp extra-virgin olive oil

2 tbsp chopped fresh dill

salt & freshly ground black pepper

Tian

2 Hass avocados, skinned, stone removed & cut into small dice

juice of 1 lime

450g (1lb) cooked white crabmeat, shell removed

10 plum tomatoes, skinned, deseeded & cut into small dice

2 shallots, finely diced

¼ tea cup chopped chives

3 tbsp lemon-flavoured olive oil

salt & freshly ground black pepper

WINE *New Zealand Sauvignon Blanc*

(1d) **To prepare the dressing**

Mix all the ingredients for the dressing. Season, pour into a jar, cover and chill.

(1h) **To make the tian**

Line a flat tray with plastic wrap. Place 10 ring moulds, 7 x 3cm (2¾ x 1¼in) deep, on the tray. Mix the avocado with the lime juice, season and divide into 10 equal amounts. Spoon into the base of each mould and smooth with the back of a teaspoon. Repeat with the white crab meat. Mix the tomatoes, shallot, chives and olive oil, season, then layer as before. Cover lightly with cling film and refrigerate.

To serve

With a palette knife or fish slice, place the tians in the centre of each plate. Remove the moulds carefully. Drizzle the dressing around the plate and serve.

SKINNING A TOMATO

To remove the skin from a tomato, cut a cross on the top and then drop it into boiling water for 10 seconds. Remove with a slotted spoon and plunge directly into cold water. The skin should now fall off easily.

Venison with Celeriac Purée & Juniper Sauce

Venison in Juniper Sauce

Juniper Berry Sauce

unscented vegetable oil

3 shallots, finely sliced

1 tbsp crushed juniper berries

1 glass dry white wine

1.8 litres (3 pints) reduced chicken stock

Venison Marinade

1.8kg (4lb) loin of venison

3 garlic cloves, crushed

3 shallots, sliced

5 sprigs of thyme

1 bay leaf

zest of 1 orange

600ml (1 pint) good red wine

150ml (¼ pint) olive oil

freshly ground black pepper

Spiced Red Cabbage

100g (3½oz) unsalted butter

750g (1lb 7oz) finely shredded red cabbage

2 red onions, finely sliced

3 garlic cloves, finely chopped

450ml (¾ pint) red wine

2 tbsp Demerara sugar

2 tsp allspice

2 tbsp redcurrant jelly

1 apple, peeled & finely grated

salt & freshly ground black pepper

Celeriac Purée

500g (1lb 1oz) celeriac, diced

1kg (2lb 2oz) Desiree potatoes, diced

150ml (¼ pint) double cream

60g (2oz) unsalted butter

celery salt & freshly ground black pepper

200g (7oz) Girolles mushrooms, cleaned, brushed & sautéed in vegetable oil

70–80 broad beans, blanched & shelled

WINE *Gigondas or a mature red Bordeaux*

(2d) **To make the sauce**

Cook the shallot and juniper berries in a little oil until the shallots are soft. Pour in the wine and reduce by half. Add the chicken stock, return to the boil, then simmer to reduce to about 600ml (1pint). Remove from the heat. Pass through a fine sieve and allow to cool. Pour into an airtight container and chill.

(2d) **To marinade the venison**

Put the venison in a bowl. Mix the marinade ingredients together and pour over the venison. Cover and refrigerate.

Cherry Clafoutis

Cherry Compote
60g (2oz) caster sugar
900g (2lb) fresh cherries, pitted
3 tbsp kirsch

Clafoutis Batter
60g (2oz) butter, melted
60g (2oz) caster sugar to coat moulds
6 large eggs
300g (11oz) caster sugar
170g (6oz) plain flour, sifted
300ml (½ pint) crème fraîche or double cream
300ml (½ pint) full-fat milk
2 tbsp kirsch
icing sugar, to dust
WINE *Muscat Beaumes-de-Venise*

 To prepare the compote
In a pan gently heat the sugar in 1 tablespoon of water until dissolved. Add the cherries and kirsch, and cook on a low heat for 15 minutes, or until the cherries are soft but still whole. Remove from the heat. Drain half the cherries, leaving the rest in the liquid. Let both cool then chill in two covered containers.

Cherry Clafoutis

 To prepare the cabbage
Heat the butter in a large pan. When sizzling, add the cabbage, onion and garlic, stir, reduce the heat, cover, and cook for 10 minutes. Add the wine, sugar, allspice and redcurrant jelly. Cover and cook, stirring occasionally, on low heat for 1 hour. Uncover and continue to cook until wine has almost evaporated. Add the apple, cook for 10 minutes then season, leave to cool, cover and chill.

To seal the venison
Remove the venison from the marinade, pat dry and season. Heat a little oil in a frying pan until smoking, add the venison and brown on all sides. Place on a roasting tray to cool, then cover and return to the refrigerator.

To prepare the purée
Boil the celeriac and potatoes in salted water until soft. Drain and pass through a potato ricer or fine sieve into a bowl. Clean the pan then return the purée to

it. Add the cream and butter. Return to the heat and beat with a wooden spoon. Season with celery salt and pepper. Remove from the heat, cover and cool.

To assemble and serve
Preheat the oven to 200°C/400°F/gas 6. Remove the meat from the refrigerator 15 minutes before cooking. Roast in the oven for 12–15 minutes, adding the mushrooms on a separate tray after 5 minutes. Boil the sauce in a pan then simmer. Heat the red cabbage and celeriac purée in 2 covered saucepans, stirring occasionally. Remove the venison and the mushrooms from the oven and leave for 5 minutes. Meanwhile cook the broad beans in boiling water for 1 minute, drain and keep warm. Pour the sauce into a jug and slice the venison. On each plate, place a spoonful of celeriac purée and red cabbage. Arrange the venison over the cabbage. Scatter the beans and mushrooms and drizzle the sauce around the plate and serve.

To make the clafoutis
Preheat the oven to 180°C/350°F/gas 4. Brush the insides of the moulds with melted butter and caster sugar, then put aside. In a mixer, whisk the eggs until frothy, add sugar; then whisk for a further 2 minutes. Add the flour, crème fraîche or cream, milk and kirsch, then whisk until well blended. Divide the drained, cooked cherries between the moulds, pour over the batter and place on a baking sheet. Bake for 15 minutes then remove the clafoutis from the oven and top up the moulds with any remaining batter. Return to the oven for 15 minutes until the clafoutis are golden in colour and firm to touch. Allow to cool and refrigerate.

To serve
Preheat the oven to 150°C/300°F/gas 2 Place the dishes on a baking tray and heat for 10 minutes. Remove, dust with icing sugar and place on the plates with a spoonful of compote. Serve.

oriental dinner

These recipes have been developed over the years to offer a range of particularly exciting oriental flavours, textures and colours. If, like me, you enjoy experimenting with different serving dishes and containers, try presenting the coconut brulée and mango sorbet in small glass candleholders – the effect is stunning. SERVES 10

Spiced Duck with Lemon Grass

Duck Marinade
2 tsp chilli flakes
60g (2oz) chopped ginger
3 garlic cloves, chopped
150ml (¼ pint) light soy sauce
4 tbsp sweet soy sauce
5 duck breasts
unscented vegetable oil

Lemon Grass Dressing
juice of 3 lemons
2 tbsp water
1 level tbsp palm sugar
1 tbsp fish sauce
1 tbsp sweet chilli sauce
2 stems lemon grass, finely sliced
2 garlic cloves, finely chopped
2 mild red chillies, deseeded & cut into
   fine strips
4 tbsp olive oil
salt & freshly ground black pepper

Slaw
300g (11oz) carrots, finely shredded
300g (11oz) red radish, finely shredded
300g (11oz) mangetout, finely shredded
1 tea cup picked coriander, washed &
   dried
salt & freshly ground black pepper

10 Wonton skins, finely shredded &
   deep fried till crispy (keep wonton skins
   covered with a cloth before frying to
   prevent them drying out)
WINE *Alsace or Oregon Pinot Noir*

(1d) **To marinade the duck**
Mix together the marinade ingredients. Place the duck breasts in an airtight container, pour over the marinade, then cover and refrigerate.

(1d) **To make the dressing**
In a saucepan, bring the lemon juice, water, palm sugar, fish and chilli sauces

Spiced Duck with Lemon Grass

to the boil, then lower the heat and simmer for 1 minute or until slightly syrupy. Add the lemon grass, chopped garlic and red chillies and simmer for a further minute. Allow to cool, then whisk in the oil and season. Pour into a jar and refrigerate.

(6h) **To cook the duck**
Preheat the oven to 190°C/375°F/gas 5 Drain the duck, then heat a little oil in a sauté pan and sauté the duck until golden brown on both sides. Place on a metal tray in the oven and roast for 8–10 minutes – the duck should be pink. Allow to cool, then refrigerate.

To serve
Slice the duck widthways and set aside. Mix the slaw in a bowl, pour over half the dressing, mix well and season. Then mix the duck into the slaw, distributing the meat evenly. Arrange in the centre of each plate, top with wontons, drizzle on the remaining dressing and serve.

Grilled Tuna with Chilli Noodles & Leeks

Chilli Noodles

salt
225g (8oz) fresh fine egg noodles
unscented vegetable oil
1 red chilli, deseeded & finely sliced
1 green chilli, deseeded & finely sliced
200g (7oz) fresh shiitake mushrooms, sliced
100g (3½oz) water chestnuts, finely sliced
200g (7oz) Chinese cabbage, finely shredded
3 tbsp light soy sauce
3 tsp caster sugar

Tomato & Lime Sauce

900ml (1½ pints) reduced brown chicken
  stock
60g (2oz) ginger, peeled & chopped
2 fresh lime leaves, finely shredded
juice of 2 limes
1 tbsp palm sugar
5 spring onions, finely sliced
5 plum tomatoes, skinned, deseeded & cut
  into large dice

30 baby leeks
unscented vegetable oil
freshly ground black pepper
10 x 175g (6oz) tuna steaks, preferably from
  the tail end

WINE White Rhône or Californian Viognier

8h To prepare the noodles

Bring a large pan of salted water to the boil. Add the noodles, bring back to the boil, then simmer for 4–5 minutes until soft. Drain under running cold water to cool. Leave to drain. Place in a bowl and toss with a little oil, then cover. Heat a little oil in a pan, then add chillies, mushrooms, water chestnuts, cabbage, soy sauce and sugar. Cook until the cabbage is soft. Remove from the heat, place on a tray and allow to cool. Mix with the noodles and season. To give 10 portions, lift a section of noodles with a carving fork, and twist around to form a nest. Place on a lightly oiled baking tray, spray with a little water and seal with foil. Chill.

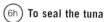
Grilled Tuna with Chilli Noodles & Leeks

6h To blanch and grill the leeks

Heat a chargrill pan. Fill a large saucepan with salted water and bring to the boil. Blanch the leeks for 2–3 minutes, then drain and refresh. Dry with a clean tea towel, brush with a little unscented oil and season. Place the leeks on the grill and remove when bar marks are visible. Transfer to a tray, forming portions of 3 leeks tied in a knot. Cover and refrigerate.

6h To seal the tuna

Heat the chargrill pan. Brush the tuna with a little unscented oil and season. Place on the chargrill pan and grill until bar marks are visible. Transfer to a tray, cover and refrigerate.

6h To prepare the sauce

Bring the stock to the boil in a saucepan, then lower the heat and simmer. Add the ginger, lime leaves, lime juice and sugar. Bring back to the boil and reduce by half. Remove from the heat and allow to cool. Store in an airtight container and refrigerate.

To assemble

Preheat the oven to 200°C/400°F/gas 6 Pour the sauce into a pan and bring to the boil, then lower the heat and simmer. Place the noodles in the oven but do not remove the foil. After 4 minutes, add the leeks and tuna. Cook for 6–8 minutes. Add the remaining ingredients to the sauce and check the seasoning. Remove the tuna, noodles and leeks from the oven. On each plate, place a nest of noodles, leeks and tuna. Pour the sauce into a jug and spoon liberally around the noodles and over the tuna. Serve.

CUTS OF FISH AND MEAT

SEVERAL RECIPES, LIKE THIS ONE, SPECIFY THE CUT OF FISH OR MEAT TO USE. TO ENSURE YOU HAVE EXACTLY WHAT YOU NEED ASK YOUR THE FISHMONGER OR BUTCHER TO PREPARE IT FOR YOU. IF YOU ARE ORGANISED IN TIME, RING UP IN ADVANCE TO ORDER IT. A GOOD FISHMONGER OR BUTCHER WILL ALSO OFFER ALTERNATIVES IF YOUR CUT IS NOT AVAILABLE.

Coconut Brulée with Mango Sorbet

Coconut Brulée with Mango Sorbet

Mango Sorbet

1.35kg (3lb) ripe mangoes
150g (5½oz) caster sugar
150ml (¼ pint) water
3 limes, juiced
30 slices of Oven-Dried Mango (see
  page 169), to garnish

SPECIAL EQUIPMENT **ice cream maker**

Coconut Brulée

1.2 litres (2 pints) double cream
2 vanilla pods, split
90g (3oz) desiccated coconut
10 egg yolks
90g (3oz) caster sugar
Macadamia Nut Brittle (see page 169), to
  garnish
WINE *Côteaux du Layon*

MACADAMIA NUT BRITTLE

This can be prepared up to a week in
advance, but the final creation should
be left until the day. Eat the brûlées
soon after garnishing.

2d **To prepare the sorbet**
Peel the mangoes, removing as much
flesh as possible from the stone. Purée
in a food processor or liquidizer and put
to one side. Place the sugar and water
in a saucepan and bring slowly to the
boil. Simmer for about 2 minutes until
all the sugar has dissolved. Allow to
cool, then add the purée and lime juice
and refrigerate.

1d **To make the sorbet**
Place 10 candleholders in the freezer.
Pour the mixture into an ice cream
maker and churn. Pipe the sorbet into
the holders, smooth the tops and return
to the freezer.

1d **To make the brûlée**
Preheat the oven to 150°C/300°F/gas 2.
Place the double cream, vanilla pods
and desiccated coconut in a heavy-
bottomed saucepan. Bring to the boil
slowly, stirring occasionally. Remove
from the heat and leave to infuse for 30
minutes. In an electric mixer, whisk the
egg yolks and sugar together. In the
meantime, bring the cream back to the
boil and add the egg yolks gradually,

whisking continuously. Pass through a
fine sieve into a jug, discarding the
coconut and vanilla. Pour into the
remaining moulds (candleholders) and
place in a deep roasting tray. Pour
boiling water into the tray to reach
halfway up the moulds. Cook for 20
minutes, or until set – the brulée should
be quite firm to touch. Remove from the
bath of water, allow to cool and then
refrigerate until ready to serve.

BOILING MILK OR CREAM

Using a heavy-bottomed suacepan is
best for boiling milk or cream as it
distributes the heat evenly over the
base of the pan.

To serve

Remove the sorbets from the freezer,
and leave to stand for 10 minutes.
Alternatively place in the refrigerator for
30 minutes. When ready to serve
decorate each sorbet with 3 slices of
oven-dried mangoes and stand a triangle
of Macadamia Brittle on each brulée.
Offer each guest 1 candleholder of each
dessert – they will not want to miss out
on either.

vegetarian dinner

Richard Cubbin is our master vegetarian menu planner and these are two of his most requested dishes. Portobello mushrooms are full of flavour and very filling but, if you cannot find them, use field mushrooms instead. SERVES 10

Millefeuille of Portobello Mushrooms & Lentils

Puy Lentil Salad
150g (4oz) Puy lentils, soaked for 12 hours
  & drained
600ml (1 pint) vegetable stock
salt & freshly ground black pepper
150g (4oz) carrots, finely diced
1 shallot, finely diced
¼ tea cup snipped chives

Mustard Oil
3 tbsp mustard seeds
¼ tsp turmeric
125ml (4fl oz) grapeseed oil

Parsley Oil
1 tea cup flat-leaf parsley, washed, dried
  & chopped
125ml (4fl oz) grapeseed oil

Millefeuille of Mushrooms
20 large Portobello mushrooms, or large flat
  field mushrooms
salt & freshly ground black pepper
olive oil to brush the mushrooms & leeks
4 large shallots, sliced into rings
1 garlic clove, finely chopped
¼ tea cup fresh thyme, chopped
300ml (½ pint) extra-virgin olive oil
40 baby leeks, washed & roots trimmed
5 large red peppers, roasted & skinned,
  seeds removed
WINE Bergerac or Languedoc Rosé

(1d) **To make the lentil salad**
Place the lentils and vegetable stock in a medium saucepan, add the salt and bring to the boil; reduce the heat to simmer for about 15–20 minutes. Refresh, drain and set aside. At the same time, cook the carrots in salted water for 2–3 minutes; drain and refresh in cold water. In a bowl mix together the lentils, carrots, shallots and chives; season to taste. Cover with cling film and place in the refrigerator.

(1d) **To make the mustard oil**
Preheat the oven to 200°C/400°F/gas 6. Place the mustard seeds on a tray and roast for about 5 minutes; allow to cool. Blend the mustard seeds, turmeric and oil in a blender for 2–3 minutes; strain through a fine sieve. Pour into a jar with a lid and place in the refrigerator.

(1d) **To make the parsley oil**
Bring a saucepan of water to the boil; fill a large bowl with iced water. Blanch the parsley for about 3–4 minutes. Remove and refresh in the ice-cold water, then dry on a tea towel or in a salad spinner. Chop the parsley coarsely and place in a blender with the oil. Blend for about 2 minutes, then strain through a fine sieve into a jar with a lid. Place in the refrigerator.

(8h) **To prepare the millefeuilles**
Preheat a chargrill pan. Remove the centre stalks from the mushrooms and score lightly across the top of each mushroom. Sprinkle with salt and leave for 5 minutes. Brush the mushrooms with olive oil and chargrill on each side until soft; leave to cool. When cold, place the mushrooms in an airtight container, covering with the shallots, garlic, thyme and oil. Season and place in the refrigerator. Bring a pan of salted water to the boil; fill a large bowl with iced water. Blanch the leeks for about 3–4 minutes. Refresh, drain and dry. Heat a chargrill pan, brush the leeks with a little olive oil and grill on all sides. Allow the leeks to cool, then add to the mushrooms.

To assemble
Place a mushroom in the centre of each plate. Place 2 leeks on top, add a little of the shallot and garlic mixture and a slice of red pepper, seasoning between each layer; repeat, finishing with a slice of red pepper on top. Sprinkle the lentil mix around the mushrooms, dress with the oils and serve. The mushrooms can be assembled up to 1 hour before; dress just before serving.

Baked Onion with Carrot & Cumin Sauce

10 x 300g (10oz) round white onions
unscented vegetable oil
salt & freshly ground black pepper
1.4 litres (2½ pints) vegetable stock
500g (1lb 1oz) cracked wheat
2 tbsp olive oil
500g (1lb 1oz) corn kernels, cooked
200g (7oz) pine nuts
8 plum tomatoes, blanched, peeled,
  deseeded & cut into 6mm (¼in) dice
¼ tea cup flat-leaf parsley, washed, picked,
  dried & chopped
¼ tea cup fresh mint, washed, dried &
  chopped
juice of 1 lime

Carrot & Cumin Sauce
unscented vegetable oil
3 shallots, sliced
1½ tsp cumin seeds
650g (1lb 8oz) carrots, chopped
1 garlic clove, chopped
300ml (¼ pint) white wine
1 litre (1¾ pints) vegetable stock
salt & freshly ground black pepper
WINE Cru Beaujolais

THE PERFECT ONION
I CANNOT RECOMMEND VIDALIA ONIONS TOO HIGHLY FOR THIS RECIPE — THEY ARE SO SWEET AND DELICIOUS.

(1d) To prepare and cook the onions

Preheat the oven 180°C/350°F/gas 4.
Line baking trays with non-stick paper.
Remove the outer skins of the onions,
leaving the root and stalk intact. Cut
the top off the onion to create a lid.
Scoop out the middle using a spoon or
melon baller. Brush the insides with
unscented vegetable oil and season.
Place on the trays in the oven and bake
for about 20–25 minutes. Remove and
leave to cool. Pour the stock into a large
saucepan and bring to the boil. Reduce
the heat, then add the cracked wheat
and simmer for about 15–20 minutes,
or until all the stock is absorbed. Add
the olive oil and stir. Add the corn
kernels, pinenuts, tomatoes, herbs and
lime juice; stir well and season. Allow
to cool, then fill the prepared onions
with the mixture and replace the onion
lids. Cover and place in the refrigerator.

(1d) To prepare the sauce

Heat a little unscented vegetable oil in
a saucepan. Add the shallots, cumin,
carrots and garlic; sauté for about 3–4
minutes. Pour in the white wine and
reduce by half. Add the vegetable stock,
bring to the boil and simmer for 20–25
minutes. Season, remove from the heat
and allow to cool. Blend until smooth,
pass through a fine sieve into a
container and place in the refrigerator.

To serve

Preheat the oven to 180°C/350°F/gas 4.
Cover the onions loosely with foil and
place in the oven for 8–10 minutes.
Heat the sauce, checking the seasoning.
Place an onion in the centre of each
plate, pour on the sauce and serve.

VEGETARIAN-FRIENDLY DESSERTS

IF YOU ARE COOKING A VEGETARIAN DINNER
YOU CAN SELECT ANY OF THE DESSERTS
FROM THE OTHER DINNERS - OR EVEN TRY
ONE FROM THE DESSERT BUFFET ON PAGES
112–15. MY FAVOURITE FOR THIS MENU
WOULD BE THE STEM GINGER ICE CREAM
WITH GLAZED PINEAPPLE ON PAGE 126.

Millefeuille of Portobello Mushrooms & Lentils;
Baked Onion with Carrot & Cumin Sauce

Often we like to entertain, not on a grand scale such as a dinner party, but informally around a kitchen table or in the garden. Perhaps we want to organize a light supper after a trip to the theatre or a concert, or a club or association meeting at home requires some informal hospitality.

for a supper party

About twice a year, I give a post-theatre supper party for a group of friends and they always request my fish pie. I set the table and place the pie in the oven, set on a timer. When we arrive home, there is time for a glass of wine and then the pie is ready. The supper is easy to serve with little fuss, friends are on hand to help with serving drinks and everyone can seat themselves. After serving out this pie keep it warm as there will always be requests for more.

Enjoying the Evening

The way to enjoy being a host is to plan simple but interesting menus that can be cooked ahead of time. Alternatively, some dishes can be prepared while guests are chatting over a glass of wine – a delicious risotto, for example. Few people can resist the warmth of the kitchen while food is being prepared so the cook is likely to have conversation and help on hand. The menus on the following pages are uncomplicated and easy to prepare. The best and simplest rule when planning menus is to cook with seasonal ingredients.

Cheating with a Chinese Supper

If, like me, you love Chinese food but are put off serving it because it demands lots of last-minute cooking when you would prefer to be socializing with your guests, why not arrange an easy supper the cheat's way? Set the table with matt-black lacquer tablemats and celedon coloured bowls, plates and serving dishes, tie the chopsticks together with chives and order your food from your favourite Chinese restaurant. When it arrives, place the food into warmed bowls and serve for a hassle-free supper.

Professional Tips

• When you know that you're going to want something to eat when you come home, set your oven on timer delay – it can be a life-saver

• Before you go out, or before your guests arrive, set the table or, if eating from laps with a fork, arrange the serving area

• Wines can be put on to chill and glasses and coffee cups arranged at the beginning of the day

• Remember, the best rule is to keep your supper simple – and the recipes in this chapter will show you how to do it with style

STORE-CUPBOARD SUPPERS

SPUR-OF-THE-MOMENT ENTERTAINING IS MADE A LOT EASIER IF YOU KNOW A RANGE OF EASY DISHES THAT CAN BE RUSTLED UP FROM THE USUAL CONTENTS OF YOUR FRIDGE OR STORE CUPBOARD.

late night supper

This fish pie is an ideal late-night supper after a theatre trip or cocktail party. I have served this on several occasions and my advice is to set the table before leaving and place the pie in the oven with the timer set on delay. On arriving home, there is just time for a glass of wine before tucking into supper. SERVES 10

Creamy Fish Pie

Pie Filling

1.5 litres (2½ pints) fish stock
200g (7oz) salmon fillet, cut into 4cm (1½in) cubes
200g (7oz) monkfish fillet, cut into 4cm (1½in) cubes
200g (7oz) halibut fillet, cut into 4cm (1½in) cubes
200g (7oz) peeled prawns
200g (7oz) cooked mussels
200g (7oz) baby scallops, shelled with muscle removed
100g (3½oz) butter
100g (3½oz) plain flour
450ml (¾ pint) double cream
3 shallots, finely sliced
2 medium-sized leeks, washed & finely sliced
unscented vegetable oil for cooking
1 glass white wine
2 tbsp Pernod
salt & ground white pepper
¼ tea cup snipped chives
¼ tea cup flat-leaf parsely, washed, dried & chopped

Creamed Potatoes

1.2kg (2lb 7oz) Desiree potatoes, quartered
300ml (½ pint) double cream
30g (1oz) unsalted butter
3 egg yolks
salt & ground white pepper

(1d) **To prepare the filling**
Bring the stock to the boil in a large saucepan, then lower the heat and simmer. Poach the fish individually, allowing about 3–4 minutes cooking time. Pass the stock through a fine sieve into a clean saucepan. In a separate saucepan, melt the butter then add the flour to make a roux sauce. Cook for 2 minutes, without browning. Add the hot stock slowly, stirring continually to prevent any lumps from forming. Cook over a low heat for about 10 minutes. Remove from the heat and add the cream. Cover with greaseproof paper and leave to cool slightly. Sauté the shallots and leeks in oil until transparent, not brown. Add the white wine and Pernod, then reduce until very syrupy. Season and transfer to a container. In an oval dish, approximately 37cm (14½in) long, 28cm (11in) wide and 6cm (2½in) deep, scatter the cooked fish, shellfish, shallots and leeks. Make sure that they are evenly distributed, then season. Add the chopped herbs to the cream sauce, stir and season. Ladle over the filling. Leave to cool, cover with cling film and chill.

(8h) **To cook the potatoes**
Cook the potatoes in a saucepan of salted water until soft, then drain. Pass through a potato ricer or fine sieve into a bowl. Bring the cream to the boil, add the butter and season. Remove from the heat, pour on to the potatoes and beat. Stir in the egg yolks and season. Allow to cool, then either pipe, using a tool with a fluted nozzle, or spoon over the pie filling. Cover and refrigerate.

To serve
Preheat the oven to 180°C/350°F/gas 4. Reheat the pie for 1 hour. If you would like the top brown, grill for a few minutes before serving.

Spiced Baked Apples

280g (10oz) sultanas
220ml (8fl oz) brandy
1 tsp ground cinnamon
½ tsp ground allspice
120g (4oz) light soft brown sugar
10 medium cooking apples (preferably Bramleys)
10 whole cloves

(2d) **To soak the sultanas**
Place the sultanas in an airtight jar, pour in the brandy and store in a cool, dry place until required.

(2h) **To prepare the apples**
Preheat the oven to 160°C/325°F/gas 3. Place the sultanas in a bowl, then add the cinnamon, allspice and sugar. Stir until combined. Core the apples, keeping them whole; do not peel them. Score the outsides around the middle. Place in an ovenproof dish, large enough that the apples will not touch – this allows them to cook evenly. Fill the apples halfway with the fruit mixture, place a clove in the centre of each one, then fill to the top with the remaining fruit. Pour about 110ml (4fl oz) cold water over the bottom of the dish , then cover and place in the refrigerator until ready to cook.

(¾h) **To cook the apples**
Bake the apples for about 45 minutes, or until they are soft and slightly puffed but still holding their shape.

To serve
Remove from the oven and leave to cool for about 5 minutes. Place each apple in a bowl and serve, pouring the syrup that collects at the bottom of the baking tray over the apples.

Spiced Baked Apples

speedy supper

When friends drop in unexpectedly, tortillas are very easy to make and quick to cook. They can be made using any left overs – meat or vegetables – and form an extremely satisfying and tasty meal. Altogether you should end up with 4 tortillas – enough for 10 people. SERVES 10

Quick-Fix Tortillas

Vegetable Tortillas

3 roasted red peppers, deseeded, skins removed and cut into large squares
250g (9oz) grated mahon cheese, or mature cheddar
¼ tea cup mixed herbs (chopped parsley, chives, and chervil, washed & dried)
olive oil
1 Spanish onion, finely sliced
250g (9oz) potatoes, finely sliced (choose a variety such as ratte or pink fir)
2 garlic cloves, finely chopped
300g (11oz) Portobello mushrooms, sliced
salt & freshly ground black pepper
200g (7oz) spinach, washed & dried
12 eggs

Chorizo Tortillas

250g (9oz) piece of cooked knuckle of ham, roughly chopped
½ chilli, deseeded & finely chopped (optional)
¼ tea cup mixed herbs (chopped parsley, chives and chervil, washed & dried)
olive oil
1 Spanish onion, finely sliced
250g (9oz) potatoes, finely sliced (as above)
1 leek, washed & finely sliced
2 garlic cloves, finely chopped
salt & freshly ground black pepper
250g (9oz) chorizo, thinly sliced & quartered
12 eggs

(2h) **To make the vegetable tortillas**
Preheat the grill. Divide the peppers, cheese and herbs between 2 bowls. Heat a little oil in a 26cm (10in) sauté pan and sauté the onions until very soft. Add the potatoes and, when soft, add the garlic, then sauté for a further 2–3 minutes. Season and divide between the 2 bowls. Clean the sauté pan with kitchen paper. Pour in a little oil, sauté the mushrooms and season. Transfer to the bowls. Reheat the sauté pan, add the spinach and cook until wilted, then season, drain and place in the bowls. Beat the eggs lightly with a fork and season. Divide and pour into the bowls. Mix well, checking the seasoning. Heat a little olive oil in a sauté pan and add the mixture. Cook on one side, then place under the grill until the tortilla is light brown and firm to touch. Leave for about 5 minutes. Slide the tortilla on to a serving platter and leave in a cool place. Repeat. Serve hot or at room temperature.

(2h) **To make the chorizo tortillas**
Preheat the grill. Divide the ham, chilli and herbs between 2 bowls. Heat a little oil in a 26cm (10in) sauté pan with a metal handle and sauté the onions until very soft. Add the potatoes and leeks and, when soft, add the garlic and cook for a further 2–3 minutes. Season and divide between the 2 bowls. Clean the sauté pan with kitchen paper. Sauté the chorizo for about 5 minutes and divide between the bowls. Once again, clean the pan with kitchen paper. Beat the eggs lightly with a fork and season. Divide and pour into the bowls. Mix well, checking the seasoning. Heat a little olive oil in a sauté pan and add the mixture. Cook on one side then place under the grill until the tortilla is light brown and firm to touch. Leave for 5 minutes, then turn on to a serving platter and set aside. Repeat.

To assemble
Cut each tortilla into 5 equal portions. Line a large wooden board with vine leaves and arrange the ham, olives, and other optional tortilla extras (below) on it. Garnish with fresh herbs and place the mayonnaise in a sauce boat. Serve hot or at room temperature.

OPTIONAL TORTILLA EXTRAS
CHILLI MAYONNAISE; CORNICHONS; CRUSTY BREAD WITH BUTTER; FRESH HERBS; OLIVE OIL; MARINADED GREEN AND BLACK OLIVES; SERRANO HAM; WHOLE SALTED ALMONDS.

Crisp Green Salad

Sherry Vinegar Dressing
2 tsp grain mustard
1 tbsp white wine vinegar
1 tbsp sherry vinegar
1 tsp caster sugar
3 tbsp olive oil
2 shallots, finely sliced
zest of ½ lemon

450g (1lb) salad leaves, washed & dried
(a selection of 4 varieties from the following: baby bok choy; baby red chard; baby spinach; escarole; green mustard leaf; mizuna; oakleaf)
½ tea cup flat-leaf parsley, picked, washed & dried
½ tea cup picked chervil, washed & dried
½ tea cup picked chives, snipped, washed & dried
a selection of edible flowers to decorate the salad: chives; nasturtiums; pansies; rose petals; rosemary; thyme

(1d) **To make the dressing**
Place all the ingredients in a bowl, mix well and season. Pour into a jar with a lid and refrigerate.

(1d) **To wash the salad and herbs**
Wash and dry all the leaves carefully, and place in an airtight box lined with a tea towel. Refrigerate.

Rhubarb Crumble with Vanilla Cream

450g (1lb) plain flour, sifted

pinch of salt

225g (8oz) unsalted butter, cut into cubes

225g (8oz) caster sugar

1.35kg (3lb) fresh rhubarb

250g (9oz) caster sugar

finely grated zest & juice of 2 medium-sized
    oranges

Vanilla Cream

600ml (1 pint) double cream

30g (1oz) icing sugar

1 vanilla pod, split lengthways, deseeded

(1d) **To prepare the crumble**

In an electric mixer, add the flour, salt, butter and sugar. Mix until the texture resembles fine breadcrumbs. Place in an airtight container in the refrigerator.

(6h) **To prepare the rhubarb**

Preheat the oven to 190°C/375°F/gas 5. Wash the rhubarb, and trim top and bottom. Cut the rhubarb into 5cm- (2in-) long pieces. Mix with the sugar, orange zest and juice, then place in an ovenproof dish. Cover the dish with foil, and bake for 30 minutes until the rhubarb is soft but still retains its shape. Leave to cool, then cover and place in the refrigerator.

To cook the crumble – 30 minutes

Preheat the oven to 170°C/330°F/gas 3 Divide the rhubarb and crumble topping between the serving dishes you are using. Bake for about 30 minutes, until you start to see the liquid bubbling out and the crumble is golden brown. While it cooks, prepare the cream.

(½h) **To prepare the cream**

Place the chilled cream in a mixing bowl, then add the icing sugar and vanilla. Whisk, by hand or with an electric mixer, until the mixture begins to thicken. If using an electric mixer, do not leave unattended, otherwise you could over-beat the cream and turn it into butter. The vanilla cream is best served as soon as it is made, which takes only a few minutes.

To serve

Place the vanilla cream in a serving bowl. With a damp cloth, clean around the bowl and serve.

add the garlic and sauté for a further 2 minutes, without browning. Add the rice and stir, making sure it is coated with butter. Pour in the wine and, when it is almost absorbed, add a little stock a ladleful at a time. When this is almost absorbed, repeat until all the stock is used. If more liquid is required, add a little boiling water. At this point the rice should be 'al dente' and creamy, not dry or runny. Stir in the butter and the Parmesan cheese, then season. Add the mushrooms and parsley, then stir, taking care not to break the grains. Transfer to a warm serving bowl, drizzle on a few drops of truffle oil and scatter over the shavings of Parmesan. Serve.

PERFECT CREAMY RISOTTO
THE SECRET IS TO COOK ON A MEDIUM-LOW HEAT, NOT SO HIGH THAT THE STOCK EVAPORATES RAPIDLY NOR SO LOW THAT IT'S NOT ABSORBED. KEEP THE STOCK BARELY AT A SIMMER AND ADD IT SLOWLY.

Wild Mushroom Risotto

tuscan supper

A few years ago, I spent a holiday in a Tuscan farmhouse with friends who shared a great love of good food and wines. These is typical of the meals we would create, from the local produce. SERVES 10

Wild Mushroom Risotto

450g (1lb) seasonal selection of wild mushrooms, large ones broken into pieces
olive oil
salt & freshly ground black pepper
3.6 litres (6 pints) vegetable stock
60g (2oz) unsalted butter
4 shallots, finely sliced
3 garlic cloves, finely diced
900g (2lb) Arborio rice
1 glass dry white wine
60g (2oz) unsalted butter
100g (3½oz) Parmesan, grated

½ tea cup flat-leaf parsley, washed, dried & chopped
a few drops of white truffle oil
shavings of Parmesan

(6h) To sauté the mushrooms
Sauté the mushrooms in a little olive oil, season and allow to cool.

(½h) To make and serve the risotto
Bring the vegetable stock to the boil, then reduce the heat and simmer. Melt the butter in a large pan, add the shallots and sauté for 2 minutes, then

Rosemary Strawberries with Biscotti

Rosemary syrup
250g (9oz) caster sugar
250ml (9fl oz) water
3 stems of fresh rosemary

1kg (2lb 2oz) strawberries, washed & hulled
lemon balm or mint leaves to garnish
40 Pistachio Biscotti (see page 123)
1 bottle Vino Santo 'the wine of the saints'

(2h) To make the syrup
Place the sugar and water in a heavy-bottomed pan; leave for 5 minutes. Add the rosemary and bring to the boil, then remove from the heat and leave to cool. Strain and pour into a bottle with a stopper. Store in a cool place.

To serve
Place the strawberries in a large serving bowl and sprinkle with syrup. Garnish with lemon balm or mint. Place the biscotti in a basket and pour the wine into glasses – guests can dip their biscotti into the wine Tuscan-style.

comfort supper

Tasty, chunky soups are popular with nearly everyone. Serve the soups straight from the pan on the stove, or ladled into large bowls. They can be prepared ahead of time, and are warm, comforting and delicious – I hope you enjoy them. For vegetarians, I have suggested how the Tuscan Bean Soup can be adapted. SERVES 10

Chicken Pot Pie Soup

3 egg yolks
pinch of salt
350g (12½oz) puff pastry

Soup
3 litres (5 pints) white chicken stock
675g (1lb 8oz) chicken breasts, skin & bone removed
4 fresh corncobs
unscented vegetable oil
1 large onion, peeled & finely sliced
2 medium-sized leeks, washed & sliced
200g (7oz) button mushrooms
400g (14oz) carrots, cut into 2cm (¾ in) cubes
200g (7oz) new potatoes, a variety such as Charlotte, washed & sliced
200g (7oz) fresh peas
60g (2oz) unsalted butter
60g (2oz) plain flour, plus extra for dusting
600ml (1 pint) double cream
½ tea cup flat-leaf parsley, washed & finely chopped
salt & ground white pepper

(1d) To prepare the pastry
Preheat the oven, 190°C/375°F/gas 5. Whisk together the egg yolks and salt. Line a baking tray with non-stick paper. On a floured board, roll out the pastry to a thickness of 2mm (⅛in). Cut out discs with a 3cm (1¼in) plain cutter and brush with the egg yolks. Place on the tray and refrigerate for ½ hour, then transfer to the oven to cook until golden brown. Allow to cool, then store in an airtight container in a cool place.

(1d) To make the soup
Bring the stock to the boil in a large saucepan. Poach the chicken breasts for about 6–8 minutes, drain, reserving the stock and allow to cool. Cut into 1.5cm (½in) cubes, cover and refrigerate. Bring the stock back to the boil, add the corncobs and cook until tender. Drain (again reserving the stock), allow to cool, then remove the corn from the cobs, cover and chill. Pour the stock into a large, clean bowl. Wash the saucepan then pour the stock (you should have about 2.4 litres/4 pints) back into it. Heat a little oil in a sauté pan and sauté the onions and leeks until soft. Add the mushrooms, sauté for a further 2 minutes, season and cool. Bring a pan of salted water to the boil, cook the carrots until tender, then drain. Repeat with the potatoes and peas. Cover the vegetables and refrigerate. Bring the stock to a simmer. In a large saucepan, melt the butter, then add the flour to make a smooth roux. Add the stock slowly, 150ml (¼ pint) at a time, mixing until smooth. Cook on a low heat for 10 minutes. Cover with greaseproof paper, allow to cool and refrigerate.

To serve
Preheat the oven to 180°C/350°F/gas 4. Warm the pastry discs. Bring the soup to the boil, add the cream, chicken and vegetables, then season. Add the chopped parsley just before serving. Float a few 'pie tops' on the soup. Serve the rest of the pies separately.

Tuscan Bean & Italian Sausage Soup

Soup
100g (3½oz) dried chick peas
100g (3½oz) dried cannellini beans
100g (3½oz) dried red kidney beans
100g (3½oz) dried pinto beans
½ large onion
2 whole garlic cloves
2 bay leaves
4 peppercorns
2 sprigs of thyme
olive oil
1 large onion, cut into chunky dice
3 garlic cloves
6 celery stalks, sliced
12 plum tomatoes, peeled, deseeded & diced
1 tbsp tomato purée
2 tsp caster sugar
1.5 litres (2½ pints) tomato juice
1.5 litres (2½ pints) vegetable stock
½ ham bone or 100g (3½oz) smoked lardons of bacon
300g (11oz) spicy Italian sausage, quartered & sliced
salt & freshly ground black pepper
½ tea cup flat-leaf parsley, washed, dried & chopped

handful of washed basil leaves, to garnish
crusty Italian bread
bowls of olive oil

VEGETARIAN OPTION
TO MAKE THIS SOUP FOR VEGETARIANS, OMIT THE SAUSAGE AND HAM BONE, OR REMOVE A PORTION OF SOUP BEFORE ADDING THE HAM BONE.

** To soak the beans**
Soak the beans separately in water overnight in the refrigerator or use tinned.

** To make the soup**
Bring a saucepan of salted water to the boil, then add the onion, whole garlic, bay leaves, peppercorns and thyme. Cook the beans separately until soft, then set aside. Heat a little olive oil in a large saucepan, add the onion, garlic and celery, and sweat for 5 minutes without browning. Add the tomato purée

and sugar and cook for 2 minutes. Pour in the tomato juice and stock, then add the ham bone or lardons. Bring to the boil, then simmer on a low heat for 30 minutes. Meanwhile sauté the sausage and set aside. Add the beans, tomatoes and sausage to the soup, and season. Allow to cool, then place in an airtight container and refrigerate.

To serve
Bring slowly to the boil, add the parsley, stir and garnish with basil leaves. Serve with warm, crusty Italian bread and bowls of olive oil.

Shrimp with Lemon Grass Laksa

50 medium-sized tiger prawns, with heads
4.8 litres (8 pints) white chicken stock
200g (7oz) rice noodles
3 shallots, finely sliced
45g (1½oz) galangal, peeled & cut
  into fine strips
3 garlic cloves, finely chopped
3 medium-sized fresh red chillies, deseeded
  & cut into fine strips
4 lemon grass stems, sliced into fine rings
1 tsp shrimp paste
100g (3½oz) chopped dried shrimp
5 tbsp fish sauce
3 lime leaves, finely chopped
1 tbsp palm sugar, or caster sugar
2 tbsp tamarind paste
3 baby bok choy, washed &
  cut into squares
½ tea cup coriander leaves, washed & dried

(1d) To prepare the soup base
Peel the prawns, keeping the heads and shells. Cover and place in the refrigerator. Bring the chicken stock to the boil, add the heads and shells, then simmer for 15 minutes. Strain through muslin into an airtight container. Allow to cool, then cover and refrigerate.

(6h) To cook the noodles
Bring a saucepan of water to the boil, then add the noodles and cook for 1 minute until soft. Drain and refresh. Cut into 2.5cm (1in) pieces, cover and chill.

To finish the soup
Bring the broth to the boil, then add the shallots, galangal, garlic, chillies, lemon grass, shrimp paste, dried shrimp, fish sauce, lime leaves, palm sugar and tamarind paste. Simmer for 5 minutes, add the shrimps and cook for 2 minutes. Just before serving, add the noodles, bok choy and coriander.

Pecan Tart with Crème Fraîche Ice Cream

Makes 2 tarts in 35 x 11cm (14 x 4¼in) fluted, rectangular flan tins.

Sweet Pastry
300g (11oz) plain flour, sifted
pinch of salt
125g (4oz) icing sugar
125g (4oz) unsalted butter, cubed
2 eggs

Crème Fraîche Ice Cream
600ml (1 pint) double cream
300g (11oz) caster sugar
600ml (1 pint) crème fraîche

Tart Filling
8 eggs
350g (12oz) caster sugar
600ml (1 pint) light corn syrup or golden
  syrup
pinch of salt
1 vanilla pod, split lengthways & seeds
  removed
450g (1lb) shelled pecan nuts
icing sugar, to dust

SPECIAL EQUIPMENT **ice cream maker**

(1d) To prepare the pastry
Mix the flour, salt, icing sugar and butter in an electric mixer until the consistency of breadcrumbs and all the butter is combined. On a slow speed, add the eggs slowly, mixing until just combined. On a floured work surface, divide the mixture into 2, cover in cling film and chill for 8 hours. The pastry is sufficiently soft to be rolled out straight from the refrigerator, and can be frozen for up to 1 month. Defrost it in the refrigerator over night when required.

(1d) To prepare the ice cream
In a heavy-based saucepan, heat the double cream gently, then add the sugar and stir until dissolved. Pour the cream into a bowl and whisk in the crème fraîche. Allow to cool, then churn in the ice cream maker. Store in a container in the freezer until required.

(8h) To ball the ice cream
Place the serving dish in the freezer. Fill a jug with hot water. Dip a scoop into the water then into the ice cream, make a ball, place in the dish and repeat for all the ice cream. Return to the freezer.

(6h) To make the pie
Preheat the oven to 160°C/325°F/gas 3. Roll out the sweet pastry, line the 2 flan tins with greaseproof paper and fill with baking beans. Allow to rest in the refrigerator for about 30 minutes. Before baking, examine the tart shells closely to make sure that there are no holes. This is important, as holes will allow the filling to run out of the tart into the mould, making the tarts very difficult to remove from the tins. If there are any small holes, plug them with a little of the remaining pastry. Bake the tart shells for about 30 minutes, then remove the beans and the paper and continue to cook for 10 minutes, or until golden brown. Remove the shells from the oven and put to one side. Now raise the oven temperature to 180°C/350°F/gas 4 for the filling. Beat the eggs lightly in a bowl, then add the sugar, syrup, salt and vanilla, and stir in the pecan nuts. Divide the filling between the 2 tart shells and cook for about 30 minutes, or until set. Allow to cool, then store in an airtight container in a cool place.

To serve
Place the tarts on a large wooden board and dust with icing sugar. Place the bowl of ice cream next to the tarts, or offer separately.

From top: Chicken Pot Pie Soup, Shrimp with Lemon Grass Laksa, Tuscan Bean & Italian Sausage Soup

Giving a party outside should be a leisurely affair. In summer, a lovely garden or terrace can be transformed into an outside dining room. Tablecloths and napkins can be bold in colour, with flowers and foliage, and perhaps even fruit and vegetables, picked from the garden and used to decorate tables.

for eating outdoors

Guests can relax on cushions, blankets and rugs distributed on the lawn. Lunch or dinner outdoors can be as simple as you want it to be – excellent pasta, mouthwatering sandwiches, cheese and fruit. The recipes that follow are for people who enjoy cooking outdoors on barbecues and sitting in a shady spot in the garden to eat easy-to-prepare, delicious food in the company of friends.

Food for Thought

Plan to take the type of foods that will survive the rigours of a car journey and heat. If necessary, the picnic must be small enough to tuck under a seat at a sporting occasion. When I first started to prepare picnics to take to cricket matches at Lords, I remember serving a great variety of foods and how difficult it was to transport and store them. I have now discovered wraps (see pages 90–91), which are extremely transportable and easy to eat in a small space.

Cooling Drinks

To chill drinks, you can pack ice in a cooler, but this is heavy to carry and bulky to store. Make fresh fruit drinks and transport them in Thermos flasks. Sleeves are available that can be kept in the freezer until required, then placed over bottles just before you leave. Wrap the bottles in their sleeves in paper to transport them. Inflatable ice buckets are another lightweight means of cooling drinks; fill them with ice when you arrive at your destination.

Best Barbecues

Keep the food simple. Light the coals on the barbecue at least three quarters of an hour before starting to grill food. Try not to use lighter fuels as they can taint the flavour of the food. Arrange the grill pan so that it can be raised and lowered over the heat. Place your buffet table and bar near to the barbecue so that guests can help themselves to salads and drinks easily.

Professional Tips

• Don't forget the essentials: bottle opener; corkscrew; insect repellent; lotion for stings and bites; sun block and hats
• Make sure that you can carry everything – blankets, rugs or quilts are very portable
• Restrict yourself to lightweight china, glassware and cutlery: plastic containers can be a godsend on a picnic
• Remember to pack paper napkins and garbage bags, too.
• A picnic that starts in daylight may finish in darkness; keep a torch handy

WINTER WONDERS

For winter picnics, prepare stews and hearty soups, storing them in wide-necked Thermos flasks so that they will be warm and reviving.

summer garden lunch

What could be more heavenly than sitting in the shade of a tree, on a lovely summer's day, enjoying a lunch with flavours from the Mediterranean? We have given this classic tuna salad a fresh and modern twist and if you can find fresh anchovies, they make it all the more sublime. Both it and the delicious dessert, cooked with olive oil, are always popular at summer lunch parties and, like most of the menus in this book, are easy to prepare ahead of time – leaving you free to relax in the company of your guests. SERVES 10

Salad Niçoise with Chargrilled Tuna

Dressing
2 tsp Dijon mustard
1 tbsp white wine vinegar
1 tbsp balsamic vinegar
1 tsp caster sugar
3 tbsp olive oil
2 shallots, finely sliced
salt & freshly ground black pepper

Salad
500g (1lb1oz) fresh tuna, preferably with the
    tail, cut into 10 equal portions
olive oil
salt
freshly ground black pepper
30 small vine tomatoes
2 garlic cloves, sliced
a little caster sugar
2 tsp thyme, finely chopped
750g (1lb 7oz) Charlotte potatoes, cooked,
    cut lengthways & chargrilled
250g (9oz) extra-fine French beans, topped
    not tailed, blanched & refreshed
1 cucumber, peeled, deseeded & sliced
200g (7oz) large black olives
36 quails' eggs, hard boiled
100g (3½oz) caper berries
5 wood-roasted artichoke hearts, cut into
    halves
½ tea cup picked flat-leaf parsley, washed
    & chopped
½ tea cup snipped chives
2 x 50g (1¼oz) tins of anchovy fillets or
    100g (2½oz) fresh anchovies, sautéd in
    a little vegetable oil

Accompaniments
crusty country bread
unsalted butter
olive oil

(1d) To make the dressing
Combine all the ingredients for the dressing in a bowl, season and pour into a jar. Replace the lid and store in the refrigerator or in a cool place.

(4h) To cook the tuna
Heat a chargrill pan, brush the tuna with a little olive oil and season with salt and freshly ground black pepper. Grill for no longer than 30 seconds each side. Place on a tray, cover with cling film and refrigerate.

(4h) To prepare the tomatoes
Preheat the oven to 160°C/325°F/gas 3. Place the tomatoes on a metal baking tray, brush with 1 tablespoon olive oil and garlic, sprinkle with the sugar and thyme, then season. Place in the oven and cook for 5 minutes. Store in an airtight container and refrigerate.

To assemble
Place the potatoes, French beans, cucumber, olives, quails' eggs, caper berries, artichokes, parsley and chives in a large bowl, then pour over ¾ of the dressing, toss well and season. Transfer to a large serving bowl, arrange the tuna, tomatoes and anchovies, then pour on the remaining dressing. Serve with warm bread, butter and olive oil.

Sauternes Cake with Poached Peaches

Make in a 25cm (10in) round cake tin.

Sauternes Cake
15g(½oz) butter for greasing
6 egg yolks
180g (6oz) caster sugar
zest of 1 large orange, finely grated
zest of 2 lemons, finely grated
120ml (4fl oz) extra-virgin olive oil
150ml (5fl oz) Sauternes
8 egg whites
½ tsp cream of tartare
170g (6oz) plain flour
¼ tsp salt
icing sugar, to dust

Poached Peaches
10 large, ripe peaches
600ml (1 pint) water
450g (1lb) caster sugar
1 bottle sweet sparkling wine
2 vanilla pods, split lengthways
zest of 1 orange, finely grated
zest of 1 lemon, finely grated
600ml (1 pint) crème fraîche

(3d) To prepare the cake
Preheat the oven to 180°C/350°F/gas 4. Grease a loose-bottomed cake tin with butter and line with parchment paper. Whisk the egg yolks and half the caster sugar in an electric mixer on a high speed, until light in colour, thick and creamy. Whisk in the finely grated

Salade Niçoise with Chargrilled Tuna

orange and lemon zest. Add the olive oil slowly, followed by the Sauternes, whisking continually. In a bowl, whisk the egg whites with the cream of tartare until the mixture holds soft peaks. Whisk in the remaining caster sugar, continuing until the mixture holds stiff peaks. Sieve the flour and salt together, then fold gently into the egg-yolk mixture; add the egg-white mixture, and mix thoroughly so that there are no pockets of flour. Pour the mixture into the cake tin, place on a baking tray in the centre of the oven. After 20 minutes, lower the oven temperature to 150°C/300°F/gas 2, and bake for a further 20 minutes, turning the cake if it appears to be browning more on one side. Remove and cool in the tin on a rack. Remove from the tin and store in an airtight container in a cool place.

(2d) To prepare the peaches

Bring a saucepan of water to the boil; fill a large bowl with ice-cold water. Plunge the peaches, 2 at a time, in the boiling water for about 20 seconds. Remove with a slotted spoon, then place immediately into the ice-cold water. Peel off the skins, then put the peaches to one side. To prepare the stock syrup, place the water and sugar into a saucepan large enough to accommodate all the peaches. Bring to the boil slowly, then add the sparkling wine, vanilla pods, orange and lemon zest. Return to the boil, then lower the heat and barely simmer. Place the peaches in the syrup and poach gently for about 15 minutes. Remove from the heat and leave the peaches to cool in the syrup; remove them from the syrup when cool. With a small knife, make a cut halfway through each peach and remove the stone gently. Place in a shallow dish and pour on a little of the syrup. Cover with cling film and place in the refrigerator. Remove several hours before required.

SKINNING PEACHES

IF THE SKINS ARE STILL A LITTLE DIFFICULT TO REMOVE AFTER THE PEACHES HAVE BEEN TRANSFERRED FROM THE BOILING TO THE COLD WATER, THEN DIP THEM INTO THE BOILING WATER ONCE AGAIN FOR A FEW MORE SECONDS.

To serve

Place the cake on a stand; dust with icing sugar. Fill a glass vase or bowl with the peaches and pour on the syrup. Divide the crème fraîche between 2 small bowls. Serve.

brilliant barbecue

Barbecues always remind me of enjoying hot, sunny weather in the company of friends. As a change from the traditional meat, I've designed my ultimate seafood barbecue. Ideally of course, I'll have helped to catch the fish that morning, but when that really isn't possible, this tantalising feast will help recreate a seaside atmosphere at home. If you really wish to replace any of the suggested recipes, try the chopped steak or grilled ribs from the buffet menus – to ring the changes, all are just as good cooked on the barbecue. SERVES 10

Vegetables with Salsa Verde

Choose 3 to 4 of the following:
10 red peppers, quartered & seeds removed
30 asparagus spears, blanched & refreshed
30 baby fennel, blanched & refreshed
4 large courgettes, cut into 1.5cm (½in)
    slices
2 medium aubergines, sliced & sprinkled
    with salt
5 medium red onions, quartered & blanched
olive oil
salt & freshly ground black pepper
a selection of fresh herbs to garnish
double quantity of Salsa Verde (see
    page 121)

To grill the vegetables
Place your chosen vegetables on a tray, brush with oil, season and grill or barbecue on both sides for 10–15 minutes until soft and bar marks are visible. Arrange on a serving dish and decorate with a selection of herbs.

To serve
Drizzle the vegetables with a little salsa verde, placing the remainder of the salsa in a bowl.

Lobster with a Tamarind Dressing

Tamarind Dressing
150ml (¼ pint) olive oil
2 tbsp tamarind pulp
2 tsp palm sugar
zest & juice of 1 lime
30g (1oz) chopped ginger
3 garlic cloves, sliced
2 shallots, finely sliced
¼ tea cup coriander, washed, dried &
    chopped
3 lime leaves, finely shredded
salt & freshly ground black pepper

5 x 675g (1lb 8oz) lobster, cooked and split
    in half with tail meat removed, sliced &
    returned to the shell
seaweed to garnish, washed and dried

(1d) **To make the dressing**
Blend the olive oil, tamarind pulp, sugar, lime zest and juice and ginger in a blender for about 30 seconds, or until a smooth liquid is formed. Pour into a clean jar with a lid; add the remaining ingredients for the dressing, season with salt and pepper and store in the refrigerator.

To grill the lobsters
Place the lobster halves on a tray and spoon a little dressing over each one. Grill, shell side down, for about 5–10 minutes until the meat is hot and the shell is brown. Remove and place on a serving platter lined with seaweed.

BBQ TIPS
MAKING SURE THAT THE COALS ARE HOT BEFORE STARTING TO COOK THE FOOD AND HAVING THE RIGHT UTENSILS TO HAND MAKES LIFE EASIER. PLACE A JUG OF HOT WATER BY THE GRILL TO DAMP DOWN FLAMES IF NECESSARY.

Swordfish with Red Onion, & Mango Salsa

Red Onion Salsa
120g (4oz) black-eyed beans, soaked in
water for 12 hours
6 ripe mangoes
5 plum tomatoes, skinned, deseeded & diced
1 tea cup coriander, washed, dried &
    chopped
½ tea cup parsley, washed, dried & chopped
4 garlic cloves, finely chopped
4 medium red chillies, seeds removed then
    diced
4 red onions, finely diced
zest & juice of 6 limes
300ml (½ pint) olive oil
salt & freshly ground black pepper

Flavoured Oil
300ml (½ pint) olive oil
1 stem of dill weed, chopped
2 star anise
½ head of garlic
2 shallots, sliced
3 lemon peel strips

10 x 180g (6oz) swordfish steaks
salt & freshly ground black pepper
dill weed flowers & stalks
lime halves

(1d) **To make the salsa**
Drain the beans. Bring a pan of vegetable stock or salted water to boil,

Lobster with a Tamarind Dressing

Grilled Swordfish with Red Onion & Mango Salsa

then reduce the heat, add the beans and simmer until tender. Drain and leave to cool. Peel the mangoes (over a sink!) and cut the flesh away from the stone. Purée half the mangoes in a blender or by hand until very smooth. Dice the remaining mangoes finely and place in a large bowl with the purée. Add the beans and remaining salsa ingredients; season. Cover and place in the refrigerator.

(1d) To infuse the oil

Place all the ingredients for the flavoured oil in a saucepan over a low heat for about 10 minutes. Remove from the heat and leave on the side to cool. Pour into a jar with a lid and store in a cool place.

To cook and serve the swordfish

Place the fish on a tray, brush with the herb-flavoured oil and season. Grill or barbecue on each side until cooked, then remove and place on a serving platter. Garnish with the dill flowers and stalks and the halved limes. Place the salsa in bowls and serve at once.

GETTING RID OF GARLIC

AS YOU WILL HAVE NOTICED I LOVE THE PIQUANT FLAVOUR OF GARLIC IN FOOD AND MANY OF THESE BARBECUE RECIPES INCLUDE IT. ITS ODOUR CAN STICK TO YOUR HANDS HOWEVER. MY FOOLPROOF METHOD OF REMOVING IT IS TO PLACE A STAINLESS STEEL SPOON UNDER RUNNING WARM WATER AND RUB YOUR HANDS OVER THE SPOON UNDER THE WATER.

Sweet Potatoes with Spring Onions

Spring Onion Dressing

150ml (¼ pint) sushi vinegar

1 tbsp caster sugar

450ml (¾ pint) unsweetened coconut milk

1 bunch of spring onions, washed, roots removed & chopped

½ tea cup chopped chives

3 tbsp toasted sesame seeds

2 tbsp sweet chilli sauce (optional)

salt & freshly ground black pepper

10 small orange sweet potatoes

(1d) To make the dressing

Blend the vinegar and sugar in a food processor for about 10 seconds. Add the coconut milk slowly and, when emulsified, remove and pour into a bowl. Add the remaining ingredients and season. Cover and place in the refrigerator.

(1d) To prepare the potatoes
Scrub the skins of the potatoes and dry with a clean tea towel. Prick the skins with a fork, wrap in foil and refrigerate.

To grill the potatoes
Place the potatoes on the grill or barbecue and, after 50 minutes, remove the foil. Return to the grill and cook until the skins are crisp.

To serve
Cut the potatoes in half, place in a serving bowl and drizzle on some dressing. Serve the remainder of the dressing in a jug.

Sweetcorn with Black Pepper Butter

Black Pepper Butter
250g (9oz) soft, unsalted butter
2 tsp crushed black pepper
sea salt flakes

10 corncobs in their husks
dried corn husks to garnish

(1d) To make the butter
Beat the butter in an electric mixer until pale. Remove, then add the pepper and salt flakes. Mix, making sure that the pepper is evenly distributed. Place in a piping bag with a 2.5cm (1in) plain nozzle and pipe onto cling film. Roll into a cylinder and place in the freezer.

To prepare and cook the corn
Remove the butter from the freezer, cut it into even slices and place in a bowl of iced water. Soak the corn in cold water for 10 minutes, then remove and drain. Place on the grill, cooking on all sides until soft. Transfer to a basket lined with dry corn husks and serve with the butter.

Marinated Prawns with Chipotle Mayonnaise

Prawn Marinade
40 skewers or vine sticks soaked in water
40 medium fresh tiger prawns
5 tbsp olive oil
5 shallots, chopped
8 garlic cloves, chopped
¼ tea cup fresh thyme, chopped
1 tbsp paprika
juice & zest of 3 limes
1 tbsp sugar
salt & freshly ground black pepper
sea salt flakes

Mayonnaise
3 tbsp white wine vinegar
juice of 2 limes
3 garlic cloves, finely chopped
2 chipotle chillies (smoked chilli), soaked & seeds removed
3 shallots, finely chopped
1 tbsp caster sugar
6 fresh free-range egg yolks
1.2 litres (2 pints) unscented vegetable oil
150ml (¼ pint) boiling water
salt & freshly ground black pepper

Sweetcorn with Black Bepper Butter

Garnish
stems of fresh rosemary or sage
fresh red chillies

(6h) To marinade the prawns
Skewer the prawns and place them on a tray. Blend all the marinade ingredients until smooth; season. Coat the prawns in the marinade, then cover and chill.

(6h) To make the mayonnaise
In a pan, heat the vinegar, lime juice, garlic, chillies, shallot and sugar, reduce by half; allow to cool. Blend the mixture, with the egg yolks, in a food processor for about 30 seconds. Pour in the oil, in a slow steady stream, stopping to scrape the sides of the bowl. When emulsified, add the boiling water and process for 10 seconds; season. Chill in an airtight container.

To grill and serve the prawns
Grill or barbecue the prawns until the shells are brown; season with salt flakes and place on a platter lined with fresh chillies and herbs; pour the mayonnaise into a bowl.

perfect picnic

Designed to be easily portable, this is my any-occasion picnic for 10 people. All the dishes are simple to prepare but truly delicious – I love the original combination of sharp feta with sweet red onions. Each cold dish can be boxed individually, with extra salad leaves added at the last moment. The squid ink pasta salad also makes a lovely main-course salad for a summer lunch at home. SERVES 10

Squid Ink Pasta with Prawn Salad

Dressing
3 tbsp white wine vinegar
1 tbsp caster sugar
5 tbsp extra-virgin olive oil

Salad
30 fresh medium tiger prawns, peeled
olive oil
salt & freshly ground black pepper
500g (1lb 1oz) fresh squid ink tagliatelle
30 asparagus spears, peeled & blanched
1 bunch of spring onions, washed, roots
 trimmed, finely sliced
10 plum tomatoes, skinned, deseeded &
 diced
2 red chillies, deseeded & finely sliced
½ tea cup snipped chives

(1h) **To prepare the dressing and salad**
Blend the vinegar and sugar in a blender or food processor for 20 seconds. Add the oil slowly in a steady stream until emulsified. Pour into a jar with a lid and store in a cool place.

(1d) **To prepare the salad**
Preheat a grill or grill pan. Brush the prawns with olive oil, season, place on the grill and cook evenly on all sides. Remove, cover and leave to cool before

Squid Ink Pasta with Prawn Salad

placing in the refrigerator. Bring a saucepan of salted water with a little olive oil to the boil, cook the pasta al dente, drain and refresh. When cold, cut the pasta with sissors into 10cm (4in) lengths. Cover and refrigerate.

To finish the salad
Place the prawns, pasta and asparagus in a large bowl and pour over the dressing. Add the spring onions, tomatoes, chilli and chives; toss well. Season and pack into containers.

Feta Cheese, Black Olives & Caper Salad

3 small red onions, each onion cut into 8
 pieces
150ml (¼ pint) aged balsamic vinegar
3 tbsp extra-virgin olive oil
2 tsp Demerara sugar
5 sprigs of thyme, finely chopped
salt & freshly ground black pepper
500g (1lb 1oz) good-quality fresh feta
 cheese, cut into cubes
300g (11oz) extra-fine French beans,
 blanched
250g (9oz) large, marinaded black olives
100g (3½oz) caper berries
20 yellow pear tomatoes, washed, dried &
 cut in half
2 tea cups picked flat-leaf parsley, washed
 & dried

(1d) **To roast the red onions**
Preheat the oven to 190°C/375°F/gas 5. Place the onions in a baking tin; pour over the vinegar, oil, sugar and thyme. Season and roast in the oven for about 15–20 minutes until the onions are soft and glazed. Transfer the onions and vinegar mixture (this will be the dressing for the salad) into an airtight container; when cold, refrigerate.

To finish the salad
Place the onions and dressing in a bowl, add the remaining ingredients, season, toss and pack into containers.

Marinated Chicken & Jewelled Rice

Chicken Marinade
30g (1oz) dried sorrel flowers
3 garlic cloves, chopped
2 jalapeno chillies, deseeded & finely
 chopped
¼ tea cup coriander, washed, dried & chopped
1 lime, sliced
5 free-range or corn-fed chicken breasts,
 skin removed
salt & freshly ground black pepper
unscented vegetable oil for cooking

Jewelled Rice
1.4 litres (2½ pints) vegetable stock
olive oil
1 onion, finely diced
3 garlic cloves, finely chopped
½ teaspoon saffron strands
5 green cardamom pods, crushed
2 cinnamon sticks
675g (1lb 8oz) basmati rice
unscented vegetable oil
peel of 2 oranges, pith removed, & very
 finely sliced
115g (4oz) carrot, finely shredded
2 tbsp caster sugar
60g (2oz) barberries (or dried cranberries),
 rinsed, stem removed & soaked for 12 hours
150g (5½oz) large golden sultanas
150g (5½oz) pistachio nuts, shelled, peeled
 & roasted
150g (5½oz) unsalted roasted cashew nuts
2 tea cups coriander leaves, washed & dried
salt & freshly ground black pepper

(2d) **To marinade the chicken**

In a large pan bring 600ml (1 pint)
water to the boil. When boiling, add
the sorrel and reduce by half. Strain
through a fine sieve into an airtight
container large enough to hold the
chicken; cool. When cold, add the
garlic, chilli, coriander, sliced lime and
chicken breasts, making sure that the
chicken is covered with the marinade.
Cover and refrigerate for 12 hours.

(1d) **To cook the chicken**

Preheat the oven to 190°C/375°F/gas 5.
Remove the chicken from the
marinade, pat dry, season and place on
a tray. Heat a little unscented oil in a
sauté pan and seal the chicken on both
sides. Transfer to the oven to cook for
about 10–12 minutes; remove and
allow to cool. Cover and refrigerate.

(1d) **To cook the jewelled rice**

Preheat the oven to 180°C/350°F/gas 4.
Bring the stock to the boil, then reduce
the heat to simmer. Heat a little olive
oil in a large, ovenproof pan and add
the onion, garlic, saffron, cardamom
and cinnamon sticks; sauté for about 2
minutes. Add the rice, stir well and do
not allow to colour. Add the hot stock,
stir, bring to the boil and cover with
non-stick paper then a lid. Place in the
oven for about 20–25 minutes, or until
the rice is tender and all the stock has
been absorbed. Allow to cool, then
cover and place in the refrigerator.
Heat a little unscented oil in a sauté
pan. Add the orange peel and carrot
and sauté on a low heat for about 5
minutes; do not allow to colour. Add
the sugar, cook for a 5 more minutes
and remove from heat. Allow to cool
and place in an airtight container.
Cover and refrigerate.

To finish the chicken and rice

Drain the barberries. Place the rice in
a large bowl, add the remaining
ingredients, season and mix well.
Pack into containers. Slice the
chicken breasts and place on top of
the rice; cover.

Spicy Vegetables

100g (3½oz) dried chickpeas, soaked
2 tsp palm oil
250g (9oz) baby onions, peeled
3 garlic cloves, sliced
2 tbsp garam marsala paste
5 plum tomatoes, skinned, deseeded &
    diced
300ml (½ pint) vegetable stock
salt & freshly ground black pepper
1 medium aubergine, diced
10 baby corn, cut in half & blanched
300g (11oz) sweet potato, blanched &
    diced
300g (11oz) button mushrooms, stalks
    removed, & cleaned
115g (4oz) baby spinach, washed & dried

Raita Dressing

300ml (½ pint) live yogurt
½ tea cup mint leaves, washed, dried &
    finely shredded
¼ cucumber, peeled, deseeded & finely
    diced
salt & freshly ground black pepper

(1d) **To make the spicy vegetables**

Cook the chickpeas until tender in a
pan of boiling salted water. Drain and
put aside. Heat the oil in a large
sauté pan, add the onions and sauté
for about 5 minutes. Add the garlic,
garam masala paste and tomato and
sauté for 5 minutes more. Pour in the
stock and reduce by half. Season and
cool. Rinse and dry the pan, then use
it to heat a little oil. Sauté the
remaining vegetables, excluding the
spinach, for about 5 minutes. Remove
from the heat, stir in the spinach,
season and allow to cool. When cold,
add the vegetables and chickpeas to
the sauce, stir and season. Place in
containers, cover and refrigerate.

(1d) To make the dressing

Place all the ingredients in a bowl, season, stir well and place in a container in the refrigerator.

To serve

Offer the vegetables and dressing separately.

ALL-YEAR ROUND

IF THE WEATHER IS LESS THAN IDYLLIC AND WARMING FOOD IS MORE DESIRABLE, WHY NOT SUBSTITUTE FOR ONE OF THE SALADS A LARGE THERMOS FILLED WITH TUSCAN BEAN SOUP (SEE PAGE 151)?

Lemon Cookies

200g (7oz) unsalted butter
120g (4½oz) icing sugar
1 egg yolk
zest of 2 lemons
2 tsp lemon juice
250g (9oz) plain flour
caster sugar

(2d) To make the cookies

Cream the butter and sugar in an electric mixer until soft and creamy. Add the egg yolk, beat until smooth, then add the lemon zest, juice and flour. Continue to mix until all the dough ingredients are well combined. Cover the work surface with a sheet of cling film and place the dough on top; cover with a second sheet of cling film. Roll the dough to a thickness of 7mm (¼in). Place in the refrigerator for 1 hour. Preheat the oven to 180°C/ 350°F/gas 4. Line a baking sheet with non-stick paper. Lightly flour a cool work surface. Transfer the dough from the refrigerator to the floured surface and use a cutter to cut out about 20 heart shapes, placing them on the baking sheet. Bake for about 10 minutes or until the heart shapes turn a golden colour. Transfer the hearts on to a cooling rack and sprinkle with caster sugar. When cold, pack carefully in airtight containers.

Top to bottom: Feta Cheese, Black Olives & Caper Salad, Marinated Chicken & Jewelled Rice

Walnut, Pecan & Chocolate Brownies

85g (3oz) plain flour
1 tsp baking powder
½ tsp salt
115g (4oz) shelled pecan nuts, roughly chopped
115g (4oz) shelled walnuts, roughly chopped
285g (10oz) extra-bitter chocolate, chopped into small pieces
200g (7oz) unsalted, soft butter
3 eggs
285g (10oz) dark brown sugar
cocoa powder for dusting (optional)

(1d) To make the brownies

Preheat the oven to 160°C/325°F/gas 3. Line a deep baking tin, about 26 x 26 x 4cm (10 x 10 x 1½in) with non-stick paper. Place the flour, baking powder, salt, nuts and half the chocolate in a bowl; mix and put to one side. Half-fill a saucepan with water, find a mixing bowl to fit on top of the saucepan and bring to a gentle heat. Place the butter and the remaining chocolate in the bowl to melt over the heat. Meanwhile, whisk the eggs and sugar in an electric mixer until creamy. Remove the bowl from the mixer and pour in the melted chocolate and butter; mix until smooth. Add the remaining ingredients and mix with a rubber or plastic spatula. Pour into the prepared tin, smooth the top and bake in the oven for about 30–40 minutes or until just set. Allow to cool for 5 minutes then remove from the tin and place on a cooling rack. When cold, remove the paper and cut the brownies into squares (you should get about 20); dust the tops with cocoa powder if using. Pack into airtight containers lined with parchment paper.

LEFT-OVER EGG WHITES

IF YOU DO NOT WANT TO WASTE EGG WHITES LEFT OVER FROM THOSE RECIPES THAT ONLY REQUIRE EGG YOLKS (LIKE THE LEMON COOKIES ON THIS PAGE), YOU CAN FREEZE THEM FOR UP TO 1 MONTH FOR USE IN OTHER RECIPES.

cheeseboard

Today the range of cheeses available can be confusing. It includes cheeses made from cows' milk, goats' milk and sheep's milk, and textures varying from hard to semi-soft and soft, with rich, smooth triple-cream types also available. In addition there are seasonal cheeses, such as Terry's favourite, Vacherin. I would recommend buying cheese from a specialised cheesemonger who will also be able to supply a good selection of biscuits and breads, as well as baskets, mats and paper leaves for serving. They will advise you on what cheese is at its peak, in season and ready to serve.

Storing Suggestions

Wrap cheese in greaseproof paper covered with a piece of muslin before storing in a plastic bag or wrapping in cling film. The best place to keep it is on the top shelf of the refrigerator (so any strong-smelling cheese will not taint other foods), in a cool cupboard or, if you are lucky enough to have a cellar, store it there in a cheese safe.

A Selection to Serve

For a buffet party, we generally provide a selection of up to 6 cheeses, depending on the number of guests. My recommendations for an interesting basket of cheeses would be a raw milk Brie with a goats' cheese (preferably a cylinder rolled in ash), a triple cream, a blue cheese, a mild washed rind and a cheese wrapped in leaves.

For a dinner party we offer a selection of 3 cheeses. Try to avoid hard cheeses that are difficult for guests to cut as well as cheeses with inedible rinds or pungent odours – not everyone will be a cheese-lover.

Cheese Basket

A Feast for the Eyes

Many years ago, I planted a grapevine in my garden, so in the summer we have glorious fresh vine leaves with which to line the cheese baskets. In September the vine produces small bunches of very sweet black grapes which I also cut to arrange on baskets. From mid-October we use colourful autumnal leaves.If you do not have access to a vine you can substitute any non-poisonous leaves from trees such as fig, maple, sea grape, plane, lemon, lime or orange. A straw or bamboo mat also makes a suitable liner for any basket or board. Arrange the cheeses to look appetising and attractive on the board, in the basket or on individual plates, surrounding them with accompaniments such as halved figs, bunches of grapes, small apples, slices of oven-dried pears (see page 169), quince 'cheese', oatmeal biscuits, fig and walnut bread or sesame wafers. If you would like to serve the cheese in individual portions on plates, arrange each serving with half a fig, a small bunch of grapes, a slice of oven-dried pear or apple, a sprig of parsley or lovage and then a few biscuits and a slice of bread.

Experiment with marinating small goats' cheeses in very good quality olive oil with herbs and spices; offer these in jars, with a pair of long cornichon tongs for easy serving. You can also add flavourings by rolling individual goats' cheeses in herbs, nuts or cracked peppercorns. It is fun to develop your own range of cheeses.

Sesame Wafers

These are easy to make and it is worth keeping a packet of spring roll wrappers in the freezer so that these wafers can be made quickly for unexpected guests. The wafers are also a delicious accompaniment for chicken liver parfait or foie gras terrine.
MAKES 40

20 spring roll wrappers, 125mm² (5in²)

1 egg white

1 tbsp sesame seeds

(1d) To make the wafers

Preheat the oven to 180°C/350°F/gas 4.
Cut the spring roll wrappers in half to
form triangles. Brush with egg white and
sprinkle with sesame seeds. Place on a
baking tray in the oven for about 10
minutes until golden brown. Remove and
cool. Store in an airtight container.

Oatmeal Biscuits

Maureen Chalander, who used to be
our head chef, developed these
delicious biscuits. They are easy to
make and store well. Makes 25

210g (7½oz) oatmeal

100g (3½oz) wholemeal flour

100g (3½oz) plain flour

15g (½oz) sugar

½ tsp salt

½ tsp baking powder

210g (7½oz) unsalted butter, cut into small
    cubes

4 egg whites

(2d) To make the biscuits

Mix the dry ingredients in an electric
mixer, then add the butter and continue
to mix until the consistency resembles
breadcrumbs. Add the egg whites and
mix until it forms a smooth dough. Roll
into a smooth ball, wrap in cling film and
place in the refrigerator for about 2
hours. Alternatively place in the freezer
for use at a later time.

(2d) To cook the oatmeal biscuits

Preheat the oven 180°C/350°F/gas 4.
Line 2 baking trays with non-stick paper
or a silicon mat. Remove the dough from
the refrigerator and place on a floured
board. Roll out as thinly as possible,
then cut into rounds with a 7.5–10cm
(3–4in) fluted cutter. Place on the
baking trays and bake for 10–15
minutes, or until golden brown. Remove
and place on cooling racks. When cold,
layer with greaseproof paper and store in
an airtight container in a cool place.

Oatmeal Biscuits with Cheese

Fig & Walnut Bread

Years ago, Terry started to experiment
with various breads to accompany
cheese and this is his favourite. We make
it in a 38cm- (15in-) long cylindrical
pudding mould. Makes 1 loaf

30g (1oz) butter, melted

280g (10oz) granary flour, sifted

280g (10oz) strong plain flour, sifted

30g (1oz) salt

30g (1oz) unsalted butter

30g (1oz) fresh yeast

1 tsp black molasses

1 tbsp liquid honey

450ml (¾ pint) milk

60g (2oz) chopped walnuts

230g (8oz) dried figs

(1d) To make the bread

Grease a mould with the butter. In an
mixer with a dough hook, combine the
flours, salt and butter. Place the yeast,
molasses and honey in a ceramic mixing
bowl. Warm the milk in a pan to blood
heat then whisk into the yeast mixture
until the yeast dissolves. Add to the flour
and continue to mix for 5 minutes or
until a smooth dough is achieved.
Transfer the mixture to a floured surface;
knead for 4–6 minutes until the dough is
firm, elastic and no longer sticky. Place
in a warm bowl and cover with cling film
or an oiled plastic bag and a damp tea
towel. Leave space for the dough to rise.
Leave in a warm place until the dough
has doubled in size. Knead the dough
smooth on a floured surface, then turn
into a 35 x 20cm (14 x 8in) rectangle.
Sprinkle on the nuts and place a line of
figs along one of the long sides. Roll the
dough over the figs like a Swiss roll and
place in the mould. Cover and leave in a
warm place until the dough has again
doubled in size (30–45 minutes). Preheat
the oven to 220°C/425°F/gas 7. Bake for
40 minutes or until golden brown and
hollow-sounding when tapped. Remove
from oven, and once the tin is cool
remove the bread. Leave the bread to
cool then store in an airtight container.

basic recipes

Vegetable Stock

MAKES 1.4 LITRES (2½ PINTS)

4 onions, cut into quarters
2 leeks, white part only, washed & sliced
5 medium carrots, peeled & chopped
½ head of garlic
10 celery sticks, washed & chopped
5 sprigs of thyme
2 bay leaves
1 bulb fennel, washed & chopped
3 peppercorns
1 star anise
2.8 litres (5 pints) water
salt & freshly ground black pepper

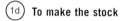 **To make the stock**

Place all the ingredients in the stockpot, bring to a simmer and cook for about 1 hour. Remove from the heat and pass through a fine sieve into a clean saucepan. Return to the heat and reduce until a good flavour is achieved. Season and allow to cool. When cold, place in the refrigerator or freezer.

Brown Chicken Stock

MAKES 1.8 LITRES (3 PINTS)

3kg (6lb 8oz) chicken bones, all fat removed
1 onion,
3 medium carrots, cut into large chunks
4 stems of celery, washed & sliced
1 leek, washed & sliced
10 sprigs of thyme
4 garlic cloves, crushed
7.2 litres (12 pints) water
2 tbsp tomato purée

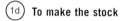 **To make the stock**

Preheat the oven to 190°C/375°F/gas 5. Place the bones in a roasting pan and roast for about 45 minutes, until the bones are deep golden brown. While the bones are roasting, place the onion in a sauté pan without oil and cook for about 10 minutes. Add to a large stockpot with the bones and remaining ingredients. Bring to the boil and simmer for about 5 hours, skimming

any scum from the top. Strain through a fine sieve into a clean saucepan. Return to the heat and reduce to the required amount (tasting to ensure the flavour is acceptable). Allow to cool, cover and refrigerate or freeze.

WHITE CHICKEN STOCK

MAKE WHITE CHICKEN STOCK IN THE SAME WAY AS FOR BROWN CHICKEN STOCK BUT DO NOT ROAST THE BONES AND OMIT THE TOMATO PURÉE.

Fish Stock

MAKES 2 LITRES (4 PINTS)

3kg (6lb 8oz) fish bones, sole are the best, cut into 3
unscented vegetable oil
1 leek, white part only, finely sliced
1 onion, finely sliced
½ bulb fennel, sliced
2 garlic cloves
5 sprigs of thyme
5 peppercorns
½ tea cup parsley stalks
1 bay leaf
1 glass dry white wine
4½ litres (8 pints) water

 To make the stock

Remove the head and any blood from the fish, then soak in cold water for 20 minutes. Heat a little oil in a stockpot and sauté the leek, onion, fennel and garlic. Cook until soft, then add the bones, thyme, peppercorns, parsley stalks, bay leaf and white wine; cover and leave for about 5 minutes. Pour in the water, bring to the boil, then reduce the heat and simmer for 20 minutes. Keep skimming from time to time to prevent scum from forming on top of the stock. Remove from the heat and strain through a fine sieve into a clean saucepan. Return to the heat and reduce until a good flavour is achieved. Allow to cool, cover and place in the refrigerator or freezer.

Pesto

MAKES 350ML (12FL OZ)

3 tea cups basil leaves
1 garlic clove, chopped
salt & freshly ground black pepper
300ml (½ pint) olive oil
15g (½oz) roasted pine nuts
120g (4oz) Parmesan, grated

 To make the pesto

Place the basil, garlic, salt, pepper and half the oil in a food processor. Process until the basil is roughly chopped. Add the pine nuts, Parmesan and remaining oil. Process for a further 10 seconds. Pesto keeps for several days covered in a layer of oil.

Red Onion Jam

MAKES 5 TABLESPOONS

unscented vegetable oil
2 red onions, finely sliced
2 tbsp brown sugar
250ml (⅓ pint) red wine
1 tbsp red wine vinegar

 To cook jam

Heat a little oil in a sauté pan over a low heat, add the sliced red onion, and cook slowly until very soft. Add the sugar, wine and vinegar, and continue to cook for about 30 minutes or until it reaches a jam-like consistency. Place in an airtight container and refrigerate.

Cassis & Red Wine Dressing

SERVES 10

2 shallots, finely chopped
150ml (¼ pint) red wine, reduced by half
1 tbsp sherry vinegar
1 tbsp crème de cassis
3 tbsp extra-virgin olive oil
salt & freshly ground black pepper

To make the dressing

Mix all the ingredients in a bowl, season and pour into a jar with a lid. Chill.

Crystallized Flowers

MAKES AS MUCH AS YOU WANT

good handful of perfect flowers or petals,
   washed & dried
1 egg white
250g (8oz) caster sugar in a sifter

(1d) **To crystallise the flowers**

If using flowers (rather than petals), cut the stems almost to the base and cut away any pieces of green. Line a baking tray with parchment paper. Place the egg white in a bowl and beat for about 20 seconds. Pick up a single flower or petal gently with the tweezers, taking care not to bruise it. Holding the flower, brush gently with egg whites and sift with the sugar; turn over and repeat. Tap the tweezer to remove any excess sugar, place on the paper and leave to dry in a warm, dry place for 8–10 hours. Store in an airtight container in a cool place.

GOOD ENOUGH TO EAT

EDIBLE FLOWERS SUCH AS ROSE PETALS, PANSIES, VIOLAS AND VIOLETS CAN BE USED TO DECORATE CAKES, MOUSSES, MERINGUES AND TARTS. THE TECHNIQUE REQUIRES PATIENCE, BUT IT IS REWARDING.

Oven-Dried Fruit Slices

MAKES 900G (2LB)

choice of fruits: oranges, limes, lemons,
   apples, pears, strawberries, mango & rhubarb
300ml (½ pint) sugar syrup (see page 000)

(1d) **To make the oven-dried fruit**

Select any of the above fruits, leaving the peel on the citrus fruits, pears and apples. Slice lengthways on a mandolin, making sure that each slice is whole and the same thickness. For rhubarb or mango, peel and slice lengthways with a knife. Preheat the oven to 110°C/225°F/ gas ¼. Line the baking tray with parchment or greaseproof paper. Dip the sliced fruit into the sugar syrup, shake to remove any excess and place on the paper; repeat. Place in the oven for 2–3 hours until the fruit is crisp and dry. Remove, leave to cool and layer with parchment paper in the container. Store in a cool, dry place.

OVEN-DRIED FRUITS

SLICES OF OVEN-DRIED FRUITS MAKE AN EXCELLENT GARNISH FOR DESSERTS OR TO SERVE WITH CHEESE.

Sugar Cobwebs

MAKES 10 (ALLOWING FOR BREAKAGES)

250g (9oz) sugar cubes
1 tbsp liquid glucose
150ml (¼ pint) water

(8h) **To make the sugar cobwebs**

Line a tray with greaseproof paper and fill a bowl with ice-cold water. Heat the sugar cubes, glucose and water in a heavy-based pan, stirring until the sugar dissolves. Bring to the boil and continue stirring over the heat to form a light caramel, or to a temperature of 165°C (325°F). Wrap your hand in a tea towel to protect it. Remove the pan from the heat, dip the base into the ice-cold water for about 20 seconds and leave to cool for 2 minutes. Dip a spoon into the caramel and make a cobweb pattern on the paper, about 10cm (4in) round. Leave to set for 5 minutes. Layer the cobwebs between non-stick paper and store in an airtight container.

Diplomat Cream

SERVES 10

300ml (½ pint) milk
600ml (1 pint) double cream
6 egg yolks
125g (4½ oz) caster sugar
75g (2½ oz) plain flour
3 tbsp Grand Marnier

(8h) **To make the diplomat cream**

Line a tray with cling film. Boil the milk with half the cream in a pan. In an mixer, whisk the egg yolks and sugar until light and creamy. Add the flour and whisk again. On a slow speed, pour in half the cream and milk mixture and whisk. Add the rest of the mixture and whisk until all combines. Return to the pan over medium heat and whisk until the mixture starts to boil. Remove from heat and pour on to the tray. Cover with cling film to prevent a skin from forming.

Allow to cool. Return the mixture to a bowl and whisk. Whip the remaining 300ml (½pint) of double cream and fold this, with the Grand Marnier, into the mixture, taking care not to over-beat. Refrigerate in an airtight container.

Macadamia Nut Brittle

MAKES 10 (ALLOWING FOR BREAKAGES)

vegetable oil for greasing tray
200g (7oz) caster sugar
75ml (2½ fl oz) water
¼ tsp vinegar
100g (3½ oz) unsalted macadamia nuts

(5d) **To prepare the brittle**

Brush a shallow metal tray (not non-stick) lightly with oil. Grease well into the corners, as the sugar will spread when hot. Brush a clean and grease-free (preferably copper) saucepan with cold water to remove any sugar crystals, as they could cause the caramel mixture to crystallize and then you would have to start again. Place the sugar, water and vinegar in the pan. Let the sugar dissolve for about 5 minutes. Bring to the boil, continuing to boil until the sugar is a deep amber colour or reaches a temperature of 160°C (325°F). Turn off the heat and leave for about 2 minutes. Add the macadamia nuts and pour on to the prepared tray. Allow to cool completely before removing from the tray. Store in an airtight container in a cool place. It does not matter if the nut brittle is broken into pieces.

(5h) **To make the brittle**

Preheat the oven to 150°C/300°F/gas 2. Line a baking tray with non-stick parchment. Using the metal blade in a food processor, process the brittle to a fine dust. Sprinkle on to the paper in an even, thin layer, making sure that there are no gaps. Place in the oven for approximately 5 minutes or until the brittle has melted – it should not continue to colour. Remove and leave for 2 minutes until cool enough to handle. Using a knife, cut the brittle carefully into tall triangles. Layer in greaseproof paper and store in an airtight container.

essential equipment

As a professional caterer and home cook, this is my wish list of equipment that I consider essential and practical in the kitchen. Some you may already own, others, you can always borrow for a one-off. Life is always made a lot easier if you have the tools of the trade. Make hints at Birthday and Christmas for those special items you really want.

Do not panic if you do find yourself without the special equipment I recommend. There are always ways to improvise. For example, if you haven't got an electric carving knife, to cut foods like cheese and butter, dip a sharp knife into a jug of very hot water before slicing. Ice cream can still be made without an ice-cream maker. Instead of putting the mixture into the ice-cream maker, once it is all combined, put it directly in the freezer and then, every hour until it is properly frozen take the mixture out and churn it up with a fork to make sure all the ingredients are distributed evenly and there no crystals.

Utensils

If you have a choice, I recommend (except where specified) that you try to buy stainless steel utensils.

airtight containers, plastic (capacity 0.25–14 litres/¼ –25 pints)
apple corer
balloon whisks, small, medium and large
500g (18oz) ceramic baking beans (or dried pulses or beans which are a good subsitute)
blow torch
bottle pourers and stoppers
box grater
cheese shaver
pestle and mortar (ceramic)
chopping boards, wooden (various sizes)
claw hammer
fish slice
flour and sugar dredgers
funnels, plastic and metal
glass jars with lids, selection of

ice-cream scoop
ladles, large and medium
mandolin
mezzaluna herb chopper
mixing bowls, set of graduated sizes
non-stick baking mats
pastry cutters, box set of round, fluted, heart and square shapes
plastic food covers
rolling pin, wooden without handles (46cm/18in)
rubber scrapers
refrigerator thermometer
salad spinner
sauce gun
scissors
silicon paper
slotted spoons
skimmers for straining
spoons
sugar thermometer
timer
tin opener
tongs
vegetable peeler
wooden spoons
zester

Knives

Buy stainless-steel knives in a variety of sizes, and store them in a wooden knife block or canvas knife wallet. The essentials are:
10cm (4in) paring knife
10cm (4in) vegetable knife
25cm (10in) carving knife
25cm(10 in) cook's knife
20cm (8in) chopping knife
15cm (6in) all-purpose knife
12.5cm (5in) serrated knife
23cm (9in) bread knife
18cm (7in) prong carving fork
20cm (8in) sharpening steel

PALETTE KNIFES

I ALSO ALWAYS KEEP A PALETTE KNIFE HANDY IN THE KITCHEN FOR LEVELLING OF THE TOPS OF DESSERTS SUCH AS THE GINGER TIRAMISU ON PAGE 135.

Pots and Pans

I recommend that you start a collection of heavy-based stainless-steel saucepans and strainers (including one that is cone-shaped). You will need various sizes. Also invest in sauté pans, non-stick milk pans, grill plates and an omelette pan.

Trays, Tins and Strainers

baking trays, non-stick (37 x 28cm/14½ x11in)
cake tins, various sizes, with removable bases
muffin tins (37 x 27cm/14½ x10½in)
cooling racks 46 x 32cm (18 x 12½in)
roasting tins, deep anodized (37 x 26 x 8cm/14½ x 10 x 3in)

Nozzles and Brushes

piping nozzles, plain and fluted, selection of plastic piping for cutting into ring moulds
poly spray bottles for oil and melted butter
stainless-steel rule
36cm (14in) plastic piping bag and nozzles
brushes,1.25cm (½in) and 2.5cm (1in)

Scales and Measures

cup measures
scales, electronic or manual (weighs to 10kg/21lb)
stainless-steel spoon measures
round weights
plastic measuring jug (2.2 litre/4 pint)
plastic measuring jug (1litre/1¾ pint)

Electrical Appliances

blender (1 litre/1.8 pint capacity)
deep-fat fryer
electric carving knife
electric juicer
electric coffee grinder
food mixer (6.4 litre/11.25 pint capacity)
food processor (1.4 litre/2.5 pint capacity)
ice cream/sorbet maker

acknowledgements

I would like to thank the following people:

My business partner, Terry Shaw, who has been the most incredible support for 18 years, his friendship, judgement, and advice will always be immeasurable. Steve Bailey, our executive chef who, with Richard Cubbin and Dave Lee, manage to put up with me and some of my crazy ideas. They run the kitchen with such professionalism and dedication, nothing is ever too much trouble. Dave Withers has been responsible for testing all the recipes apart from the desserts. He has worked tirelessly for six months with creativity and so much attention to detail and skill. We have both had the most wonderful time.

Paul North and Liz Taylor for testing the seasonal desserts and dessert buffet. Jane Grafton for interpreting my ideas on desserts so brilliantly and testing them. John Hopkins and Will Yap for running around town picking up all the bits and pieces I wanted. Luis for his hard and loyal work. Phillipa Candy for keeping the office going, being so patient and minding the books. Nicola Edwards has worked with me on this project from the beginning – she is the most wonderful assistant, nothing is too much trouble and her efficiency is legendary. Her wit, humour and ideas have been a great source of support. All the team have been extremely encouraging through the months it has taken us all to develop these recipes. Their loyalty and enthusiasm know no bounds.

Sir Elton John and David Furnish for giving us the opportunity and trust to create very memorable parties, and for letting us raid the contents of their china and linen cupboards and for the generous use of their home. George Quinlan for letting us disrupt his day and being so incredibly kind and helpful. Bob Stacy for his help and great sense of humour. Bryan and Nanette Forbes for their support and encouragement and letting us use their lovely lake and gardens.

Kyle Cathie who made this all possible, my editor Sophie Bessemer who, for the past 18 months, has held my hand through what I feel is uncharted waters – thank you for being so patient. Samantha Gray, my copy-editor, for lots of encouragement and Mark Latter at Vivid for his innovative design and constant good humour through everything. Wei Tang, whose styling is so inspiring – we have both had a tremendous time and you have taught me what works through a camera lens. Jeremy Hopley for the most wonderful photographs and for making the days in the studio enjoyable for all. I have gained so much from just being there.

To Charlie Woodward Fisher, a good friend and support, and his team at Fisher for being true professionals. Ken Turner, Detta Phillips, Michael Mathews, Simon Lycett and Rob Van Heldon – all creative floral designers from whom I have gained much knowledge and the memory of wonderful parties.

John Reid, who has been the most incredible support over the last 15 years, and who is always a great source of encouragement, guidance and advice. Lady Elizabeth Anson at Party Planners – we have had years of wonderful parties and enjoyed every moment, especially our away-day picnics! Joseph, Franklin and Maurice Ettedgui for letting me create L'Express and Joe's. All our customers over the years for their loyalty and trusting us to create their dreams. Our oldest customer, in the nicest way, John Bayman, for always being fun and a friend, watching the children grow up – we did the christenings and 18th birthday parties.

Gabriel and Lynne, Olivia and Lauren Alvarez, who are always there for me; Gabriel for introducing me to Mexican food; Rod and EM Grimes Graeme for being wonderful friends, great supporters and testers of recipes. Rod taught me everything I know about barbecuing. Roddy Grimes Graeme helped me to understand the mysteries of e-mail and the Internet. Frank and Carolyn Mercurio who have brought so much into my life. Joan White for proof-reading and being a good friend for nearly 30 years. Alison and Stephen Camacho for the rum punch recipe and their encouragement. Bill Minors for teaching me to fish although I still cannot eat the barracuda we catch. Irene Hopton Scott for reading the first drafts. Christine for always being happy, helpful and keeping my home together for me. John Hird for encouragement and patience. Sarah and Brian St Pierre for their advice and help. My friends, who I have not been able to see, thank you for being so understanding. Sheila Keating who wrote the article that started this project.

Tiles of Newport, for the loan of tiles for our Moroccan evening. Lucy and Phillip at The Icebox, for the ice bar. Guinivere, Mark, Heather and Kevin Weaver for letting us borrow such wonderful items from your Aladdin's cave in the King's Road. Graham Jones, Terry Jones, Sophie and Jerry of Jones Hire, for listening and their generosity in letting us rummage through their warehouse and borrow equipment. William and Annie Mellon of Top Table who listen and supply beautiful china, glassware, cutlery and linen – thank you for taking us seriously. Trade and Care for the loan of their beautiful lacquerware. Also all at Wedgewood for much of their china that we used in the photographs and VV Rouleaux for their fabulous ribbons. Julian Posner at Banana Split for letting us photograph their magnificent marquee. Julian Chamberlen for the wine suggestions. Pedro Oliveira for testing the cocktails and Steve White for folding the napkins.

index

Apples
spiced baked apples, 146, **147**
spiced waffle topping, 108
Apricot & pumpkin seed waffle
topping, 108, 109
Artichokes
asparagus & artichoke salad,
121, **121**
Asparagus
asparagus & artichoke salad,
121, **121**
crostini with asparagus and
wild mushrooms, 85, **85**
Autumn menu, 124-126
Avocado
Parma ham & avocado wraps,
90, **90**
Awkward silences, overcoming,
60

Banana & coconut sunset, 75
Band, finding, 58
Bar
equipment, 64
large parties, for, 64
small and informal gatherings,
for, 64
staff, 36
Barbecues, 158-161
Beans
refried beans, 111
Tuscan bean & Italian sausage
soup, 151, **153**
two-bean salad with sesame
dressing, 107
Beef
chopped steak with chunky
tomato sauce, 97
hot salt beef & pickles, 110
Thai beef cups, 84, **85**
warm beef salad with orange
dressing, 104, **105**
Bellini, 68
Bitter chocolate tart, 129, **129**
Black challans chicken with
spring rolls, 124, 125, **125**
Bloody Mary, 68
Blueberry muffins, 110
Bread, quantities, 79
Brioche & butter pudding, 113
Brown chicken stock, 168
Brulee cream, 114
Brunch buffet, 108-11
Buckwheat blinis with smoked
salmon curls, 84, **85**
Budget, 12
Buffet
china on, 34

space for, 24
Buffet party
brunch buffet, 108-11
desserts buffet, 112-115
East-West buffet, 104-107
food for, 95
food quantities, 95
Moroccan buffet, 101-**105**
street food buffet, 96-99
tables, arranging, 95
Butternut squash coup, 124,
124

Cabbage
port wine duck with cabbage
parcels, 128, **128**
Caipirinha, 73
Canapes, 33
buckwheat blinis with smoked
salmon curls, 84, **85**
cheese souffle tartlets, 83
chicken dumplings, 83
crostini with asparagus and
wild mushrooms, 85, **85**
number of, 81
prawn dumplings, **82**, 83
salmon fish cakes with spicy
tomato dip, 82
Thai beef cups, 84, **85**
tomato and Mozzarella
shortbreads, 84, **85**
Candlelight, 44, 45
Carrots
baked onion with carrot &
cumin sauce, 143, **144**
carrot & orange salad, **100**,
102
Cassis & red wine dressing, 168
Celeriac
venison with celeriac puree &
juniper sauce, 137, **137**
Champagne berry jelly with
summer fruits, 123, **123**
Champagne cocktail, 69
Cheese
cheddar & mustard muffins,
110
cheese souffle tartlets, 83
feta cheese, black olives &
caper salad, 163, **165**
goats' cheese & basil muffins,
110
goats' cheese & rocket wraps,
90, **90**
goats' cheese, fig & red onion
jam tart, 133, **133**
Mozzarella & red pepper
focaccia topping, 98, **99**

Parmesan choux sticks, 92, **92**
Parmesan tuiles, 92
serving selection, 166
storing, 166
tomato and Mozzarella
shortbreads, 84, **85**
vine leaves, on, 166
Chefs and cooks, 36
Chermoula marinaded seabass,
102
Cherry clafoutis, 138, **138**
Chicken
black challans chicken with
spring rolls, 124, 125, **125**
brown chicken stock, 168
chicken pot pie soup, 151,
153
chicken satay sticks, 98
chicken with lemon & olives,
100, 102
dumplings, 83
marinated chicken & jewelled
rice, 163, **165**
Massaman chicken, 104, **105**
pan bagnat, 96
Children, 60
China, 14, 34
buffet, on, 34
hiring, 35
plate sizes, 76
Chinese duck with plum sauce,
87, **87**
Chinese supper, 145
Chocolate
bitter chocolate tart, 129, **129**
hot chocolate mousses, 132,
132
three-chocolate mousse with
chocolate shapes, 112, **112**
walnut, pecan & chocolate
brownies, 165
Chopped steak with chunky
tomato sauce, 97
Chorizo tortillas, 148
Christmas tree decorations, 18
Circus theme, 17
Citrus peel, 68
Clams
Manhattan clam chowder, 96,
96
Classic Margarita, 72
Cleaning post-party, 15
Cocktail party
drink, quantity of, 66
drinks, 81
food for, 81-92
seats, 24
space for, 24

Cocktails
Bellini, 68
Bloody Mary, 68
Caipirinha, 73
Caribbean, 69
Champagne cocktail, 69
classic Margarita, 72
Cocktails 69
Cosmopolitan, 72
frozen Margarita, 72
Long Island ice tea, 72
Mai Tai, 72
Moscow Mule, 72
Singapore sling, 73
strawberry Daiquiri, 70
Terry's dry Martini, 72
watermelon Margarita, 70
West Indian rum punch, 69
winter whisky warmer, 68
Coconut brulee with mango
sorbet, 141, **141**
Colour co-ordination, 17
Comfort supper, 151, 152
Corn chowder soup sips, 88
Cosmopolitan, 72
Couscous, 103
Crab
spiced Indian crab, 86, **87**
tian of crab, **136**, 137
Crisp green salad, 148
Crostini with asparagus and wild
mushrooms, 85, **85**
Cucumber
pickled cucumber & pawpaw
salad, 106, **106**
Cutlery, 14
choosing, 34, 35
hiring, 35

Dairy products, quantities, 79
Date, setting, 13
Days for entertaining, 13
Decorations, making, 16
Desserts buffet, 112-115
Desserts, quantities, 79
Dinner parties
autumn menu, 124-126
do-ahead dinner, 130-132
effortless dinner, 136-138
Mediterranean dinner, 133-
135
Oriental dinner, 139-141
preparation, 117
seating, 24
spring dinner, 118-120
summer menu, 121-123
vegetarian dinner, 142-144
winter menu, 127-129

Diplomat cream, 169
Disco dancing, 58
Do-ahead dinner, 130-132
Drinks
  banana & coconut sunset, 75
  cocktail party, for, 81
  cocktails. See Cocktails
  cooling, 64, 66
  ice, 66
  large parties, for, 64
  mango & passion fruit cooler,
    75
  melon, apple & lime coolade,
    74
  paw paw & pineapple cooler,
    75
  quantity of, 66
  raspberry & redcurrant frappe,
    74
  small and informal gatherings,
    for, 64
  sugar syrup, 74
  types of, 64
  watermelon & lime cooler, 74
Drinks party, budget, 12
Drunken guests, dealing with,
  61
Duck
  Chinese duck with plum
    sauce, 87, **87**
  port wine duck with cabbage
    parcels, 128, **128**
  spiced duck with lemon grass,
    139, **139**

East-West buffet, 104-107
Effortless dinner, 136-138
Eggs
  huevos rancheros, 111, **111**
Entertainment, 58

Fantasy themes, 16, 17
Feta cheese, black olives &
  caper salad, 163, **165**
Fig & walnut bread, 167
Fireplace, festive, 17
Fish
  creamy fish pie, 146
  fish stock, 168
  quantities, 79
Flowers
  crystallised, 169
  professional, 42
  roses, 41
  seasonal, 41
  types of, 41, 42
Focaccia bruschetta, 98, 99,
  99
Foliage, 42
Food quantities, 79
Formal dining, 49
French theme, 17
Frozen Margarita, 72
Fruit
  Champagne berry jelly with

summer fruits, 123, **123**
oven-dried fruit slices, 169
quantities, 79
summer fruits with raspberry
  sauce, 114

Garden party, 25
Gazpacho soup sips, 88, **88**
Ginger
  ginger tiramisu, 135, **135**
  stem ginger ice cream with
    glazed pineapple, 126, **126**
Glassware, 14
  choosing, 34, 35
  hiring, 35
  quantity of, 66
  style of, 66
Glazed lemon tart, 114
Goats' cheese & basil muffins,
  110
Goats' cheese & rocket wraps,
  90, **90**
Goats' cheese, fig & red onion
  jam tart, 133, **133**
Grains, quantities, 79
Green pea soup sips, 89, **89**
Guest list, 29
Guests, 60, 61

Hardware, 14
  hiring, 35
  mix and match, 34
  multi-purpose styles, 34
  serving, for, 35
Hash brown potatoes, 110
Hiring hardware, 14
Host, duties as, 60
Huevos rancheros, 111, **111**

Ice, 66
Ice bowls, 35
Ice cream
  pecan tart with creme fraiche
    ice cream, 153
  stem ginger ice cream with
    glazed pineapple, 126, **126**
  strawberry tart with rhubarb
    ice cream, 120, **120**
Introductions, making, 60
Invitations
  form of, 29
  formal, 29
  maps, 30
  printed, 30
  refusals, percentage of, 30
  replies, 30, 60
  time for sending, 14, 29

Kitchen equipment, 76, 170
Kitchen guide, 79
Kitchen, stocking, 78

Lamb
  lamb with potato cake &
    thyme sauce, 119, **119**

Moroccan lamb, 101
Late arrivals, 60
Late night supper, 146
Lemons
  glazed lemon tart, 114
  lemon cookies, 165, **165**
Lentils
  millefeuille of Portobello
    mushrooms & lentils, 143,
    144
Linen, 14
Lobster with a tamarind
  dressing, 158, **159**
Long Island ice tea, 72

Macadamia nut brittle, 169
Mai Tai, 72
Mango
  coconut brulee with mango
    sorbet, 141, **141**
  mango & passion fruit cooler,
    75
  swordfish with red onion &
    mango salsa, 158, **160**
Manhattan clam chowder, 96,
  96
Marquees
  dance floor, 39
  dismantling, 27
  entertainment, space for, 58
  extension of home, as 25
  lighting, 25
  lining, 25
  loos, 27
  sites for, 25
  transformation of, 38, 39
  windows, 27, 39
Massaman chicken, 104, **105**
Meat, quantities, 79
Mediterranean dinner, 133-135
Melon, apple & lime coolade,
  74
Menu
  budget, 32
  combination of dishes, 32
  dinner party, for, 117
  elements of, 32
  food quantities, 76
  golden rules, 76
  ingredients, 32
  planning, 14, 32, 33
  preparation, 32, 76
  presentation, 32
  table, for, 49
  tradition, breaking with, 32
  variety in, 32
  vegetarians, 33, 78
  written, 49
Mint tea, 102
Moroccan buffet, 101-103
Moroccan lamb, 101
Moroccan setting, 55
Moscow Mule, 72
Mozzarella & red pepper
  focaccia topping, 98, **99**

Mushrooms
  crostini with asparagus and
    wild mushrooms, 85, **85**
  millefeuille of Portobello
    mushrooms & lentils, 143,
    144
  mushroom, tomato & rocket
    focaccia topping, 98, **99**
  wild mushroom risotto, 150,
    150
Music, 14, 58
Mussel & saffron broth, 130,
  130

Names, remembering, 60
Napkins, 46, 57
New York waffles with a
  selection of toppings, 108,
  109, **109**
Night lights, 45

Oatmeal biscuits, 167, **167**
Onions
  baked onion with carrot &
    cumin sauce, 143, **144**
  goats' cheese, fig & red onion
    jam tart, 133, **133**
  red onion jam, 168
  sweet potatoes with spring
    onions, 160
  swordfish with red onion &
    mango salsa, 158, **160**
Orange
  carrot & orange salad, **100**,
    102
  warm beef salad with orange
    dressing, 104, **105**
Oriental dinner, 139-141
Outdoor eating, 155
Outdoor lighting, 45
Oven timings and temperatures,
  76

Pan bagnat, 96
Parma ham & avocado wraps,
  90, **90**
Parmesan choux sticks, 92, **92**
Parmesan tuiles, 92
Party etiquette, 60, 61
Passion fruit pyramid, 115,
  115
Pasta
  quantities, 79
  squid ink pasta with prawn
    salad, **162**, 163
Pawpaw
  paw paw & pineapple cooler,
    75
  pickled cucumber & pawpaw
    salad, 106, **106**
Peaches
  Sauternes cake with poached
    peaches, 156, 157
Peas
  green pea soup sips, 89, **89**

Pecans
  pecan tart with creme fraiche ice cream, 153
  walnut, pecan & chocolate brownies, 165
Pesto, 168
Pheasant supreme with crispy potato, 131, **131**
Picnics, 163-165
Pina colada, 69
Pineapple
  stem ginger ice cream with glazed pineapple, 126, **126**
Place cards, 46, 49
Planning
  checklist, 15
  date, setting, 13
  list of requirements, 12, 13
Plant pots, 42
Plate sizes, 76
Pool party, 17
Pork
  baby pork ribs, 107
Port wine duck with cabbage parcels, 128, **128**
Potatoes
  hash brown potatoes, 110
  lamb with potato cake & thyme sauce, 119, **119**
  pheasant supreme with crispy potato, 131, **131**
Poultry, quantities, 79
Prawns
  dumplings, **82**, 83
  marinated prawns with chipotle mayonnaise, 161
  marinated tiger prawns, 98, **99**
  spicy, hot & sour prawns, 106, **106**
  squid ink pasta with prawn salad, **162**, 163

Quails' eggs with caviar, 86, **86**
Quesdillas with tomatillo salsa, 97
Quick-fix tortillas, 148

Raspberry & redcurrant frappé, 74
Red mullet
  spicy red mullet on a bed of Asian greens, 107
Red onion jam, 168
Rhubarb
  rhubarb crumble with vanilla cream, 149, **149**
  rhubarb ice cream, 120, **120**
Rice
  loin of veal with lemon risotto & spinach, 134, **134**
  marinated chicken & jewelled rice, 163, **165**
  wild mushroom risotto, 150, **150**

Rice paper wraps with a spicy soy dip, 91, **91**
Rim of glass, salting, 70
Roasted vegetable terrine, 118, **118**
Rocket
  goat's cheese & rocket wraps, 90, **90**
  mushroom, tomato & rocket focaccia topping, 98, **99**
Room transformations, 38
Rosemary strawberries with biscotti, 150
Rosewater cream, 103, **103**

Salad
  asparagus & artichoke salad, 121, **121**
  carrot & orange salad, **100**, 102
  crisp green salad, 148
  feta cheese, black olives & caper salad, 163, **165**
  pickled cucumber & pawpaw salad, 106, **106**
  quantities, 79
  Salad Nicoise with chargrilled tuna, 156, **157**
  two-bean salad with sesame dressing, 107
  warm beef salad with orange dressing, 104, **105**
Salmon
  fresh salmon wrapped in smoked salmon, 127, **127**
  salmon fish cakes with spicy tomato dip, 82
Sausage
  chorizo tortillas, 148
  Tuscan bean & Italian sausage soup, 151, **153**
Sauternes cake with poached peaches, 156, 157
Savoury muffins, 110
Seabass
  chermoula marinaded seabass, 102
  seabass with sweet potato mash & fennel, 122, **122**
Seating cards, 49
Serving dishes, 35
Sesame wafers, 166, 167
Shrimp with lemon grass laska soup, 152, **153**
Silks and spices room setting, 22
Singapore sling, 73
Smoked salmon
  bagels, 109
  buckwheat blinis with smoked salmon curls, 84, **85**
  fresh salmon wrapped in smoked salmon, 127, **127**
Smoking, 61
Soup

butternut squash coup, 124, **124**
chicken pot pie soup, 151, **153**
corn chowder soup sips, 88
Gazpacho soup sips, 88, **88**
green pea soup sips, 89, **89**
mussel & saffron broth, 130, **130**
shrimp with lemon grass laska soup, 152, **153**
tomato & lemon grass soup sips, 89
Tuscan bean & Italian sausage soup, 151, **153**
Speedy supper, 148, 149
Spiced Indian crab, 86
Spoons, food on, 86, 87
Spring dinner, 118-120
Squid ink pasta with prawn salad, **162**, 163
Staff, 36, 37
Stem ginger ice cream with glazed pineapple, 126, **126**
Strawberries
  rosemary strawberries with biscotti, 150
  strawberry Daiquiri, 70
  strawberry tart with rhubarb ice cream, 120, **120**
Street food buffet, 96-99
Street scene, 21
Sugar cobwebs, 169
Sugar syrup, 74
Summer fruits with raspberry sauce, 114
Summer garden lunch, 156, 157
Summer menu, 121-123
Summer theme, 17
Supper parties
  comfort supper, 151, 152
  late night supper, 146
  preparing, 145
  speedy supper, 148, 149
  Tuscan supper, 150
Sweet potatoes
  seabass with sweet potato mash & fennel, 122, **122**
  sweet potatoes with spring onions, 160
Sweetcorn with black pepper butter, 161, **161**
Swordfish with red onion & mango salsa, 158, **160**

Table settings, 15
  centrepieces, 46
  Christmas, 18
  edible decorations, 46
  elegant, 50
  individual place settings, 52
  Moroccan, 55
  napkins, 46
  Oriental, 46

place cards, 46, 49
runners, 46
themed, 17
Table snacks, 81
Terry's dry Martini, 72
Thai beef cups, 84, **85**
Thank you notes, 61
Three-chocolate mousse with chocolate shapes, 112, **112**
Tian of crab, **136**, 137
Tomato juice, 68
Tomatoes
  mushroom, tomato & rocket focaccia topping, 98, **99**
  tomato & lemon grass soup sips, 89
  tomato & Mozzarella shortbreads, 84, **85**
Tuna
  grilled tuna with chilli noodle & leeks, 140, **140**
  rice paper wraps with a spicy soy dip, 91, **91**
  Salad Nicoise with chargrilled tuna, 156, **157**
Tuscan supper, 150

Ultra-violet effect, 21
Veal
  loin of veal with lemon risotto & spinach, 134, **134**
Vegetable crisps, 92
Vegetable stock, 168
Vegetable tortillas, 148
Vegetables
  quantities, 79
  roasted vegetable terrine, 118, **118**
  spicy vegetables, 164
  vegetables with salsa verde, 158
Vegetarian dinner, 142-144
Vegetarians, 33, 78
Venison with celeriac puree & juniper sauce, 137, **137**
Venue, 14
  away from home, 25
  budget, 27
  finding, 27
  garden, 25
  questions to ask, 27
  seats, 24
  space, 24

Walnuts
  fig & walnut bread, 167
  walnut, pecan & chocolate brownies, 165
Watermelon & lime cooler, 74
Watermelon Margarita, 70
West Indian rum punch, 69
Wine, planning, 14
Winter menu, 127-129
Winter whisky warmer, 68
Wraps, 90, 91